MOTHER-LOVE
AND ABORTION

A Legal Interpretation

ROBERT D. GOLDSTEIN

University of California Press
BERKELEY ■ LOS ANGELES ■ LONDON

University of California Press
Berkeley and Los Angeles, California

University of California Press, Ltd.
London, England

Copyright © 1988 by The Regents of the University of California

LIBRARY OF CONGRESS

Library of Congress Cataloging-in-Publication Data

Goldstein, Robert D.
  Mother-love and abortion: a legal interpretation /
Robert D. Goldstein.
    p.   cm.
  Bibliography: p.
  Includes index.
  ISBN 0-520-06084-9 (alk. paper)
  1. Abortion—Law and legislation—United States.
2. Unborn children (Law)—United States. 3. Mother
and child—United States. 4. Fetus. I. Title.
KF3771.G65   1988
344.73'0419—dc19   87-30895
[347.304419]   CIP

Printed in the United States of America

1 2 3 4 5 6 7 8 9

Contents

Preface

Justice Powell announced his retirement from the United States Supreme Court as I write this. His vote had provided the bare majority of five justices who, in the past few years, were firmly and expressly committed to upholding *Roe v. Wade*. In that 1973 case, the Supreme Court, then with only two dissenters, established the constitutional liberty of women to choose to abort their pregnancies until the fetus becomes viable. This same majority has been equally committed to upholding those cases, following *Roe*, that substantially limit the power of government to restrict this liberty through burdensome, costly, and discouraging regulation of the time, manner, and place in which the medical profession may provide abortion services.[1] This bare majority contained the four oldest men on the Court, including Justice Powell. In the year of his departure, the remaining members of this group ranged from 79 to 81 years of age.[2] However, other and younger justices on the Court would overrule *Roe* and return to the states the power to outlaw abortion altogether or, at a minimum, to regulate it so substantially as to make legal abortion unavailable as a practical matter to many, especially to those who are young and not wealthy.

What will happen to *Roe v. Wade* and the constitutional liberty of choice turns on the vagaries of the age and health of the remaining justices; on whom the President nominates to fill vacancies; on what standard of review the Senate applies in determining whether to consent to those nominees;[3] and, finally, on the decisions new justices make once the responsibility of judgment is theirs, giving due regard to the procreational choice *Roe* protects, its place in the canons of privacy cases, and the obligations of the doctrine of *stare decisis*.

But how a newly constituted Supreme Court may in the next few years treat existing precedent is not of consequence to the arguments of this essay. For this is not a book on the constitutional legitimacy and longevity of *Roe*. Rather, it is an exploration and interpretation of the legal regime of choice that began in some states in the 1960s and that *Roe* extended across the nation and attempted to explain. Thus, when *Roe* is referred to in this volume, it is only as an exemplification of the law of abortion-choice, albeit the one that has shaped the terms of the abortion debate for the last fourteen years. Were *Roe* to be overruled, an understanding of the current legal regime would become crucial, because battles over the status of abortion would then be fought, year after year, in multiple legislative bodies and in far more numerous political campaigns. Were the regime of *Roe* to remain unchanged in the coming decade, then the continuing task of understanding it would remain. Indeed, the duty of explicating the law of abortion to our youth would be especially important, because those who come to sexual maturity, even now, may fail to understand the constraints on abortion—and indeed contraception—that existed not very many years ago; and they may, accordingly, fail to comprehend the liberty that is now theirs.

Any interpretation of the law of abortion occurs against rapidly changing landscapes of life and death, and life's reproduction. With technological virtuosity, men and women can translate age-old wishes into reality. Women may abort pregnancies safely and cheaply, and with an effectiveness that unfortunately surpasses our contraceptive capability. Gone is an earlier time when for many the intention to induce the menses or end a pregnancy remained in the realm of wish; or, even if certain primitive steps were taken, a resulting abortion might nonetheless be felt not to have been fully intended, or, if intended, procured at a price amounting to punishment. In other circumstances, where before there was barrenness, couples may now conceive or otherwise have children through the use of fertility drugs, artificial insemination, embryonic implantation, and surrogate mothers. The premature infant may be successfully, indeed perfectly, sustained; and the handicapped newborn, who once would have quickly died, may now be treated through means ranging from the extraordinary and heroic to the routine. Because of the rapidly developing capacity for early fetal observation and diagnosis, a fetus may be delivered prematurely for medical care, or treated *ex utero* and returned to the womb, or, in other cases, aborted.

But each technical advance requires more explicit and refined ethical analysis. Debates attempting to clarify these changing landscapes continue insistently in legislatures, in prosecutors' offices, in courtrooms, in houses of worship, and in the journals. The asserted obligation of pregnant women to follow the prenatal advice of their physicians has become the impetus for a criminal prosecution, for findings of child abuse, and for civil injunctions empowering physicians to control pregnancy by compelling a blood transfusion or a caesarian delivery against the woman's wishes.[4] Parental consent to medical treatment of premature or handicapped neonates has become the subject of federal regulation and scrutiny. Lawsuits pit surrogate mothers against genetic fathers for custody, and court decrees send children shuttling among a variety of caretakers. The legal uncertainty physicians confront about life's beginnings, about when late second trimester fetuses may be aborted and when they instead become patients, is matched by their uncertainty about life's departures, about when those who have lost all potential for consciousness may be relieved of their living organs that another near death may be revived.

In these varied forums the debates alternate between substantive criteria and procedural solutions, between valuing private choice and public control, between the rhetoric of rights and individual liberation and of duties and communal obligation, between emphasizing a woman's equality in the public arena and her special family role in procreation, and, finally, between the foolishness of human narcissism and its boldness, and the deadly constrictions of guilt and its animating virtues.

The technological and social changes that underlie these developments appear to validate the individualistic categories in which the abortion debate has been conducted, as it contrasts a woman's right to equality and autonomy with a fetal right to

life. For is not the fetus observable and treatable, a patient—
whether person or not—in its own right? And is not its location
in any particular womb a happenstance that our doctors may
alter and social arrangements, such as surrogate mothering,
may adjust?

Against such trends that disaggregate begetting, bearing, and
rearing from each other, I intend to mount an old-fashioned interpretation and defense of procreational choice and the privacy
of that first and most basic community of woman and fetus. The
analyses of abstract and universal rights—to self-determination
and to life—require supplementation for they omit the particularity of mother-love and the love for the mother that conjunc-
tively define the identity of a woman and her offspring. I propose
a number of fundamental themes in support of this defense of
procreational choice: The privacy and autonomy that *Roe* protects belong not only to the woman as an individual but also to
the dyadic, indeed symbiotic, unit of woman and fetus. This
dyad constitutes the relevant community for understanding the
abortion decision. The woman is the decision maker with respect to this community, in consultation with a physician whose
presence tests her procreational decision in interpersonal dialogue. The larger community's interest in the next generation is
realized through the woman's decision whether to bear her child.
The state is, as a matter of fact, otherwise unable to protect the
fetus except through a caretaker's intervening determination to
love her offspring. An abortion prohibition would therefore constitute an exploitation of a woman's mother-love. And, finally,
the impersonal efforts of others to represent the fetus are un-
availing because it is the woman who can best interpret the
meaning of fetal silence. This essay no doubt has implications
for some of the aforementioned biomedical issues; but the question of abortion is more than enough to occupy the present
volume.

■ ■ ■

To preserve the essay form, I have reserved much material for
the notes, trusting that the interested reader will not be deterred

after completing the essay from turning to those notes that are pertinent. In addition to standard citations, the notes serve to guide readers to the relevant literature; afford a flavor of the work of those on whom I rely, as I am prone to giving extensive quotations for that purpose; provide a detailed account of the current state of Supreme Court decisions on abortion; and allow for extended discussions of such topics as the potential demand for adoptive infants, the psychological meaning of abortion, the current age of viability, the demographics of abortion, the relationship of psychoanalytic object-relations theory to infant research, and so forth.

The invaluable encouragement of my wife and the supportive openness of the Law School of the University of California at Los Angeles have enabled me to move from an idea to its expression. My colleagues have helped by asking more questions than each successive draft answered. These readers, some of whom may dissent from this work, include: Richard Abel, Alison Anderson, William Forbath, Carole Goldberg-Ambrose, Kenneth Karst, Christine Littleton, Carrie Menkel-Meadow, Herbert Morris, Fran Olsen, Arthur Rosett, Gary Schwartz, Murray Schwartz, Steve Shiffrin, Jonathan Varat, and Stephen Yeazell. Drs. Justin Call, Spencer Eth, Milton Greenblatt, Bernard Towers, and Louis J. West have also provided useful advice for which I am most appreciative. The staff of the UCLA Law Library, and in particular Jan Goldsmith, Myra Saunders, and Eric Wade, have been most helpful in responding to my numerous requests. Defeating successive software problems, Philip Trull and Rita Saavedra typed the manuscript with a good cheer that was beyond the call of duty. For financial support, I would like to thank the UCLA Academic Senate, Dean Susan Prager, and the Law School Dean's Fund. Students Sandra Segal, David Kaplan, and Hallie Hochman checked citations for accuracy, and Lisa Hauser and Judith Wilson performed other research tasks as well. To those who have taught me the method of mother-love, a more private appreciation is due than can appropriately be expressed here.

Even in the dreams of men, a book may appear as a child being born, even a book about abortion. I hope that what follows bears a fair relationship to the actual procreational experiences of at least some women, and that it has developed sufficiently to be of service to those who—privately in internal and familial colloquy and publicly in their professional lives—take upon themselves, for whatever personal reasons, the unhappy burden of carrying on the abortion debate.

Los Angeles, June 1987

Introduction

As the subject of abortion passed beyond the whispers of women into the public realm, it occasioned an outpouring of philosophical, legal, and political debate. Dwelling on this debate disturbs. Treating the matter abstractly, the philosophical literature elaborates and educates, without advancing resolution. The political essays from each side of the debate inhabit different worlds. The case studies of abortion clinics leave one troubled to the core about the hardness of many women's lives.[1] Whether that leaves one as troubled as the annual number of abortions or the at-risk children born to inadequate, uncommitted, overextended, or ambivalent parents is a matter of some individual difference.

This intense, vigorous, repetitious, vile, sometimes intelligent, sometimes crazy—even criminal—abortion debate does not now appear susceptible to an intellectual or political solution[2] satisfactory to both the groups that would regulate market access to abortion and the groups that support its continued deregulation. (To avoid the usual phrases, I shall refer to those who would prohibit or substantially regulate the availability of abortion as "regulators," and those who substantially favor the present regime of lawful elective abortion as "deregulators."[3])

In his sustained criticism of *Roe v. Wade* and the abortion liberty, John Noonan, Jr., the leading regulator among the legal professoriat and now a federal judge, argues that *Roe* represents the triumph of a positivist and totalitarian position: that personhood is solely a construct of the law. As it gives, so the state may take away that personhood—and with it the right to life. Drawing upon his work on slavery and the manner in which the law dehumanized slaves by treating them as chattel, Noonan asserts that deregulators mask the existing human fetus behind the

1

forms of the law and, by thus avoiding plain facts, look away from the realities of the practice of abortion.[4]

Such a masking of a shared reality, by one side or the other, could of course account for the lack of common ground in the debate. An unmasking, accordingly, might facilitate a reclamation of shared understandings among ongoing disputants.

This essay is motivated by a sense that a different reality is denied and masked. What is denied is that the fetus and then infant, utterly and helplessly dependent, lacks an identity and existence apart from its relationship with the mothering one who chooses to care for it. What is masked is the centrality to human existence of mother-love and the love for the mother.[5]

• • •

In exploring this claim, it will first be helpful to get our bearings by reviewing and clarifying, at some substantial length in chapter 1, the parameters of the abortion debate in certain of the philosophical and legal literature. Because the particular resolution of the abortion issue in *Roe v. Wade* may become vulnerable to the changed composition of the Supreme Court, it is especially important to understand these parameters, for they set, in the current discourse, the legitimate limits on alternative abortion policies.

But the primary purpose of this extended review is to understand the way in which the debate treats the relationship of fetus and woman. In the literature, the permissibility of abortion turns on identifying rights-bearers, specifying the rights they bear, and resolving conflicts among these rights; this literature first describes persons and then, secondarily, the minimalist duties they owe each other. Thus the fetus is typically treated as a creature entirely separate from the woman who carries it. Their interaction is structured by absolute negative rights, in one account, and, in another, by affirmative obligations of a good samaritan nature. In both versions, the rhetoric is individualistic: woman and fetus stand as strangers apart, in arm's length opposition to each other, the bonds between them, their commonality, slighted. But such atomistic assumptions prove inadequate for comprehending human procreation. This approach, especially when combined with the current technological mentality that sees in the potential development of artificial placentas a means of resolving the abortion controversy, leads to a troubling denigration of mother-infant attachment, for it is governed by a logic of separateness.[6]

This review prepares the way, in chapter 2, for a search for an alternative and less atomistic description of procreation that would focus attention first and foremost on the relationship of attachment between the fetus and the woman carrying it. Such an account would locate the personhood of an offspring in its developing and constitutive relationship with its mother and would describe the rights and duties of each in terms appropriate to that unique dyad. Current work in political philosophy, feminist theory, and psychology encourage this project.

Then, in chapter 3, this essay describes one human developmental theory to demonstrate how such a relational approach can illumine the law of abortion. The theory used here for illustrative purpose derives from psychoanalysis, especially from those investigations conducted by its object-relations school. While not without problems, it has the virtue, among others, of giving a most careful and respectful account of the development of self from its relationship with others. That body of work can be used to describe the fetus in relational terms as a constituent part of a dyadic whole; for, in this theory's view, infantile existence cannot be disentangled from the infant's relationship with a caregiver and from her vital commitment to it, her mother-love.

This perspective affords an interpretation and defense of the legal regime of procreative choice that *Roe v. Wade* reflects. The law's privacy doctrine, upon which it built, protects this relational field, through which the infant may eventually emerge as an autonomous rights-bearer. By offering her a reasonable period of time in which to make her maternal choice, the law also protects the woman's decision of whether to commit herself to the intensity and life-changing identity of motherhood and respects her judgment of whether she is then ripe for this symbiotic relationship. In our society, a woman's commitment of love belongs to the realm of freedom: the state cannot coerce and ought not exploit her love by denying to her a meaningful period of choice.

In closing, this essay will briefly consider, from the competing perspectives of chapters 1 and 3, claims about the kind of society that countenances abortion and the manner in which the silent fetus may find representation in that society. It will do so by reflecting upon two historical comparisons, which some draw, between antebellum slavery and totalitarianism and our present regime of procreative choice.

1

Individual Rights
and the
Logic of Separateness

THE PREDOMINANT PHILOSOPHICAL AND LEGAL ANALYSES IN THE secular abortion debate attempt to explain who are rights-bearers and to define the rights that they bear; then, to the extent made necessary by their answers, they seek to work an accommodation between the rights of the woman and fetus. The individualistic and atomistic assumptions about personhood that underlie these efforts pave the way for the recent appearance of arguments that see in the technological possibilities of early separation of woman and fetus a means of resolving the conflicting interests of the two. This chapter will explore the structure of the philosophical and legal debate in order to clarify its understanding of the relationship of woman and fetus and its resulting logic of separateness.

THE PHILOSOPHICAL ARGUMENT

In the philosophical debate, two great questions dominate analysis and delimit the strategies of argument. Their resolution shapes, or at least rationalizes, the author's position on abortion. The first question is, When, if ever, does a fetus become a person and, accordingly, a being with moral standing and a bearer of a right to life? The second question is, To what does this right, if it exists, entitle the fetus? This latter question may be re-cast as, What is the nature of the relationship between fetus and woman?[1]

The Nature of the Fetus: Who Holds a Right to Life?

Some assert that abortion is permissible because during many or all of its gestation the fetus lacks a right to life. It lacks that right because it is not the kind of living being, indeed not the kind of living *human* being, that has moral standing as a rights-bearer. Although alive and although a form of human life, as ova and sperm are forms of human life, it is not yet a person. Analysis then requires the elaboration of the criteria by which we come to include living organisms in the class of "persons" or rights-bearers.[2]

The multiplicity of answers as to when personhood arises and which criteria define it, and the inability of philosophers to put forward compelling reasons for preferring one answer over another, lead some to reject the relevance of the following in-quiry altogether.[3] Yet, the question of personhood returns and returns again in the literature, in the political debate, and in the consciousness of women and men, shaping or at least providing an opportunity for the coalescing of their attitudes on abortion.

Some refer to cognitive psychological qualities to determine the personhood of the fetus. Among philosophers, Michael Tooley has taken the cognitive criteria to their outer limit by adopting particularly restrictive requirements for admission into the class of rights-bearers. A being, according to this perspective, must have a continuity of consciousness of itself as having wants or purposes, before it can have a right to a life in which it can further those purposes and before it can be said that its death is a harm to a person. That point arises sometime after birth, according to Tooley's reading of the cognitive psychological literature.[4]

Not consciousness of self and purposes but *sentience*, or the "capacity for feeling or affect," is the essential characteristic of a rights-bearing creature, argues the philosopher L. W. Sumner in his useful book on the morality of abortion.[5] Since the best estimate of embryologists is that sentience does not arise before mid-second-trimester forebrain development, Sumner locates some point in the second trimester as the time at which the fetus becomes a rights-bearer.[6] He accepts viability as a rough indicator of this point and therefore as a rough indicator of moral standing. One virtue of the criterion of sentience, argues Sumner, is that it avoids the line-drawing problem that confronts "liberals" who seek to justify abortion after viability without also justifying infanticide, and that confronts "conservatives" who wish to condemn early abortion without also condemning contraception.[7]

Regulators by contrast rely exclusively on biological criteria, existing at or shortly after fertilization, for defining personhood. Many of them argue that the right to life is a species right, available to the diploid form of the species but unavailable to sentient or intelligent creatures that are not *homo sapiens*. This species right first attaches to a single cell called a zygote—a cell created in a woman's oviduct by the penetration of a sperm into her ovum, both of which constitute the haploid phase of human life. These regulators explain that this single cell has a new and unique diploid chromosomal makeup, different from its parents, that will determine its future growth. They further claim that no line can be drawn after fertilization which can rationally distinguish this resulting new genotype of human life from the infant.[8]

However, that single cell may give rise to twins, in which case it is not yet the cellular entity that will develop into one and only one unique being; indeed, it may develop into something other than a person as well, including a form of cancer. For this reason other regulators instead focus their interest on that moment in development, at approximately fourteen days past fertilization, after which no twinning and no recombination of twins into a single unit will occur. For at that point the embryo both contains a unique genetic makeup and can be said to be launched on the road of unique bodily development determined by that genetic code.[9] It is *indivisum in se*. Moreover, unlike its predecessor the zygote—almost half of which spontaneously miscarry within those two weeks—it has a not unsubstantial chance after the second week of successfully traversing the road to birth.[10] The requirement that the substantial potential for development into an infant must indwell within a unique physical entity may explain why some regulators do not also require protection for the potential of egg and sperm, which have some characteristics in common with the zygote.

For practical reasons, people choosing this moment of development may align themselves with those who choose as the moment of personhood the process of implantation by the blastocyst, as the embryologists call it, in the uterine wall. Implantation, which begins six to seven days after fertilization, is the time when the blastocyst, some interpreters say, enters into a human relationship, with the woman.[11]

The focus on twinning or implantation over fertilization as a criterion of personhood permits those who rely on it to justify— as not interfering with a person—those contraceptive devices that prevent implantation, immediate preventive measures for rape victims, and gynecological or other abdominal surgery after ovulation without waiting for the onset of menses to prove the absence of pregnancy.

Other biological milestones have also been suggested as marking the metamorphosis of the embryo (as it is called between weeks three and eight) and the fetus (as it is called thereafter) into a person and as completing the process of development from becoming human into human being. Some note moving heart tissue at four weeks; the functioning of a heart and the development of other organs at six to seven; the capacity of lung function between twenty and twenty-four weeks, or the completion of the primary histological differentiation of organs at between twenty-six and thirty-six weeks. Arguing that it is the human brain that sets human beings apart from animals and makes us interpersonal and moral beings, others make distinctions based on brain development. They point, for example, to first brain activity (although its electrical activity differs from postbirth activity and appears random) at eight weeks or after; early stimulus-response behavior which depends on some central nervous system development, at ten to twelve weeks; the fuller development of subcortical forebrain capacity—more or less what Sumner identifies as sentience—which permits sufficient system integration to support viability, at about twenty to twenty-four weeks; or, some weeks later, higher cerebral activity, which may support the capacity for a minimal sort of wakeful consciousness. Depending on whether one looks to first signs of organ development or to organized biological systems as evidence of sufficient complexity to deserve respect, one will stress either heartbeat and brain waves or cardiovascular system and brain functioning. Depending on whether one adopts traditional or newer definitions of death, one will stress a functioning cardiovascular system or a functioning brain as the *sine qua non* of a person's life.[12]

Other points have been proposed as well. Quickening, the time in the second trimester when the pregnant woman first feels the moving fetus, is a period significant to the common law. Viability is accepted by some as the point at which a sensible distinction between fetus and new born can no longer be drawn. Believing that the best picture of the human soul is the human body, some would reinforce respect for human beings by according respect to the fetus at a point after its middevelopment, when its form more resembles a newborn; but others understandably see this resemblance as early as the eighth to tenth week of gestation. Finally, according to *Roe,* birth is the moment when the Constitution of the United States extends, as do some other traditions, the recognition of personhood.[13]

Sumner rejects these last four points—quickening, viability, resemblance, and birth—since he claims they do not derive from any inherent characteristic of the fetus that we could agree is of the essence of a person.[14] They are instead products of the adult world's response to the fetus and its potential for interaction. I shall return later to the claim that the rights of a fetus should be determined apart from its interaction with an adult, and to the underlying assumption that its essential nature may be comprehended wholly apart from its relational connection with the woman carrying it; and I shall make criticism of this claim a central theme of this essay.

For the present, it suffices to note that the interpersonal nature of birth has biological dimensions that are themselves important to understanding the relational nature of the fetus. At birth the fetus is separated from the placenta, the amniotic sac, and the umbilical cord. These tissues developed from one part of the blastocyst, the other part eventually developing into the fetus. That blastocyst had in turn developed from a woman's fertilized ovum; that ovum, in the course of only one week, had first been extruded from the woman's ovaries, then resided along with a myriad of the woman's other cells in her oviduct, and then, if fertilized, had joined with her uterine wall. If these tissues developing from the blastocyst are treated as a part of the fetus, then fetal form and function radically differ from the infant into which it metamorphosizes. If not, then they are separate living human tissues without any claim to personhood and conjoined equally to woman and fetus. Especially because an abortion technique might operate more directly on the placenta than the embryo or fetus, it is surprising that the status of the placenta has received so little attention—as if the individualistic category of personhood directs the attention of regulator and deregulator alike away from fetal interconnectedness with the woman.[15] These connective tissues, which are shed only at birth by each, bridge woman and fetus and embody the mysteries of uniqueness but sameness, self but other, that surround the fetus and the philosopher's efforts to describe what or who it is.[16]

The Duty Correlative to the Right to Life

At least since the publication of MIT philosopher Judith Thomson's work on abortion, it has seemed very likely in the current debate that an affirmative answer to the first question—that the fetus *is* a person—will not, without additional claims, lead to the conclusion that abortion of that fetus is wrong in some or all circumstances.[17] Thus, any analysis of abortion that accords personhood to the fetus at some stage of gestation must address the second essential question: What rights flow to the fetus from that personhood or, put differently, what duties fall to the woman? The literature generally agrees that persons are entitled to respect, amounting to a right to life. But there is far less agreement on what duties a fetal right to life, should it exist, would impose upon the pregnant woman, and in particular whether a right to life includes a welfare right against the woman to supply needed sustenance.

Many regulators have long accepted, at law and in principle, abortion in a few well-delineated circumstances. A study of such exceptions to an abortion prohibition discloses the different answers that these regulators have given to this second question posed by Thomson. Their different answers alert us to the ways in which the relationship of woman and fetus is understood.

When the Woman's Life Is Jeopardized. The most widely but not universally agreed-upon exception to a doctrine prohibiting abortion is the right of the woman to save her own life. Some would deny abortion even in this circumstance,[18] holding that the right to life protects a person so long as he is morally innocent of putting another's life at serious risk. As a being incapable of forming intention and not morally responsible for the physical danger it may pose to the woman, the fetus, it is said, may not be aborted.[19]

Nonetheless, teachings of the Catholic Church, by focusing on her intent and the doctrine of double effect, allow the woman and her physician to undertake certain acts that lead to fetal death. This doctrine permits the woman to occasion the death of the innocent fetus, provided that her intent is to save her life and the means adopted to achieve that end do not aim at or have as their primary therapeutic action fetal death but only incidentally bring it about. The removal of a cancerous uterus or associated radiation treatment prior to viability is permitted, although the fetus dies. The treatment of ectopic pregnancies is assimilated to this doctrine, although not without significant strain: the operation aims at the removal of the diseased fallopian tube, not the fetus growing within.

In contrast, a woman threatened by pregnancy's drain on her body, as a result of diabetes, cardiovascular problems, difficult labor, or the like, is without recourse because the purpose and means of treatment aims at pregnancy termination.[20]

With respect to these latter cases, which the doctrine of double effect does not cover, others nonetheless claim that neither its right to life nor moral innocence protect the fetus from abortion. Assimilating a right of self-protection to a right of self-defense, they assert that the common law properly recognizes the right to use force against one who threatens but may be innocent. As the source of the threat, the fetus is treated as a technical aggressor (in the sense of being the physical cause of the threat) who may be stopped by the woman and her agents.[21]

These two versions of the exception for the woman's life, the doctrine of double effect and of the fetus as technical aggressor, are of enormous import to the woman at risk and her family. But with modern medicine these doctrines affect only a few, given the availability of relatively safe caesarians and neonatal care. Still their existence shows that a right to life does not, without further explanation, protect the fetus from even the intentional acts of the pregnant woman.

∎ ∎ ∎

The rhetoric of this exception is that of absolute rights. The relationship between woman and fetus is rendered in negative and antagonistic categories as if they were living in two separate worlds—except that they inhabit the same space.

When the Woman Has Been Raped. A second exception, for pregnancies resulting from rape, is not unusual among abortion regulatory schemes. But the theories of the woman's life exception and the rape exception inhabit different realms of discourse.[22] While the theory of self-defense is cast in negative rights, the theory of the rape exception employs the rhetoric of affirmative relationship, of good samaritan obligations, between fetus and woman.

Asserting that the fetus has a right to life, those regulators who justify the rape exception may argue as follows. A right to life, as you and I enjoy, does not create a general welfare right against others to supply the wherewithal of survival. Generally, a woman need not lend her body to a fetus, or to anyone else who is in need of sustenance, and certainly not for the length of time and with the risks and burdens attendant on pregnancy. The state presumably cannot compel a woman to become a surrogate mother for an orphan zygote or, were it feasible, to donate her body parts to a born child, even if she is the cause of injury as in child abuse.[23] This is, of course, the central message of

Thomson's well-known hypothetical: the right to life of an ailing world-class violinist does not justify a group of music lovers in kidnapping a woman and hooking her up to the innocent and dying violinist to provide him with kidney function and other essentials of life for nine months until he heals. Nor does it prevent the woman from subsequently separating herself from the violinist, to his permanent detriment.

However, some critics of her work assert that Thomson's kidnapped woman unwillingly attached to the dependent violinist is in a very different position from that of the pregnant woman. The latter has a unique relationship to the fetus that gives rise to a special obligation to be a good (and on Thomson's scale of moral behavior, a very good) samaritan, to the extent of providing nine months of sustenance at some personal risk and detriment. This special relationship arises because the woman either intentionally or negligently created the conditions that placed the fetus in the dependent condition requiring sustenance. It is not that a woman creates dependence by virtue of being an ovulating and womb-bearing creature, but rather because she has chosen to engage in sexual intercourse, so the argument goes. No obligation exists in the case of rape since the woman has not voluntarily undertaken the responsibilities that flow from intercourse.[24]

With this argument one can also account for maternal life and health exceptions to an abortion prohibition, without having to address the moral innocence of the fetus. The obligation is to be a good samaritan, not a heroine. Even the good samaritan need not risk death or serious harm. Accordingly, an exception can and should be made where the woman's life or health is at stake. With a similar argument one can justify abortion in cases where a pregnant girl is below the age of consent, and thus not responsible for a resulting pregnancy.[25]

Deregulators agree that, absent special circumstances, a fetal right to life (should it exist) does not entail a welfare right to sustenance and the correlative good samaritan obligation. But they assert that intercourse does not create those special circumstances. Two accounts are available to them.

Some feminists claim that heterosexual intercourse under patriarchy may not be deemed the free will of the woman, absent a radical reconstruction of the power relations between the sexes, the elimination of economic dependence of women on men, and the control of male violence against women (as children assaulted by relatives and child-care personnel, as adults assaulted by strangers and acquaintances, and as married adults assaulted by husbands).[26] This strong claim does not and will not win broad assent, although the evidence of violence and domination upon which the claim is based must be given consideration.

Others, such as Thomson, argue from general notions of when a person may be held responsible for her intentional acts and her acts with unintended but foreseeable consequences, whether negligent and blameworthy or nonnegligent and blameless. Thomson would apparently hold to her choice the woman who consciously sought impregnation (assuming the fetus to be a person). When a woman neither intends to become pregnant nor fails to take reasonable contraceptive precautions, Thomson appears to suggest that she may not be obliged to continue the pregnancy. Good samaritanism is not a matter of strict liability. For if the use of reasonably effective contraception did not satisfy a person's responsibility, then Thomson asks why the rape victim cannot be said to be responsible in that she preserved her fertility by failing to be sterilized. However, it is not clear that her argument would justify abortion in the case of a woman who carefully used a postfertilization device that prevents implantation, given Thomson's working assumption (which finally she rejects) that the zygote is a person. What of the woman who neither sought pregnancy nor employed contraception? In the abstract, negligent actions may create samaritan duties of some duration and burden. But according to students of female sexual acculturation, the misinformation that young women have acquired by education and experience—and the pressures upon them for sex that our culture appears to condone—lead them to believe that impregnation is so unlikely that the nonuse of contraception cannot by itself be said to make impregnation an intended or reasonably foreseeable outcome of any one act of intercourse.[27]

It should now be clear that an acceptable theory of the nature, rights, and obligations of sexuality is essential if a would-be regulator is to move from the claim that a fetus, as a person, has a right to life to the claim that abortion is wrong except in the case of rape and related exceptions. Yet the question of the personhood of the fetus has obscured and displaced, in the abortion debate, this equally important question about the nature of sexuality; because of this, it is uncertain what sort of account of sexuality may develop. To succeed in imposing a good samaritan duty on women, such an account ought to have the following characteristics: It must be as plausible to women as to men; thus, it would have to be able to justify, in light of a long history of abuse, the resulting double standard in which the burdens of procreation are imposed substantially on women. It should acknowledge the instinctuality that makes sexuality driven and the natural and necessary contribution sexuality makes to intimate association, personal identity, and the pleasure of life. For purposes of the law, it ought to be able to distinguish contraception from abortion. It should take into account a woman's different knowledge and capacities for consent to intercourse and procreation at different stages of her life. Additionally, it ought to excise the punitive motivation of those who would exploit and use children by treating them as a means to punish sexually active women, even when monogamous.[28]

Finally, any claim that sexuality must be employed exclusively for procreative purposes and that any unintended conception brings with it an obligation to the resulting fetus should be given a form that is capable of being properly addressed to the secular and pluralist state. To the extent that such a claim about sexuality has its mainstay in certain religious attitudes that conflict with other religious and secular views, the argument that deregulation of abortion is the appropriate response for our religiously diverse society might be put forward. However, substantial criticism has been leveled at a similar argument that, because beliefs about the personhood of the fetus often have religious origins, the state ought not establish, by prohibiting abortion, one among a plurality of religious views.[29]

However, a failure to provide an acceptable theory of sexuality or otherwise to establish a good samaritan duty arising from intercourse would not be a regulator's last move. He may claim that the woman, although without affirmative obligation to the fetus, has no permissible way to assert her right to autonomy after implantation. Such an argument based on negative rights (assuming the zygote is a person) would allow preimplantation methods of pregnancy avoidance for all women but deny postimplantation abortions in all cases including rape, except where the woman's life is at stake.[30]

This regulator may claim that there is a crucial difference between pre- and postimplantation acts in that postimplantation abortions kill the embryo or fetus by injuring or invading its bodily integrity, whereas preimplantation acts merely allow the blastocyst to die unimplanted. Any fetal right to life has at its core a right to be free from destructive invasions of bodily integrity.[31] After implantation, the right to life, viewed solely as a negative right, suffices to preclude the woman from avoiding a relationship with the fetus except in self-defense. The regulator might add: Thomson's examination of the right to life as a welfare right was superfluous in the postimplantation setting.[32]

Thomson's story ends with the kidnapped victim reaching around and unplugging herself; she does not first dismember the violinist. Among the noninvasive methods of relationship avoidance may be the intrauterine device (IUD) and certain birth-control pills. These methods apparently make a woman's womb unavailable for samaritan service, and are the equivalent of walking away from one in need. The blastocyst simply never engages with the woman and is carried out with her menses.

By contrast, once the woman has begun to render aid to the fetus, after implantation, she can cease her aid only by direct invasion of its bodily integrity. The dilation and evacuation (D&E) abortion procedure, typically used in much of the second trimester, not only disconnects the fetus but dismembers and destroys the fetal body. Suction or sharp curettage (D&C) procedures in the first trimester—which are used in most abortions—will also typically attack the bodily integrity of the fetus as well as the placenta.[33]

But a regulator making this argument would not have characterized all postimplantation abortifacients. At some points in her pregnancy, a woman can have recourse to an "unplugging" method that separates the fetus from her without invading its physical integrity. After the first third of her second trimester, she may receive a prostaglandin injection or suppository that brings on uterine contractions. Although prostaglandins may sometimes depress the fetal cardiovascular system to the point of death, reports Noonan, the fetus in at least some cases does not survive being thus expelled primarily because it is not viable outside the womb.[34] A hysterotomy also effects a separation, but this is so invasive of the woman, akin to an early caesarian, that it is seldom performed. More significantly, a progesterone antagonistic agent like RU 486 may soon become available in suppository or oral form for use in the first half of the first trimester. It permits a woman to terminate uterine receptivity (which she would otherwise temporarily create and maintain by her body's special production of progesterone after fertilization); as such, she can cause separation apparently without any direct action on the embryo.[35] Death results entirely from its own nonviability. The pregnant woman thereby asserts a right to her own body without invading any right to bodily integrity that the fetus may have.

The moral significance of a distinction between invasion and noninvasion of the fetus may be doubted by regulator and deregulator alike. The regulator may claim that there is no distinction of importance between the woman who sets in motion events that separate the nonviable fetus from needed care and sustenance and the woman whose agent directly and invasively attacks the fetus in a way that kills it. In both cases the pregnant woman is the author of the events that lead to death; she does more than merely let the fetus die of its own nonviability.[36] However, such an argument would also disallow preimplantation acts of pregnancy avoidance, since the act-omission of separation is probably not meaningfully distinguishable from the act-omission of preventing implantation. But the disallowance of preimplantation omissions ultimately depends on an anterior judgment that the woman had an obligation not to omit her extraordinary aid; whether such a good samaritan obligation exists has already been discussed.

By contrast, the deregulator (assuming a fetal right-to-life but no samaritan obligation) may reject the pre- and postimplantation distinction by asserting that the woman may take defensive steps to prevent the fetus from unjustifiably, and thus parasitically, forcing her into a samaritan position. Such steps may be analogized to those permitted in bodily self-defense against one who threatens not only substantial physical injury but any substantial bodily impairment or control. The woman, who also possesses a common law right of bodily integrity and autonomy, may repel invasions by direct action against the fetus.[37] Here regulator and deregulator again deeply and inconclusively diverge with respect to the importance that they attach to a woman's control over her body and the extent to which they accept her use of self-help (the law affording no other remedy for nine months) to preserve her autonomy.[38]

■ ■ ■

The samaritan analysis pictures a distant relationship between woman and fetus, most affirmatively characterized as one of duty arising from sexual intercourse. Such relationship as there is grows not from a deep attachment of mother and offspring but as an incidental sequela of another passion.

When the Woman Is Unduly Burdened: Noncapricious Treatment of the Fetus. In addition to rape and the woman's life and health, regulatory schemes worldwide often include exceptions to an abortion prohibition for incest, for substantial fetal abnormality, and for poverty and other family conditions.[39] These exceptions may all be comprehended within the theory of the good samaritan obligation or as an acknowledgement that the fetus is not yet a person.

In some jurisdictions, pregnancies resulting from incest are categorized with rape as "jural exceptions" because of the illegality of the intercourse that gave rise to them. Those who ascribe personhood to the fetus and wish to defend this exception may properly treat most incestuous intercourse as involuntary so as to assimilate incest to the rape exception and its analysis of the good samaritan obligation.[40]

The "fetal indications" exception would permit abortion where there is a reasonable likelihood of serious fetal malformation. Those who accord the fetus personhood can justify a broad fetal-indications exception, by arguing that the good samaritan obligation arising from intercourse does not extend to the fetus whose severe abnormalities increase the burdens on the woman beyond what may be reasonably imposed, given the limited benefit that she would be conferring on it.[41] Many regulators would of course hesitate before adopting this approach because it permits an argument that the burdens of poverty and other family difficulties (and possibly any substantial interference with a woman's life goals, such as educational or employment plans) also exceed the scope of the good samaritan obligation.[42] Generous application of the good samaritan theory thus leads to a multiplicity of exceptions, and possibly to deregulation.

More convincingly, in the alternative these exceptions are compatible with treating the fetus as a human organism that is only a potential rather than an actual person because, being in a stage of its life cycle that precedes the human-being stage, it is only in the process of becoming a person. To the extent that such a potential person can have interests that should be respected, those interests appear to require that it not be denied a future life as a person for no reason or for trivial reasons; but whether they require more is far from clear.[43]

The response of those who wish to preclude these exceptions has been to urge the concept of "abortion for convenience" and to suggest that women typically have abortions for inconsequential reasons.[44] But without more evidence than an occasional anecdote supporting it, this move fails to counter the far more plausible conclusion that most women do not obtain abortions for trivial or whimsical reasons. However much human inadequacy may be in evidence in some of the case studies of abortion clinics, decisions made for convenience are not. Accordingly, requiring that abortions only be performed for nontrivial reasons, indeed for serious reasons, is entirely consistent with a legal regime of complete deregulation for some period of pregnancy. Of course, where a woman offers what appears to some as a trivial explanation, she is simultaneously expressing one of the weightiest of reasons: she does not love the potential within.

• • •

These philosophical arguments generally describe an all-or-nothing ascription of rights, a battleground of woman and fetus contending for ascendancy and of rights in conflict seeking to trump each other, a zero-sum game. The logic inquires into what minimum obligations may be imposed on the woman, and if, when, and how she may appropriately sever her fetal connection. Sometimes employing the rhetoric of negative rights, sometimes that of welfare rights, the analyses treat the fetus and woman as independent creatures, indeed strangers, and avoid the extraordinary dependence and intertwined interconnectedness of their relationship.

THE LEGAL ARGUMENT

Legal analyses reflect these philosophical debates, refracted through the prism of judicial review. As a result of its atomizing logic, current analyses, especially when joined with a technological mentality, are coming to favor as the appropriate legal solution fetal separation from the woman and subsequent incubation or transfer in lieu of abortion.

Roe v. Wade

In seeking to understand how the law of abortion-choice and its critics accept the terms and consequences of the philosophical arguments, it is useful to distinguish the relatively noncontroversial aspects of *Roe* from the controversial ones. The latter consist entirely of the Court's evaluation of the disputed philosophical issues: the status of the fetus (as valued by the state) and the nature of the woman's right to avoid a relationship with it.

The (Relatively) Uncontroversial *Roe*.   *Roe* does not pit woman-right against fetus-right directly, but woman-right against state interest. For according to *Roe* the fetus is not a bearer of rights in our fundamental law, a status that the fourteenth amendment reserves for the born. Absent a constitutional amendment to the contrary, *Roe*'s holding on the meaning of "person" in the four-teenth amendment seems secure for the present. Not only do the textual and historical arguments appear to favor *Roe*'s conclusion but institutional concerns favor it as well. The transformation of fetal interests, which the state may choose to protect, into a constitutional right, which the courts must protect, could require the judiciary to reach its own evaluation of fetal rights in a variety of situations extending beyond the abortion context, a task the Court avoided in *Roe*. Moreover, as the prior discussion of good samaritanism implies, a contrary conclusion that the fetus is a person within the meaning of the fourteenth amendment would not succeed in outlawing abortion *simpliciter*.[45]

The personhood debate reappears, however, in the analysis of the state interests that weigh against a woman's choice. Both the Court and its critics could have acknowledged a variety of interests that a state might assert for regulating abortion. But neither *Roe* nor the consensus in the ensuing debate has recognized any interest that could substantially limit a woman's access to an abortion, performed in accordance with prevailing medical practice, other than the interest in protecting the potential life of the fetus.[46] Following the philosophical debate, the ground that a state may advance against a woman's liberty interest is narrowed to the interest in a future member of the human community.

This narrowing appears to reflect a general recognition of the importance of the woman's liberty: no utilitarian calculus may trump her right to procreative liberty but only the government's interest in actual or potential new life.[47] This recognition that a woman has a constitutionally protected liberty interest (of some dimension) has gained broad acceptance over time.[48] It seems likely that as the constitutional status of parental privacy and authority over the family has survived more than sixty years—since the Court gave it recognition in *Meyer v. Nebraska* and *Pierce v. Society of Sisters*—so too will its recognition of pro-creative autonomy in the privacy cases survive, even if in the short run some justices on a reconstituted Court might seek to limit this recognition.[49] Technological advances and tendencies of a bureaucratic state will no doubt produce instances of state coercion in family matters that will provoke a judicial response founded on privacy principles. Such principles safeguard equally against prohibitions on contraception and reproduction, and against enforced sterilization and the state's use of women as breeders.

Based on her liberty interest, *Roe* implicitly struck at least one balance between a woman's right and the state interest that is relatively noncontroversial in the secular abortion debate: a state may not prohibit abortion when a woman's life is in jeopardy. Even (now Chief) Justice William Rehnquist, dissenting from *Roe*, wrote:

The Due Process Clause . . . undoubtedly does place a limit, albeit a broad one, on legislative power to enact laws such as this. If the Texas statute were to prohibit an abortion even where the mother's life is in jeopardy, I have little doubt that such a statute would lack a rational relation to a valid state objective.[50]

This conclusion treats the law of abortion in a manner consistent with the common law of self-defense and good samaritanism, neither of which compels a person to sacrifice her life when another places it at risk without justification.

The right of a woman to protect her health, at least in some serious circumstances, is also relatively uncontroversial. This conclusion presumably derives not only from her liberty interest but from the fact that a woman is a fourteenth-amendment person, while a fetus is not, and that her immediate life interests may not be thus jeopardized on its behalf.[51]

If it is uncontroversial that an exception to an abortion prohibition based on a threat to life, and possibly to health, is constitutionally mandated, then *Roe*'s basic due process methodology should be secure. At its simplest, *Roe* insists only that a state's coercive interference with a person's liberty be supported by a governmental purpose that is legitimate and sufficient to outweigh the individual's interest, and that a state's coercive means be rationally related to its purpose and not too unnecessarily burdensome of the infringed right. The easily stated test of course is exceedingly difficult of application; and doctrines of judicial deference, separation of powers, and federalism diminish its force.

Finally, *Roe*'s holding with respect to the state's interest in protecting maternal health also appears unexceptional when analyzed apart from its holding on the state's interest in fetal life. The Court has indicated it will reject as irrational a state's claim that its interest in maternal health justifies regulations that make early abortions substantially less available than they would be if simply performed according to prevailing medical practice. Such limitation in the name of medical safety would irrationally increase the medical risk to women by forcing them to endure the much greater risks of childbirth (or illegal abortion). For ease of application, the Court designated "approximately the end of the first trimester" as that point after which safety regulations burdening access to abortions performed by physicians would not be presumed to be irrational.[52]

The Controversial Roe. What is controversial in *Roe* is the relative importance that the Court attached to the state interest in potential life and to the woman's privacy interest. It deemed the latter fundamental and deemed the former insufficiently compelling, until fetal viability, to trump the woman's interest in choice.[53] Critics maintain that the Court failed to offer proper constitutional support—textual, structural, or historical—for this conclusion.[54] Such criticism and the appropriate rules of constitutional interpretation and adjudication, however, are outside the scope of this essay, which is concerned not with what branch of government announced the doctrine of abortion-choice but with its interpretation.

Roe may also stand for the controversial proposition that a woman's interest in health (which always trumps the state's interest in fetal life) includes her interest in avoiding the increased statistical risk of undergoing childbirth as compared to abortion. Whether, pursuant to a theory of good samaritan obligations, the state may force a woman to endure this greater statistical risk, on behalf of a being who is not a fourteenth-amendment person, remains unclear under *Roe*. For at present the state lacks the power, due to fetal nonviability, to prohibit elective abortions during the period of such greater statistical risk; when the state has the power to prohibit them under *Roe*, in the third trimester, the statistical safety of abortion has disappeared.[55]

Roe Criticized Within the Court

Criticism of *Roe* on the Court has substantially increased since President Reagan appointed Justice Sandra Day O'Connor, the first female Supreme Court justice, to replace a retiring supporter of *Roe*, Justice Potter Stewart. In a 1983 dissent joined by Justices Rehnquist and Byron White, she put forward the claim that *Roe* miscalculated the weight of the competing interests of the state and the woman (and by implication misconstrued the status of the fetus and the woman's good samaritan duties to it).[56]

She begins her critique by asserting that *Roe*'s trimester structure has fallen to two technological developments. As a result of medical advances, most second trimester abortions are now so much safer than childbirth as to undermine *Roe*'s treatment of the second trimester as a time of permissible state medical regulation. Second, advances in neonatology have led to sustaining for an indefinite time (but with a substantial risk of injury) some premature infants of weight and age below that noted in *Roe*. Accordingly, the date of viability is gradually moving back into the second trimester.

Her technological premise is, as of now, problematic. While the evidence on which she and the Court find abortion to be safer than childbirth is largely unquestioned, her inference about a significant downward trend in the age of viability is not. *Roe* identified viability "at about seven months (28 weeks)" or approximately 1000 grams in weight, but recognized that it "may occur earlier, even at 24 weeks."[57] The twenty-eight week old, weighing at least 1000 grams, now often has in the studies at least a 70-percent survival rate if born in or near a good hospital; and a majority of these survivors appear normal after several years of followup.

Since *Roe*, many hospitals have developed a substantially increased capacity to sustain infants between twenty-six to twenty-eight weeks gestation (since last menstrual period, or "LMP") and weighing 750 to 1000 grams, although with negative physical sequelae for some. However, the data generally indicate that below twenty-six weeks a majority, and on some readings of the data a substantial majority, will die despite the expenditure of enormous sums of money and effort to save them. The survivors have a very significant chance, approximating 20 to 30 percent, of suffering moderate to severe physical and neurological detriment, defect, and injury. Despite reports of several infants surviving at twenty-two weeks, uncertainties in determining gestational age make reports of survival below twenty-three weeks LMP dubious. In short, there has been only a moderate change in the typical age of viability since *Roe*—from two to four weeks; and *Roe* itself had acknowledged the possibility of viability at twenty-four weeks, a possibility that may now be approaching twenty-three weeks.[58]

From these data, O'Connor surprisingly concludes: "It is certainly reasonable to believe that fetal viability in the first trimester of pregnancy may be possible in the not too distant future."[59] This conclusion appears to be overly eager and unappreciative of the biological limitations on the current technology. Only in weeks twenty to twenty-four, the precise time depending on individual growth, does lung development permit oxygen exchange. Prior thereto, a delivered fetus would require an artificial placenta for life support. While technological predictions are risky, there do not appear to be substantial grounds for claiming that allocational choices, either rational or irrational, will soon lead to the development and general availability of such placentas. For they would not only present substantial technological problems but also require an improved theoretical understanding of placental function.[60]

Accepting twenty to twenty-four weeks as the absolute inside limit for viability in the near future, one must conclude that *Roe*'s trimester scheme remains robust. Although many physicians avoid potential legal problems by refusing to terminate pregnancies when the fetus is arguably within two weeks of viability, the present downward trend in viability should nonetheless have little practical impact on most women, since less than 1 percent of abortions annually occur after twenty weeks.[61]

Moreover, under present law only some of the abortions which now occur after twenty weeks would be affected by the survival of a few infants in that gestational range. For the Court has mandated that the legislature may not compel physicians to adjust their medical judgment of viability to a preestablished standard of "any chance of survival" based on the one smallest infant to have ever survived. Preserving access to abortion services late in the second trimester, the Court has instead held that viability is a medical decision, based on statistical probabilities and clinical judgment, made on a case-by-case basis by the attending physician.[62] Substantially more than 60 percent of the few infants born before twenty-five weeks of gestation now do not survive because of individual variation in lung development, weight, and other reasons. Thus, there will continue to be many pregnancies in that period in which a physician could accurately and in good faith predict that the fetus is not viable and cannot survive, whether intact or with substantial injury. Sound medical judgment does not keep pace with heroic medical experimentation. As a result, the data on which O'Connor relies should have only a limited impact on the performance of abortions.

But assuming *arguendo* that O'Connor's factual assumptions were some day to prove correct and the age of viability were to drop well into the second trimester, then the period of greater statistical safety of abortion as compared with childbirth would extend into the period of viability. This would require the Court to determine the unresolved question of whether the state may forbid an abortion undertaken to protect the woman's health, a power generally denied by *Roe*, in the event that the medical conclusion about her health were based solely on the greater statistical safety of abortion. Only in this one limited sense is *Roe*, in O'Connor's phrase, "on a collision course with itself."[63] In all other respects, *Roe's* structure would withstand changes in the age of viability. Furthermore, short of viability extending into the first trimester, over 90 percent of the decisions to terminate a pregnancy made today would continue to be protected.

But O'Connor argues that it is best to jettison *Roe* now because these technological tendencies will someday undermine *Roe's* trimester system altogether, as if eroding *Roe's* trimester scheme would erode *Roe's* balancing of interests as well.[64] With her proposed abandonment of that balance and its focus on viability, O'Connor asserts that there would be no logical point at which to conclude that the state interest in fetal life becomes compelling other than at the beginning of pregnancy.[65] Such a compelling interest would entitle state regulation of abortion throughout pregnancy to the deference that courts generally accord ordinary legislation when they impose only the minimal requirement that it bear a rational relationship to its legitimate purpose. Most any regulation that made access to abortion more problematic would survive such minimal scrutiny because it would bear a rational relationship to the purpose of protecting potential life—which becomes a legitimate purpose in the first trimester under O'Connor's proposed analysis. Accordingly, she suggests, the state may establish any number of barriers that inhibit the woman's choice from the start of pregnancy. Such barriers could be especially high since it is in the nature of the lowered judicial scrutiny O'Connor proposes that a court's review would only be from the perspective of what is burdensome to the well-to-do, rationally calculating, iron-willed woman.

Justice O'Connor asserts that she would reserve a more intense or strict scrutiny (of the kind the Court now applies to most abortion regulation) for those instances in which a state imposed "severe limitations" or "unduly burdensome" intrusions or an absolute prohibition on a woman's abortion choice.[66] However, given her view of the compelling nature of the state's interest in the fetus throughout pregnancy, it is unclear what values should guide a court in undertaking such stricter scrutiny and whether, even applying such scrutiny, it could ever justify favoring female autonomy over a legislative preference for fetal life.

Even when the state has a compelling interest in fetal life and asserts it, *Roe* identifies one superior value that affords protection of female autonomy: the woman's interest in her life and health, broadly conceived. Were O'Connor to accept this aspect of *Roe* and were she to conclude that the state may compel a woman to assume good samaritan obligations to a fetus despite the greater statistical risk of carrying it to term, then her analysis would actually return the law to a pre-*Roe* regime, found in some states, which forbade all abortions except those protecting the woman's interest in her life and health when pregnancy posed a particular threat.

Any such return to pre-*Roe* days, by the rejection of its allocation of decision-making power to the woman and her physician, would entail that former regime's exceedingly troubling procedural and equality problems. *Roe* was, after all, in part a response to the problems of procedural due process, vagueness, and equal protection associated with other regulatory schemes. Some of these schemes in practice allocated to hospital committees the exclusive power to review the reasons of women for aborting. Such committees sometimes had quotas on the number of abortions they would approve, excluded nonstaff physicians from the abortion evaluation, denied adequate representation to the woman, and rendered unreviewable decisions. Such a procedure did little to protect a woman's right to be heard and to have an independent judgment rendered in her case, and it involved a substantial invasion of her interest in informational privacy. Problems of vagueness in the criteria for lawful abortion, and the related problem of selective prosecutorial enforcement, contributed further to unfairness. These schemes allowed the availability of abortion to be so capricious that some medical settings were fifty-five times more likely to perform abortions than others; such a discrepancy is procedurally troubling to the extent that it is more the product of arbitrary and unpredictable differences in decision making and enforcement schemes than the product of differences among the states in the legal criteria for abortion. Of course, such inequalities involved substantial discrimination against the poor. As the discussion of good samaritan obligations implied, those restrictions on abortion also involved a substantial disparity in the imposition of good samaritan duties on women as compared to men; it would accordingly appear that any future limitation on abortion that the Court might permit should in fairness lead to a society-wide decrease in autonomy in favor of obligations of mutual aid.[67]

Justice O'Connor has left uncertain whether she would go further than she had proposed in her dissent and join with Justices White and Rehnquist who have urged that *Roe* be overruled altogether and that states be permitted, should they choose, to prohibit abortion completely. But significantly she has noted that she would only "assume," for purposes of her dissent, without committing herself to the proposition that "there is a fundamental right to terminate pregnancy in some situations."[68] What a demise of that fundamental right and *Roe* would entail for the privacy cases protecting contraceptive rights and family autonomy, she has not undertaken to assess.[69]

Separation

Justice O'Connor too quickly assumes that abandoning *Roe's* evaluation of when state interests become compelling leads to the conclusion that a state may substantially interfere with abortion. For if technology were to eclipse *Roe's* trimester system, it could also provide a new solution to the *Roe* equation. The technology that would lower viability might also create the conditions, at least theoretically, for a regime not of abortion but of elective separation and fetal incubation in the hospital. (I say theoretically not only because the availability of such technology is speculative but also because the risk of fetal injury during separation would probably be substantial. To the extent such risks would weigh against allowing transfer, they should probably also weigh against a finding of fetal viability early in gestation.)

This potential was apparently not appreciated by the Court that rendered *Roe*, which seems to have identified abortion of a viable fetus (in the third trimester) with fetal death. However, experience led the Court to permit a state to change that third trimester regime from one of therapeutic abortion, with attendant fetal death, to therapeutic separation of the fetus from the woman, provided that the woman's health is not jeopardized by this change.[70]

The law's emphasis upon viability may now, with O'Connor's technological focus, be understood as recognizing that viability is significant because only then does the state have the wherewithal to achieve its interest in potential life without exploiting the woman by forcing her to become a good samaritan. For the first time since conception, it can realize its interest by requiring separation where the woman would otherwise abort.

But if this is the significance of viability, why did *Roe* permit the state to further its compelling interest in the viable fetus by using (through an abortion prohibition in the third trimester) the healthy woman as an incubator and require the state to permit separation only in those rare cases involving the woman's health? This is because *Roe's* reliance on viability had earlier afforded the woman an opportunity (for approximately six months) to avoid, through abortion, being thus used by the state. After affording real choice, *Roe* did not further insist that the state realize its interest in the fetus by a means so narrowly drawn as to accommodate some woman's wish to choose not abortion in the first six months but only a nontherapeutic separation in the last three.

Roe's recognition of the state's power to ban elective abortion at viability, after approximately six months, coincides with a woman's untrammeled right to elective abortion for a substantial period prior thereto. If the latter were denied, then so might the former, in favor of a new regime of elective separation. For if technological development permitting early viability would also permit separation, constitutional considerations might require it as a significantly less burdensome accommodation of the two competing interests.[71]

Should a state assert an interest in a first trimester or early second trimester viable fetus by prohibiting abortion at a time so early in pregnancy as to preclude effective choice, a woman would, with some basis, be heard to say: "I want my separation now." With such separation, the woman could realize at least some of the interests that *Roe* protects. She could avoid many of the health risks and physical burdens of pregnancy, which concentrate in the second half of pregnancy. If performed early before public knowledge of her pregnancy, the separation could entirely protect her interest in informational privacy, in her public identity as a nonparent, and in the avoidance of the stigma of premarital pregnancy or of giving up a child for adoption. And it would spare her some of the unwanted intimacy of association with the fetus, which grows in intensity after quickening.

Accepting the philosophical claim that abortion involves hostile and competing interests of individuals or potential individuals, the commentary on *Roe*—including the work of such dissimilar commentators as constitutional scholar Laurence Tribe and the abortionist turned regulator, Dr. Bernard Nathanson—increasingly accepts elective separation as an appropriate resolution of the abortion question to the extent technology were to permit it. Even so careful a critic as Guido Calabresi, dean of Yale Law School, believes separation and mandated transfer to another woman is a solution to be desired.[72]

If it were to become not the occasion for private consensual and donative fetal transfers to committed caregivers but rather the basis for state coercion through an abortion prohibition, this technological accommodation of competing interests could create a Huxleyan horror. The ancient phrase *parens patriae* would acquire new and pathetic meaning. The country's most important "parents" could become the states of New York and California, with thousands of abandoned fetuses (many only a couple of inches long) filling neonatal units at enormous expense. Departments of human services would make medical decisions for them, involving the most serious of allocational choices and the most serious of consequences for the fetus' future life. It could be anticipated that a new due process of orphans would develop since each of those choices would involve state action. Without mothers and fathers involved in these decisions, how would the state decide who is to survive and what treatment is to be administered? A technological version of *Roe*, like Justice O'Connor's, tends toward this technological nightmare.

If this is an exaggeration, a theoretical and macabre imagining only, then it must be because women, if denied abortion, would generally prefer to rear their own children than put them out to state hatcheries, as many presently prefer abortion or raising their own children to adoption. This points to a central aspect of human procreation that the individualistic categories of the abortion debate fail to capture: the deep, constitutive, identity-defining attachment between women and their offspring. This attachment generally leads women, with their mates if possible, to rear the children they bear until maturity leads to independence.

2

A Search for a
Logic of Attachment

NOTING DEFICIENCIES IN THE SUBSTANCE AND LANGUAGE OF THE debate reviewed thus far, some would altogether reject its individualistic, rights-based categories. They ascribe its language to an atomistic society comprised of self-interested and apparently self-sufficient rights-holders, held together by nothing more than a social contract. Disagreeing with liberal contractarian theory, which postulates individuals as antecedent to community, they prefer to understand society as a web of communal obligations that predate individuals and give them meaning. This approach begins with a rhetoric of solidarity, employing such terms as *commitment, caring,* and *community* as well as the concepts of *natural, nature,* and *necessity.* Calling the deregulator's language that of the amoral consumer of microeconomic theory, exercising her subjective preferences as if they were sovereign, these critics prefer the language of a welcoming connectedness that understands the tragic centrality of suffering and sacrifice in human life. They would therefore recast the language of rights into the language of duties, the duties owed by a moral person to others and especially the needy and the innocent.[1]

Yet the question of abortion cannot simply be answered by shifting from an analysis of rights to an analysis of the duties individuals owe one another. The same questions arise in reverse, albeit with a different valence: what is the nature of the duty; at what point in fetal development is the duty owed; and how do the life circumstances of the pregnant woman affect the proposed duty? Nor can the ethic of care be justly or effectively implemented without respect for the caregiver. To seek to replace the language of rights with the language of duty is to risk excluding women from the respect and autonomy that the language of rights affords, for rights and liberties are the currency by which our society and law extend recognition and respect to a person and her autonomous will.[2] Finally, if antiabortionists intend to regulate, to impose their moral evaluation of abortion on others, then they must make their argument amenable to the language of rights. For at law, especially constitutional law, the discourse of rights dominates to the exclusion of all else. Thus Noonan, the law professor and judge, continues to insist upon the rights of the fetus, even as he blames deregulators for the logic of a debate that leads to separation and abortion, and even as he calls for the "surpassing of such [abortion] liberty by love."[3]

While the language of rights cannot be abandoned, this criticism of the rhetoric of the debate merits further consideration. For the foregoing analyses, of whether the woman and fetus are discrete rights-bearing individuals with antagonistic interests, lead to a characterization of procreation and to descriptions of the woman and fetus that are partial at best. As noted in chapter 1, the concept of personhood, used to assess the status of the fetus, fails to comprehend their interconnectedness. To the extent that the personhood some attribute to the fetus suggests the autonomy and individuality typically associated with a rights-holder, it is an abstraction that as likely dulls our appeciation of the fetus' extreme dependence and vulnerability as sharpens our respect for it. In treating their relationship as one of negative rights, deregulator and regulator alike convey that woman and fetus are strangers to each other despite fetal need and the intensity of many a woman's response to pregnancy, to her own flesh and blood. Also unsatisfactory is the exclusive derivation of the woman's good samaritan duty to her offspring from the obligations arising from genital heterosexuality, that is, from matters partially extrinsic to the maternal relationship; for by implying that what the offspring needs the woman can simply be coerced to give, the regulator risks omitting love and nurturance. Perhaps most troubling of all, were medical-funding choices eventually to result in artificial placentas, an exclusively rights-based analysis could logically lead to a regime of separation in which abandoned fetuses are raised in state hatcheries. This specter of solipsistic anonymity should heighten appreciation for what is left out: that between woman and fetus the attachment is not merely strong but constitutive of their individuality, their identity.

To understand abortion more fully, a supplementary approach would be useful that does not omit the constitutive attachments within and through which fetuses become the particular children of particular parents and then rights-bearing citizens themselves. Such an account would explain the development of persons in families in relation to each other and acknowledge that they are implicated in each other's lives, without yielding the individual respect that is a person's due. It would presumably not define personhood as if it were a solitary achievement of the fetus and its DNA that precedes rather than presupposes participation in the primary community of woman and fetus. Thus, it would attempt more fully to articulate the fetus-woman relationship and more adequately to account for the metamorphosis of fetuses into persons and women into mothers through this attachment. What that relationship requires would be relevant to defining the obligations of its members to it. The method must accordingly explain what maternity requires of a woman, and inquire into the conditions under which she may appropriately provide what is needed. An account with these characteristics could more fully comprehend procreation and illuminate the law of abortion-choice.

The impetus to develop such a supplementary account has been encouraged by recent work—in such fields as political philosophy, feminist theory, and developmental psychology—that attempts to locate the person within his or her relationships in a preexisting community. This communal precondition, this fundamental interconnectedness, was evocatively conveyed by John Winthrop, first governor of the Massachusetts Bay Colony, in his shipboard sermon long ago, when he referred to "our community as members of the same body." Since membership in a family and citizenship in the state are determined primarily by who, having once been part of her same body, emerges from the womb of one of the women members, the questions of abortion and communal membership are closely linked.[4]

The emphasis in political theory on communal membership as a necessary precondition of the self and source of rights is in recent evidence, for example, in the work of the political philosopher Michael Sandel. He has directed his attention toward the constitutive quality of relationships and communities for the person and toward the intersubjective nature of the self. Because persons are in part constituted by their communal memberships, he questions the liberal postulate that the self exists exclusively *a priori*, apart from its attachments to others. Accordingly, he has criticized the account of the autonomous ego of Kant's and Rawl's deontological liberalism with which the theory of personhood in the secular abortion debate is sometimes linked. Empirically, persons are nowhere so disembodied, so unattached, so unmolded by their historically and culturally rooted experience as, he asserts, liberal theory's vision of the self requires. Nor would such a "thin" self, some argue, be worthy of the moral respect that liberal theory accords the autonomous ego.[5] Indeed, the neonatal unit filled with orphan fetuses bound to artificial placentas appears as the caricatured and embodied approximation of the Rawlsian original position as Sandel describes it: without a sponsoring tradition, history, or family.

The philosopher Ferdinand Schoeman has developed a not unrelated argument that focuses more narrowly on the problematic ascription of rights to children in families. In a particularly compact and felicitous essay (that does not deal with abortion), he suggests that the language of rights "may obscure" understanding of the parent-child relationship and may even be destructive of family bonds. Rights-based arguments stress distance and boundaries between persons but are "short on caring and intimacy and insensitive to the state of dependency and vulnerability into which children are born and remain for several years." The "traditional moral boundaries, which give rigid shape to the self," fail to comprehend the "relationship between parent and infant [which] involves an awareness of a kind of union between people. . . . We *share our selves* with those with whom we are intimate."[6]

The family project of childrearing requires intimacy, a "blurring the boundaries of individual identity." Intimacy in turn requires privacy and autonomy from state intervention. To preserve the necessary intimacy, and the privacy it requires, Schoeman would reserve rights language for the interaction of family members with the outside world. But for intrafamilial matters, he urges that "[p]arents can be seen as representing the interest of the family as an integrated whole in addition to representing their own particular interests . . . even when what is at issue is a conflict in interest between the parent as individual and the child as individual."[7]

One strand of feminist theory has similarly criticized the emphasis in ethical and political theory upon the autonomous individuated ego and its rights, an overemphasis it attributes to masculine values.[8] The critique has even extended to the dominant modes of scientific thought, including the description of DNA as the master of organismic individuality, as if an organism were not fundamentally shaped by interaction with its environment.[9] Some are beginning to apply this criticism to the abortion debate, trying to transcend its rights-based categories with a relational approach in ways akin to this essay.[10]

Those studying the psychology of women have been especially alert to this critique. For example, Carol Gilligan writes that masculine psychologies tend to emphasize the autonomous identity of individuated selves; and masculine moralities tend to emphasize justice, which is defined as the rules of the game by which a fair accommodation of distinct selves may be achieved. But these masculine accounts do not adequately capture the full experience of women, who tend to define themselves far more than do men by their relationship with significant others, and their morality far more by their capacity to care for those to whom they are attached. Gilligan writes:

[T]he morality of rights differs from the morality of responsibility in its emphasis on separation rather than connection, in its consideration of the individual rather than the relationship as primary.[11]

Accordingly, women psychologists have started to delineate a theory of the "the relational self," with the person defined more by her attachments than by the concept of ego identity with its implication of a self-defining and largely individuated autonomy.[12]

Finally, advances within developmental psychology suggest that the importance of the infant-caregiver bond as constitutive of the infant must be given the attention that custom and folkways have long accorded it. Academic infant psychology has moved well beyond purely perceptual and cognitive studies, which treated the infant as a separate and individuated being, to attempt to account for the development of the self through human relatedness. Though of no great surprise to mothers and fathers, this research has illuminated the rich world of the baby's interaction with its caregivers, finding perceptual and cognitive capabilities and vulnerabilities far beyond what had previously been described. With slow-motion photography researchers have captured, frame by frame, an extraordinary synchrony of interaction between mother and infant, leading some experimenters to speak of a mother and infant regulatory unit. In other research, longitudinal studies have detailed the significance of maternal attachment and its deprivation.[13]

This then describes the project of the remainder of this essay: to develop a supplementary approach to abortion, as described above, that comprehends the constitutive relationship of woman and fetus through which personhood develops; and then to interpret the law of abortion-choice, exemplified by *Roe v. Wade*, as establishing a rights-based regime which takes account of that relational understanding.[14]

We shall see that when we follow the advice to supplement the debate on rights with an ethic of love, the result may not be what some expect.

3

Abortion and
Symbiotic Attachment

To UNDERSTAND THE FETUS PROPERLY THE "DISTINCTION BETWEEN persons,"[1] at their origins, must be reevaluated. Inquiry into its status should begin not with the fetus in isolation but with the relationship in which the offspring develops into a person. That relationship is of a different order from those whose participants social convention and ordinary language treat as distinct selves. Instead, common wisdom understands that mother and offspring belong together, as, for example, the mother-infant motif in a myriad of paintings attests. Constituting a whole, they may not be readily understood apart from each other. For their relationship, central to an understanding of potential life, is constitutive of the offspring's eventual self. By treating the fetus not as a person or as a potential person but rather as a constituent and constituted part of a whole, a relational approach may supplement the individualistic language that has attended the abortion debate and counteract its logic of separateness, as it tries to locate rights in one or the other of woman and fetus.

To explore this claim and to indicate what a relational account of personhood might look like, I shall employ for illustrative purposes one available relational description of human nature. That account derives from psychoanalysis and, in particular, from the investigations of its object-relations school, for it provides a workable and compelling description of the relationship between the woman and her offspring. After setting

38

forth that account in the next section, I shall turn to its application to the law of procreative choice.

PSYCHOANALYTIC THEMES: INDIVIDUALITY, DEPENDENCE, AND FUSION

A Note on the Use of Psychoanalysis

While not without methodological problems and many doubters, psychoanalysis has among its virtues several that recommend its use here to illustrate a relational approach. First, Freud's work has the quality of according respect to persons by placing at its therapeutic center a self capable of freedom, to at least a limited degree, through rational introspection, self-knowledge, and choice. This links it to at least some of the theories of personhood reviewed in chapter 1. At the same time, psychoanalytic object relations theory provides an account of the self's origin in intimate and fused relationship with others and, in particular, with its caregiving mother. Developed by certain second-generation analysts through the careful and prolonged study of and involvement with patients' lives, this theory describes human growth as a process of separation and individuation from an original maternal matrix. Freud's work, when combined with this later-developed object-relations theory, maintains a critical tension between a respect for individuality and a protection of commonality.

In addition, the language of psychoanalysis is especially attuned to the task of describing the infantile state. Its development of a special terminology of dependency for describing human infancy, though off-putting to some, serves as a potent reminder that ordinary language and thought should not be presumed adequate for describing this preverbal period of extraordinary dependence and immaturity.

Finally, in its analyses of parent and child, psychoanalysis is rooted in the study of intergenerational tensions, of the needs of

children for committed adult care as they struggle for independence, and the needs of adults to care for others, often through
reproduction and care of their own children and their children's
children. In studying the present delicate balance between the
individual struggle for autonomy and freedom and the cultural
struggle for an intergenerational ecology, psychoanalysts attempt to provide an account of regeneration.[2] Thus its developmental theory centers upon tensions found in the dilemmas of
abortion.

What follows is an account of the origins of the self in infantile symbiosis with the mother, drawn selectively from the work
of a few of the more evocative of those psychoanalytic writers
who first helped to develop an object-relations point of view. It is
put forward at some length and technical detail not because all
the details are essential to the subsequent interpretation of the
law of procreative choice, nor because all the details are obviously correct, but precisely to evoke what is now at the periphery of the abortion debate: mother-love and love for the mother.

I would encourage those who doubt the psychoanalytic enterprise, both as a form of knowledge related to the social sciences and as a contribution to ethical discourse, not to dismiss
the following analytic description altogether. It should at least
be treated as a metaphorical attempt to take certain difficult
questions about human procreation seriously and to communicate about a degree of dependence and human need, adult and
infantile, that common observations confirm but that our language is ill equipped to describe—because among other reasons
that condition occurs most intensely when words are absent.
The following analytic account affords a language for those common observations on which the remainder of chapter 3 builds.[3]

An Object-Relations Account of Personhood

Freud's psychoanalytic psychology appears intensely individualistic. The road to mental disease is an internal one of personal and inescapable conflict; and the road to health is, if
it exists at all, similarly found from within. Freud aimed his
therapy at the symptoms and inhibitions that interfere with a

patient's realization of his own goals, which express an aspect of his identity. Flight from individuality through the loss of self in others was viewed with analytic suspicion—whether that loss occurred as love of the analyst in transference, in overidealization of a mate, in subordination of one's judgment to a group, or in subjugation to a *führer* and his *volk*.

Because of this heightened individualism, some read Freud as providing "considerable support for our reigning notions about freedom and privacy" in which freedom is the absence of social constraint, happiness is the satisfaction of private desire, and human relations, as with Hobbes, are fundamentally "forms of antagonism."[4] These are the terms of the philosophical and legal arguments discussed above, in which the woman and fetus are described atomistically, their interests are said to conflict, and a woman is perceived as realizing her freedom only at the expense of the fetus.

The very existence of personhood Freud at first took for granted.[5] But late in his life, Freud began to explore the origins of the individuality that his therapy sought to strengthen. When he did, different themes—of attachment and fusion—began to emerge. As Freud explored the origins of the "I," or the ego, the central role of the mother came steadily into focus. As early as 1905, he had postulated:

[A] child sucking at his mother's breast has become the prototype of every relation of love. The [adult] finding of an object [relationship] is in fact a refinding of it.[6]

The mode of this first loving relationship, he concluded, is the infant's incorporation of the mother physically by sucking and mentally by a psychic taking in, which Freud called identification. This "type of love . . . is consistent with abolishing the object's separate existence."[7] The ego of the infant develops through identification with the mother, with whom at first it is at one; only as time passes is she increasingly experienced as the "other."

If central to the development of the self is an attachment in which the boundaries of self and other are absent and in which satisfaction arises not despite or through the other but *in* the other, then a very different Freud emerges, possibly with a different moral and political outlook. It begins to appear that respecting persons and protecting the autonomous ego require recognition and acceptance of a prior condition of interrelatedness. A new, less individualistic frame of reference becomes available.[8]

This other Freud provides the foundation for the more recent emphasis, among many psychoanalysts, on fusion in accounting for the origins of individual personhood. As a result of their observations and therapeutic work, these analysts have concluded that, in each human being, there is a very deep layer of experience, dating back to the earliest days of infancy and even into the womb during the last stages of pregnancy, that may be characterized as nonindividual existence.[9] The offspring experiences the world as part of itself, and itself as part of its primary caretaker; the infant is unable to tell what is inside, within its body, and what is outside and from another. Developmentally, this means that at the beginning, during some number of months around the time of birth, there exists a period of human symbiosis with the mother.[10]

This term "symbiosis," borrowed from biology and transmuted in the borrowing, is meant to suggest a dependence so great that it can be said that the fetus-infant, as it may be called, does not exist as a separate being but in fusion with the mother.[11] Without specifying its exact parameters, I shall use the phrase "fetus-infant" to emphasize the infant's gradual development from symbiosis into an individuated state. It implies not fetal personhood—as regulators urge when they deny any coherent dividing line between fetus and infant—but rather emphasizes the dependent interconnectedness of fetus and infant alike with the woman-mother.

A story in Plato's *The Symposium* long ago gave expression to the centrality of this fusion. In relating the following myth, Aristophanes explains that the origin, goal, and nature of love is the reunification of incomplete persons with each other:

Suppose Hephaestus with his tools were to visit them as they lie together, and stand over them and ask: "What is it, mortals, that you hope to gain from one another?" Suppose too that when they could not answer he repeated his question in these terms: "Is the object of your desire to be always together as much as possible, and never to be separated from one another day or night? If that is what you want, I am ready to melt and weld you together, so that, instead of two, you shall be one flesh; as long as you live you shall live a common life, and when you die, you shall suffer a common death, and be still one, not two, even in the next world. Would such a fate as this content you, and satisfy your longings?" We know what their answer would be; no one would refuse the offer; it would be plain that this is what everybody wants, and everybody would regard it as the precise expression of the desire which he had long felt but had been unable to formulate, that he should melt into his beloved, and that henceforth they should be one being instead of two. The reason is that this was our primitive condition when we were wholes, and love is simply the name for the desire and pursuit of the whole.[12]

The person experiences separate individuality as a defect, and the joy of love not as an active loving individual but rather as part of a dyadic whole.

Analysts developing object-relations theory have reached the same conclusion as Aristophanes, except that by "primitive" they do not mean the prehistory of the race but the preindividual history of the person. Furthermore, they assert that this preindividual history in symbiotic fusion is essential to the subsequent development of personhood. Thus, fusion is the precondition for the infant's becoming a person, as *Roe* aptly put it, "in the whole sense."[13]

For example, based on lengthy observation of infants and toddlers, the analyst Margaret Mahler describes the "psychological birth of the individual," from physical birth through the third year of life, as a process of separation and individuation from a state of union with the primary caregiver. Following a symbiotic period of fusion comes a period of "hatching" out of the "maternal matrix," which begins at five to six months after birth. Brief at first, these hatching experiences require many repetitions before the infant gradually comes to experience and tolerate separateness. Indeed, not until three years of age is the "I" firmly established. In accord with other analysts, Mahler makes "*the* central dimension of psychological development" in the human being "the move from a state of complete dependence and relative lack of differentiation between self and other to increasing definition of self and to increasing independence."[14]

The analyst and pediatrician D. W. Winnicott describes symbiosis this way:

[T]he infant and the maternal care belong to each other and cannot be disentangled. These two things, the infant and the maternal care, disentangle and dissociate themselves [over time] in health; and health . . . to some extent means a disentanglement of maternal care from something which we then call the infant or the beginnings of a growing child.[15]

Indeed, "the inherited potential of an infant cannot become an infant unless linked to maternal care."[16] During symbiosis, the mother conforms herself to the infant and devotes herself to meeting the infant's needs as exactly as possible, so that it can take the world for granted and enjoy a brief experience of having needs promptly satisfied—what Winnicott calls an experience of "omnipotence"—until it is strong enough to tolerate the frustration of her gradual nonconformity to its infantile desires. Following the disentanglement, the child achieves, in Winnicott's phrase, the capacity to be alone in the presence of his mother; he exists with an individuality that comprehends separateness, an inside and out, because the earlier fused relationship with the mother has been internalized.[17]

While most mothers are, in Winnicott's phrase, "good enough" to supply just what infants need, some are not.[18] Where this initial entanglement is absent or unsatisfactory, the impact on the child may be significant. The psychoanalyst Rene Spitz studied those infants who lacked that "good enough" mother, indeed had no mother at all: babies left in institutions for months without any special persons to care for them, having to make do with the physical care of the staff. Denied their needs for mother, for the love of the one (as distinguished from the impersonal ministrations of the many), they became subject to a variety of disturbances. Without a degree of personal care, some grew depressed and more depressed, and some succumbed. This syndrome, "hospitalism," is marked, says Spitz, by a mortality rate far in excess of that of infants bonded with caregivers.

Another analyst, Selma Fraiberg, has studied infants who are starving to death while in the care of their mothers—the "failure to thrive" infants. These infants are subjected to such ambivalence, rejection, failures of acceptance, and incompetence that they start losing weight and become at risk of irreversible damage, including severe personality problems, learning disabilities, mental retardation, and possibly death.

Even when the infant does not appear to be physically at risk, failures in early caregiving may, depending on individual vulnerabilities, cause psychic trauma, producing a variety of disturbances in the sense and coherence of self. These disturbances include failures of personalization and realization—the incapacity to live within one's body as a self in relation to an external world; and the impairment of the capacity to become attached and related to others—the disorders of nonattachment. The consequences have been known under such diagnostic labels as borderline, schizoid, and narcissistic. Such persons may complain of fundamental dissatisfaction with life: a deep withdrawal from reality, from their own affective life, from their bodies, and from others, all leading to feelings of unreality. Their lives seem unlived.[19]

Because years of traditional psychotherapy had failed to touch such patients, some analysts came to the conclusion that a deeper level, a more intimate contact between patient and therapist had first to be reached through regression to the earliest infantile period of symbiosis before a cure could be effected. Cure required not the traditional psychoanalytic work of exploring the patient's conscious and unconscious self through his thoughts and feelings, but rather the provision, within the constraints of the analytic setting, of an experience of fusion that the patient wanted. This had to be provided from without, not analyzed from within, because of the nature of symbiotic need for the other.

For example, the analyst Michael Balint, who wrote especially vividly of this, notes that some patients' ills arise not from their personal difficulties in controlling impulses or resolving conflicting affect but rather from "something missing" in their earliest experience. To convey the seriousness of this deficiency, Balint describes it as a "basic fault" in the psyche, which he attributes to a "considerable discrepancy" between an infant's psychological needs and its environmental provision. This environmental deficiency leaves in some patients "an unquenchable and incontestable feeling that, if the loss [or deficiency] cannot be made good, the patient himself will remain no good and had better go mad or even die."[20] This basic fault has consequences which "appear to be only partly reversible" and then only if the person can make a "new beginning" of his life. In therapy, a new beginning depends on the analytic situation recreating a maternal matrix of "primary love." To achieve this, the patient and analyst must go through, in Balint's evocative phrases, a "phase of the undifferentiated environment . . . of the primary substances . . . of the harmonious interpenetrating mix-up," akin to "[f]oetus, amniotic fluid, and placenta . . . [which are] a complicated interpenetrating mix-up of foetus and environment-mother."[21] At such a time, the environment has hardly any structure and no sharp boundaries; environment and individual are one.[22]

The analyst must give himself over to the patient in the world of primary love: "there must not, and cannot, be any clash of interests between subject and environment,"[23] between patient and analyst. An analyst unwilling consciously or unconsciously to tolerate the intimacy and strains of such a regression to primary love forestalls cure. These strains include the toleration of those powerful affects that adults do their psychic best to avoid or deny, including intense hate evoked by the infantile demands of the patient, and anxiety about the loss of ego boundaries and the related fear of self-annihilation that precede the return to primary love. Thus the analyst's provision of this primary love requires his full consent and participation:

[The analyst] must—tacitly or explicitly—consent to be used, otherwise the patient cannot achieve any change: without water it is impossible to swim. . . . The substance, the analyst, must not resist, must consent, must not give rise to too much friction, must accept and carry the patient for a while, must prove more or less indestructible, must not insist on maintaining harsh boundaries, but must allow the development of a kind of mix-up between the patient and himself.

All this means consent, participation, and involvement.[24]

But this consent and participation does not elicit the patient's appreciation. For regressed to the period of primary love, he takes for granted the extreme efforts of the analyst to meet his needs. Indeed, he acts and feels as if his caregiver altogether lacks any separate individuality:

This primitive—egoistic—form of love works according to the principle: what is good for me is right for you, i.e. it does not recognize any difference between one's own interests and the interests of the object; it assumes as a matter of fact that the partner's desires are identical with one's own.[25]

In summary, these experiences in treating severe pathologies have led analysts deeper and further back, to the earliest mother-infant relationship and to the paradigm of the fused symbiosis before boundaries coalesce and personhood develops. Never fearing a paradox, Winnicott summed up this perspective when he said: "There is no such thing as a baby."[26] "[A] baby is always part of someone."[27] He added:

[I]f you set out to describe a baby, you will find you are describing a *baby and someone*. A baby cannot exist alone, but is essentially part of a relationship.[28]

To repeat, there is no such thing as a baby, there is only a dyadic mother-infant unit. Our particular individuality exists because, first, some caregiver, sufficiently unambivalent, chose to care for us and merge with us and let us merge with her.[29]

THE RULE OF MOTHER-LOVE

The dyadic language that psychoanalysis has developed for describing our secular origins comprehends, I shall argue, the relationship of woman and fetus. The resulting understanding of the fetus in a relational field not only can clarify the status of the fetus at common law but also can deepen the meaning of the procreational privacy that the law protects. As discussed shortly, clarified also are analyses of the two competing interests that the law of procreative choice has identified: the woman's liberty interest, her mother-right, and the state's interest in potential human life. From this enhanced understanding comes an interpretation of the legal regime of choice that focuses not on fetal viability but on the reasonable period of time a woman needs to act on behalf of the dyadic unit as its representative, and to choose whether to make her constitutive commitment to it of mother-love. In the unlikely event that technological change were to undermine the reasonable period of choice that viability has thus far afforded, then this interpretation could be used to replace the viability standard.

The Nature of the Fetus and the Dyadic Unit

For at least the first several months after birth, as psychoanalysts suggest, it is more appropriate to speak of a mother-infant dyadic or symbiotic unit than of an infant. It is appropriate similarly to understand the fetus, which is physically attached to the woman, as a part of this dyadic whole. For if anything the term "symbiosis" is more appropriate to the interconnections of woman and fetus: the fetus is more dependent, more intertwined, and less arguably possessed of an even partially differentiated self than the infant. Nor does the period of infantile symbiosis or dyadic unity, as psychoanalysts apply these terms to infants, mark an abrupt break from an earlier fetal period of individuated development; rather, the prior fetal condition of attachment appears to lead epigenetically into the fused postbirth symbiotic state of the infant. Indeed, one of the purposes of the symbiotic concept is to emphasize the extreme immaturity and dependent nature, the fetus-like character, of the infant. This concept is capacious enough to include both the biological and the psychological interconnections of the fetus-infant and woman.[30] At first the dyad maintains itself primarily biologically, although the woman's sexual and procreative inclinations usually play a major part in its formation. But the woman's autonomous decisions become increasingly important as pregnancy develops until, after birth, her chosen commitment (or that of one acting as her proxy) to the dyad becomes essential to its survival and growth. It is this dyadic unit which the woman maintains that provides the biological and psychological substrate for the later individuation and personhood of the infant.

Given this description of woman and fetus, it is plausible to suggest that the law, for at least some purposes, may acknowledge the dyad of woman and fetus, rather than each separately, as the appropriate unit of analysis. Such acknowledgment, at least for heuristic purposes, would prove profitable, for it would not only augment understanding of the law of abortion but also clarify the status of the fetus at common law and *Roe*'s relationship to that law.[31]

Moreover, such a description preserves much of the relevance of rights-language even as it understands the fetus in relational terms, an advantage noted in chapter 2. Although object-relations theory may encourage some reevaluation of our atomistic conception of individuality, it nonetheless treats human beings as autonomous individuals for much of their life cycle and thus as bearers of rights of respect. Only at the very beginning of life does it identify not an individual but instead a dyadic unit, which itself has interests against third-party interference that the law may protect by according it rights.

The Dyad at Common Law.   Over the past several decades, the law has shown a growing solicitude for the fetus by increasingly allowing tort recovery and criminal vindication for injuries suffered *in utero*, where previously the law had denied such protection. The relationship of the law of abortion-choice to this development is the source of some perplexity for those who see in this trend the just recognition of fetal personhood. When faced with trying to reconcile the law of abortion-choice with these common law developments, some courts, similiarly perceiving a contradiction, have mistakenly used *Roe* to rationalize their denial of legal protection to the fetus. As one court, in refusing to permit a wrongful death action on behalf of a previable fetus, asserted:

If the mother can intentionally terminate the pregnancy at three months, without regard to the rights of the fetus, it becomes increasingly difficult to justify holding a third person liable to the fetus for unknowingly and unintentionally, but negligently, causing the pregnancy to end at that same stage.[32]

Understanding the fetus not as an individual creature with interests but instead as a constituent member of a dyadic whole, which in turn possesses rights that the law should protect against third-party interference, could eliminate such perplexity. From this perspective, the law of abortion-choice and these developments in tort and criminal law are both part of the same trend of extending to the dyad the legal protection it deserves. *Roe* protects its autonomy from state interference, and tort and criminal law from wrongful interference by third persons.

This common law development has primarily involved actions in tort to recover for automobile accidents, medical malpractice, and other injuries inflicted upon the fetus. Recovery for such injuries has been allowed even for a negligent blood transfusion given a woman prior to conception. After it is born alive, the child (or, if it subsequently dies, the child's estate) then sues for these prebirth injuries. If the fetus dies *in utero* as a result of such wrongs, some recent legislation and judicial decisions permit the representative of the fetus, typically a parent, to sue in a wrongful death action. If the law has spoken in more customary individual terms by naming the after-born fetus, or its estate, as the plaintiff, that need not obscure the live object of protection: the woman-fetus dyadic couple and the emotional expectancy of the pregnant woman and her mate in that couple.

More recent common law developments have included wrongful birth actions. In such an action, a parent seeks recovery not for any injury to the fetus but for the very fact of its conception or birth. Thus, a woman may sue a physician whose negligence proximately caused an unwanted conception, through a faulty sterilization or other negligent provision of birth control, or through improper genetic counseling that failed to alert the plaintiff to the risks of conception. Or she may sue a physician whose negligence led to an unwanted birth through an incomplete abortion or through a failure of fetal diagnosis that forestalled the termination of the pregnancy. These actions may be understood as protecting the dyad's autonomy against third-party injury and, more specifically, as protecting the choice of the woman acting as dyadic representative, a concept that will be developed later.[33]

But pursuing the law's atomistic logic of treating the fetus as an independent entity to its final conclusion, some children have recently sought a remedy analogous to their parents' wrongful birth claims, on the ground that they have suffered a separate and independent wrong. Mostly without success, they have asserted that their very existence is a wrong to them and a compensable injury. Such "wrongful life" actions complain not of any prenatal physical injury but of an intentional or negligent act that resulted in an "unwanted" life. Those who wrongfully and proximately caused the plaintiff to be conceived or not aborted are the defendants. These actions may lie primarily where a technicality, such as an elapsed statute of limitations, bars the parents from recovering through a wrongful birth action. But they have the potential for radically expanding and altering tort liability in this area; for they expand not only the kinds of harms that are compensable but also the range of possible defendants. Some courts have even invited a child to sue his parents for their failure to abort or avoid conception when, as a result of genetic or congenital defect or miserable life circumstance, his life is a trouble to him.[34]

The dyadic concept affords a rationale for precluding such wrongful life actions against parents; for it estops the minor plaintiff who is bound by the choice of the dyadic mother to give birth, a decision which the minor bears as his own. More generally, the dyadic concept provides a rationale for the current uneasy rejection by courts of most wrongful life actions: for the protected interest belongs to the dyadic unit and not to the separate selves of parent and child.

Finally, the dyadic concept may usefully clarify the legal status of zygotes created as a result of *in vitro* fertilization. In a typical procedure, multiple ova are chemically induced in a donating woman and then fertilized in the laboratory in order to increase the likelihood of a successful outcome. Because not all of the resulting zygotes are then implanted in the gestational mother, a zygote will have been created that is not intended to and never will become an infant and is not sponsored by an adult who intends to care for it. A zygote created *in vitro* but never implanted for gestation would under a dyadic approach possess no individual interest entitling it to be preserved, apart from the decision of the woman donor acting as dyadic representative. To endow such a zygote with a right to life, as if it had an existence independent of the adult who intended its conception and nurture, or, at the opposite extreme, to treat it only as property of the clinic, or as an escheat to the state, could create serious problems.[35] Destruction of these zygotes, in accordance with the donor's intent, would be the appropriate end for an entity that lacks the maternal commitment of one who has originated it and is prepared to enter into a symbiotic relationship with it. While their adoption could be arranged without maternal authorization, it would more effectively affirm the principle of human bondedness to permit this only when the donor, or possibly the intended mother as her proxy, has provided for this eventuality. The principle of maternal sponsorship limits the *Brave New World* potential of this technology.

The Dyad and the Law of Abortion: The Mother as Dyadic Representative. Recognizing the relevance and reconciling capacity of a supraindividual unit like the dyad is, of course, no innovation in the law. Nor is acknowledging a unit's decision-making capacity with respect to matters affecting it. Thus, decision making on behalf of the dyadic unit, and its future, may be located in it. But the manner in which supraindividual units reach decisions affecting the interests of their members, and the limits upon such decisions, are matters of much legal complexity. Such units as partnerships, corporations, labor unions, and other associations typically do not substitute for the individuals who comprise them; and their decisions are constrained by the rights of their constituent members.

With respect to personal relationships, the common law has, in the past, treated the husband-and-wife relationship as a fusion of two persons into one common supramarital identity represented solely by the husband, thus suppressing a female individuality and decisional capacity. Mindful of this history the Supreme Court has taken pains to eschew such a characterization of marriage in its privacy doctrine:

[T]he marital couple is not an independent entity with a mind and heart of its own, but an association of two individuals each with a separate intellectual and emotional makeup.[36]

In partial contrast, in analyzing the relationship of parents and their born children, the Court has emphasized that there is a presumption that an identity of interests exists between parent and immature child or that parents act in their child's best interest. Indeed, the constitutional doctrine of privacy compels the state to respect that presumption unless rebutted, and to give deference to parental choices on behalf of their immature children.[37]

The law of procreative choice does not merely presume irrebuttably an identity of interests between a woman and a separate fetus. It may rather be understood as treating the woman-fetus couple as an independent entity, and as accepting the woman as the sole legal representative of the unit and of its nonindividual constituent.[38] The law, so interpreted, further insists that the woman, as the unit's complete representative, be left unconstrained in making the unit's fundamental decisions respecting its continuation and dissolution.[39] By treating her as the exclusive decision maker, the law may take cognizance of the fact that the pregnant woman is the only part of the unit with any reality-testing and decisional capacity. For unlike the married couple and the parent and maturing child, the woman-fetus dyad does not consist entirely of individuals with separate biologies and largely separate personalities.

But why should fetal dependency and fusion preclude recognizing the fetus as having a sufficient interest under the law to justify the regulation of the manner in which the woman may cause the dissolution of the unit? For if simple dependence were the test of whether a person has rights, all rights would disappear. No man or woman is an autarky; all society is a mutual interdependence. Remove the farmer and I may soon cease to exist; but that does not give the farmer rights over my existence. As the political philosopher Charles Taylor has observed about theories in which rights are primary, the vision of autonomous rights-bearing persons does not presuppose individual isolation and self-sufficiency.[40] Indeed, the contractarian theory of rights recognizes that the vulnerability of persons requires the modification of natural rights; and, in their stead, it develops a system of rights in furtherance of mutual interdependence.

One difference between my relationship with the farmer and the fetus-infant's relationship with its mother is this: my well-being and the farmer's as citizens require only our equal respect as autonomous rights-bearing persons; the farmer is not himself a direct constituent of my identity. But the fetus-infant, in its natural state of physical and psychological fusion and vulnerability, needs not simple respect but a personal and prolonged devotion of care amounting to love. Put differently, respect for the nature of the fetus-infant requires recognition of the dyadic unit of which it is a fused part.

Some criticize *Roe* for erroneously applying the privacy doctrine to the woman's choice because her choice involves another as well.[41] But the privacy the law of abortion-choice protects is not the Millian privacy of classical liberal theory: the sufficient-self's right to be let alone, which stops where another's right begins. Rather, it protects the intimacies of an extraordinary fused relationship, within which its adult constituent is disposed to provide mother-love because she has been accorded freedom and privacy with respect to it. Through such intimacy, her offspring eventually comes to have an autonomous personhood, with rights of his own.

Mother-Right

The woman's right, what *Roe* treats as her fourteenth amendment, due-process liberty interest, is the right to determine whether she will enter into a physical and emotional symbiosis with the fetus-infant and, more generally, into a love relationship of parenting.

This is not a simple matter of bodily autonomy. Mother-right substantially differs from the right to separate from the fetus, toward which the logic of the abortion debate appears to move.

Mother-right is not fully captured by an interpretation of *Roe* as a case about the power of the state to coerce intimate acts. The state presumably may not order persons to perform sexual acts, or use contraception, or marry as a remedy to paternity suits, or return home as a remedy to a bill of divorce claiming abandonment. Similarly, the law professor Philip Bobbitt asserts that the state may not order the woman to carry a fetus:

[C]arrying a child within one's body and giving birth must be a profoundly intimate act. . . . I can conceive of no other relation as intimate as that between woman and developing embryo, a relation so intermingling that all other acts that seem intimate to us are by contrast momentary and detached. If the state cannot coerce women into conceiving in its behalf, how can it be claimed that the state can coerce a woman into carrying an embryonic form until she is forced to give it birth?[42]

This focus on discrete acts, apart from the intimate relationship in which they occur, risks undermining the claim of the act's intimacy.

Better is the description by Kenneth Karst, a constitutional scholar, of the right of intimate association that focuses on the intimacy of the relationship in which such acts may occur. This associational right defines the nature of the abortion right: "the values of nonassociation, protect . . . particularly women . . . against the enforced intimate society of unwanted children, against an unchosen commitment and a caring stained by reluctance, against a compelled identification with the social role of parent."[43]

Because of this right's first amendment doctrinal underpinning, Karst stresses the expressive and self-defining aspects of the associations one makes and "the importance of those values [of intimate association] to the development of a sense of individuality."[44] (Whose individuality, the mother's or the infant's?) The right's expressive and self-defining elements are, of course, significant, for the identity of parenthood is one of the most fundamental of all identities. When the state is otherwise constitutionally disabled from coercing persons into particular work, religious, and credal identities, for it to coerce women and men into this identity by forbidding abortion would signify a failure to appreciate the fundamental constitutive position of parenthood for identity in the life cycle.[45] There are, after all, few matters closer to the soul.

But the nature of the activity of associating is of greater salience here than the expressive and self-defining aspect, the withwhom, of intimate association. It is thus especially important to focus on the commitment made necessary by association, the fidelity that commitment requires, and the inner resources that it demands. The activity linked with the making of an association of mother and fetus-infant is called mother-love. Love is generally thought to be outside the competence of the state.

The commitment of psyche and soma of motherhood, the inner strength and capacity that allows a woman to mother, the grace required by a demanding child of gargantuan loving (and subsequently, hating) proportions, all belong to the realm of free will. Not the self-definitional aspect alone but the givingness of intimate association requires freedom. As Balint put it, the extraordinary demands of primary love—to be completely used as a taken-for-granted indestructible maternal environment—are such that the consent of the caregiver is necessary for her active participation.[46]

That love belongs to the realm of freedom is ontological and definitional: it arises from the nature of love. The attempt to coerce even beneficence and altruism among family members is "despotism," Charles Fried, the current solicitor general of the United States and Harvard law professor, wrote in a discussion of contractual obligation: "For the sharing within a family is and must be voluntary."[47]

An empirical hypothesis about the scope of freedom in our society may also be advanced. But first it is well here to recall Erik Erikson's caution that every society has its own sense of freedom.[48] There have of course been societies that have liberated the energy of women on behalf of infants and children without granting them much say in marriage or procreation—although the practice of abortion was probably known in such societies as well and may have afforded some choice.[49] There is, however, little in our society that would support (and much that would undermine) a woman, deprived of free choice, in mastering necessity in a manner that liberates human love. In a modern society like ours—in which kinship ties are otherwise very weak and in which a woman's security, resources, and social status bear a less and less positive relationship to her mothering—choice may be an important source of commitment, and privacy the protection that may encourage personal involvement in wise family arrangements.

As already noted, some argue that love may belong to the realm of freedom but that consent to motherhood should be found once the woman has freely chosen to engage in sexual intercourse. They claim that through genital heterosexuality, she leaves the realm of free choice for the realm of obligation (which is misnamed after the Samaritan who freely gave of his own accord). That conception begins, in most circumstances, in the intimacies of intercourse contributes to the attachment and love of parents for children; but the motive for engaging in each act of intercourse can hardly be said to always (or even often) include the kind of deep, complex, and realistic wish for and commitment to a child on which society or a child would want to rely.

The claim of obligation from intercourse denigrates what a mother gives and what a fetus-infant needs. It denies that the caretaking that is appropriate within and after the symbiotic relationship transcends compliance to an externally imposed obligation and requires an abiding vital strength.

The State Interest

The state interest in limiting abortion has come to be identified exclusively with its interest in affording protection to a potential human being. Weighing this interest against the woman's privacy interest in procreational choice, *Roe* held that the former did not become sufficiently substantial until fetal viability to permit the prohibition of elective abortion.

But the mere uncritical repetition of the phrase "governmental interest in potential life"—which is all that it has received from courts and commentators—leaves the nature of that interest unclear. Is it the kind of interest that the government can further through the coercion of the criminal and civil law; or is it most appropriately realized through the government's use of its spending power to create a more favorable material, social, and symbolic climate for childrearing? As the Supreme Court noted in the abortion-funding cases:

There is a basic difference between direct state interference with a protected activity and state encouragement of an alternative activity consonant with legislative policy. Constitutional concerns are greatest when the State attempts to impose its will by force of law; the State's power to encourage actions deemed to be in the public interest is necessarily far broader.[50]

The government can accomplish many things through coercion. It can summon the army and punish criminals. It can shape aspects of the family by jailing couples who use violence against their children or engage in certain sexual practices. Through restrictions on divorce, it has in the past effectively compelled people to remain married who otherwise would not. But it could not compel husband and wife to care for each other.[51] As adults they are capable of surviving, with varying degrees of success, without their mutual love and acceptance, and of finding alternative sustaining sources in children, religion, friends, and work.

Infants, however, lack that capacity and flexibility, and must look to a mothering one for nurturance. When that care is missing or when their need confronts a degree of intolerable ambivalence, hostility, or nonacceptance, infants may grow ill in mind and body, although some can transcend their early experience. Such illness may occur at different psychological levels depending on the infant and mother. Some will appear to survive, but deeply suffer inside; others will survive enough to inflict the lovelessness of their origins on others. The failure-to-thrive infants will actually curl up and, without intervening care, die. The fate of these infants means there is a concrete, minimum, rock-bottom form of human interaction, beyond mere provision of bodily need, that human life requires. This psychosoma need is a fact that sets an absolute limit to government coercion. Those who survive physically intact the early absence of committed care still need a basic acceptance that rises above the level of administration. Without it they may suffer a destruction of spirit, of their capacity for interaction and attachment. If the state's interest is in the potential of newborns to become contributing, hopeful members of our culture—what Justice White appears to call the "governmental interest . . . in protecting those who will be citizens if their lives are not ended in the womb"[52]—then the attachment needs of infants even more substantially constrain the power of the state.

The state cannot assure the survival and growth of infants any more than it can command good poetry. There must be an intervening act of human grace and creativity.[53] In caring for the infant, human involvement is required that goes beyond mere ministration to bodily need—that the government could order, a bureaucracy could perform.

That the need of infants for committed care sets a limit on what the government can accomplish directly obviously does not imply that all children who would have been aborted but for a prohibition will tend to be abused, neglected, or substantially harmed; for many women, although not all, tend to care for the children they are compelled to bear.[54] In using coercion to discourage abortion, governments do not achieve their aim directly, but rather exploit the good grace of many women to love their babies and to suffer and transcend their ambivalence in procreative communities whose existence, membership, or size is not of their own choosing. But the power to exploit women who would otherwise choose abortion should not be confused with the power to protect potential human life. That is a "power" that is confined to the one who makes a personal commitment to the child.[55]

Here mother-right meets state interest. Society's extraordinary interest in childhood depends first of all on the woman's choice of vital participation with her offspring.[56]

A Reasonable Period of Choice

The law may be understood as implementing dyadic autonomy by providing the dyad's adult constituent with the opportunity to make a procreative decision on its behalf during some reasonable period. The fetal-viability standard, which Roe adopted, established this period as lasting approximately six months. During that period of privacy, the woman can discover her pregnancy and exercise her dyadic responsibility by making an associational choice of whether to enter into a symbiotic relationship with the fetus and newborn and, more generally, into a relationship of parenthood.

Statistics show that the law has protected a procreational choice that women are prepared to make. Women who wish to commit themselves to motherhood are doing so in substantial numbers, with, for example, 3.6 million births in this country in 1983.[57] Among those who are not prepared for this commitment, over 1.5 million women annually, or approximately one-quarter of those pregnant, make a choice against dyadic development through abortion.[58]

Because about 91 percent of all abortions occur within the first trimester, it further appears that for many women the first three months of pregnancy afford a sufficient opportunity to make a determination for the dyad.[59] While the first trimester may suffice for the overwhelming majority of women in any one year, this period does not afford choice to all these same women throughout their fertile years. For during her life, a woman may find herself facing a procreative decision in a context for which three months simply do not suffice.

For example, women at the beginning and end of their fertile years may have difficulty identifying their pregnancies due to irregular menses: older women nearing menopause may misinterpret a missed period; and the very young girl may not only be irregular but also suffer the disadvantages of ignorance, inexperience, and dependency. Other women will be slow to identify pregnancies throughout their fertile years because of variable menses. Prior advice of sterility, medical misdiagnoses of pregnancy symptoms, periodic bleeding during pregnancy, and other physical and medical factors also lead to the late identification of pregnancy. There are even reports that a few young women do not comprehend their pregnancy until the end of the second trimester or later. Poverty, rural residence, and other factors that substantially limit access to medical services and counseling may retard dyadic decision as well by slowing the identification of pregnancy and decision making with respect to it. Lack of money and difficulty in locating and scheduling abortion services may also delay implementing a decision to abort.

At certain times in their lives, some women may have special difficulty determining procreative intentions on behalf of the dyad. This group includes minors and the emotionally stressed and troubled, who delay not solely from the failure of early detection but also from a wishful denial that only the inexorable progress of pregnancy pierces. The very young, still as much children as adolescents, are especially prone to such difficulties, and to very late abortions; so too are the poor and poorly educated. As a result of the male's desertion in response to the growing reality of pregnancy, some women face the same context of decision as do those who never relied in their decision making on maintaining a durable procreative unit with the father; but they face this context of decision much later in pregnancy.[60] Finally, late second trimester abortions involve those women carrying fetuses suffering from severe abnormalities that cannot be identified before pregnancy's fifth month, at least until safe and reliable techniques are developed to permit screening at a significantly earlier stage than amniocentesis now allows.[61]

Improved education, increased medical care for the poor and young, lowered cultural and social impediments to a woman's prompt identification of pregnancy, further contraceptive development, early genetic screening, and greater availability of first trimester abortion services[62] including an antiprogestational agent like RU 486—all may make women less reliant on second trimester abortions. Nevertheless, it may be anticipated that such later abortions will always be sought in a small number of cases because of the particular contexts of decision facing some women.[63] But with such social and technological advances, the reasonable period of choice may possibly contract up to the fifth month of gestation, or, with substantial change, even more.

Thus, the nearly three months that the viability standard presently affords beyond the first trimester protects the dyadic choice of women who find themselves during a particular pregnancy in a context of decision that requires additional time. As a more robust concept than is currently credited by some judges and commentators, viability can probably do the work of protecting the procreative choice of most women for the foreseeable future.[64]

Were technology to shorten the period of fetal nonviability substantially into the second trimester, and were a state to choose to confine elective abortion to that period, most women could still effectively exercise procreational choice on behalf of the dyad. But such a state would thereby deny, in a discriminatory manner, choice to those dyadic representatives, in the following particular classes, who find themselves unable to adjust to a shorter period of choice. It would have the effect of discriminating against women with a physiology that involves very irregular menses, a natural condition for which a woman is not responsible; it would similarly affect minors beginning their fertile lives and older women nearing menopause, conditions which they cannot control but which confront most women. It would disfavor the poorly educated, including substantial numbers of the poor and minorities. That state would also arbitrarily discriminate against women who for other personal and unique reasons face circumstances in which they are unable to detect their pregnancies and make a procreational choice forthwith, although such reasons would be unrelated to any interest the state might have in forbidding only these particular women from acting on behalf of the dyad. Finally, it would altogether eliminate decision making for women carrying fetuses with severe abnormalities.

Should some extraordinary technological advance in the future permit physicians to maintain early second trimester or even first trimester fetuses outside the womb with alternative placentas that are generally available throughout a state or to transfer fetuses to recipient women, then protection of dyadic autonomy would require the restructuring of the laws in those states that preclude abortion of the viable fetus. This task of preserving dyadic autonomy could be accomplished through a state legislature's determination to adopt a regulatory scheme that allowed nontherapeutic abortions after the moment of viability,[65] or through a state judicial reinterpretation of the period of choice, now afforded by the viability standard, using various theories[66] including the one advanced here. But for the immediate future, the viability standard will be sufficiently effective to protect most women in their choosing whether to enter into a relationship of maternal love.

THE DYADIC REPRESENTATIVE: CRITICAL QUERIES

The dyadic concept has, at least for some, an intuitive and commonsense appeal. In clarifying the relationship of abortion law to other recent developments in tort and criminal law, it serves a useful purpose. That the woman is the appropriate and exclusive representative of the dyad with the decisional capacity and power to determine its future is the far more controversial claim. It rests, thus far, on several grounds: that the dyadic concept constitutes a fair description of pregnancy and the early postbirth period; that offspring need (and the state wants for them) a continuity of personal committed care which is aptly described as mother-love; and that a commitment of love, at least in our society, is a private decision beyond state coercion both as a matter of right and, to an extent, of fact.

This claim on behalf of the woman's decision-making power may be further explored by considering the following three questions: granting the dyadic concept, why does adoption not suffice as a way of allowing a woman to opt out of the dyadic relationship? why may the woman not terminate the dyadic unit through infanticide if she may do so through abortion? and why is the woman the exclusive decision maker for the unit?

Why Not Adoption?

Since the theory of symbiotic attachment relied on here focuses on, among other values, providing the infant with a loving environment and the woman the freedom not to love, why may not the state prohibit abortion and rely on adoption, immediately at birth, to reconstitute the dyad and reconcile the needs of both woman and neonate? This would also enable others who deeply wish to parent the opportunity to do so.[67]

One short answer is that the states in this country do not claim to be, nor are they, prepared to guarantee to each woman that they will arrange an adoptive equivalent of her biologically rooted care for each of the millions of now-aborted fetuses. While data are difficult to come by, it appears that even prior to the deregulation of abortion in the late 1960s, which partially contributed to the reduced availability of infants for adoption, adoption services did not provide adequate care for many children, and especially for nonwhites and those who suffered some handicap.[68]

To this answer some may respond that such failures are not dispositive, for this essay exaggerates the importance of a particular committed caregiver for each infant. For example, it is said that there are communities, such as kibbutzim, in which society provides communal care from birth that meets the needs of the infant and child. Assuming this to be true for argument's sake, the affective economy of the kibbutz is such that mutual identification may make each child the child of all, so that, through a common maternal identity, caretakers provide the personal care children need.[69]

We do not have that kind of communal society. We are an individualistic nation of strangers; ours is a "culture of separation."[70] Here even paternalism is suspect (and maternalism is seldom mentioned). Without a society committed to communal provision and mutual identification—that is, to more than unreliable foster-care systems—the mere theoretical possibility of a communal responsibility for all children is irrelevant.

But between the inadequate impersonal ministrations of the state in our culture of separation and the care of the biological mother, there are particular persons who could enter the dyad and provide committed care for some infants: strangers overwhelmingly eager to adopt children, as well as grandparents, aunts, uncles, and others. Might not the state sunder begetting and bearing from rearing, and compel a woman to carry a pregnancy to term in those cases where a particular caregiver was available?

Invocation of a woman's individual claims—that she has a right to bodily autonomy with respect to the burdens of pregnancy and the use of her genetic procreative power; that she should not be subjected to the health risks of pregnancy against her will; that she should not be forced into the intimate association of pregnancy; and that she should not be the subject of sex discrimination under the law of good samaritan obligations, or otherwise deprived of the equal protection of the laws—all may be resorted to as responses to an argument favoring adoption over abortion, even in those cases where an adequate adoptive alternative exists. It may be added that a woman's opportunity to protect these interests in any particular pregnancy should not depend so unpredictably on the varying availability of adoptive parents.

But as compelling and sufficient as the invocation of such individual interests may be, it is appropriate to explore how this essay's perspective not only affords a relational understanding of the fetus in a dyad, but also accords the pregnant woman a privileged position as dyadic representative that is superior to that of other would-be dyadic participants.

To do this appears to require claiming a privileged status for biological motherhood in human procreation.[71] That status derives from the fetus-infant's needs; from the woman's psychic and somatic capacities and experiences of fertilization, pregnancy, birth, and infant care; and from the reinforcing support of the religious, mythological, and group-psychological history of our culture, which creates special maternal meanings, turns predispositions into ideals, and commits women (as it commits men) to certain social uses.

The Supreme Court, I think, tacitly recognized and accepted this privileged status and the centrality of biological motherhood to procreation. In protecting the woman's choice, it respected the unity of motherhood, in contrast to the centrifugal forces of production and consumption, of technology, and of our intellectuals that are tending to disaggregate begetting, bearing, and rearing from each other.[72] The Court may be understood as implicitly expressing its unified understanding of motherhood when in *Roe* it identified some of the burdens of pregnancy and child care, mixed up together, as part of a whole:

The detriment that the State would impose upon the pregnant woman by denying this choice [of abortion] altogether is apparent. Specific and direct harm medically diagnosable even in early pregnancy may be involved. Maternity, or additional offspring, may force upon the woman a distressful life and future. Psychological harm may be imminent. Mental and physical health may be taxed by child care. There is also the distress, for all concerned, associated with the unwanted child, and there is the problem of bringing a child into a family already unable, psychologically and otherwise, to care for it. . . . [T]he additional difficulties and continuing stigma of unwed motherhood may be involved.[73]

The Court, moreover, did not consider adoption as an alternative to the burdens of childrearing or as an antidote to the "distress" of an unwanted child.[74] For, as it must have concluded, the unwanted child, even if put out for adoption at birth, can involve for the woman who would not choose adoption at least the misappropriation of her genetic procreative power, her body and its strength during pregnancy, her associational capacity, and her attachments and identity as a mother. Adoption does not cure these unwanted infringements.

The integrated and whole view of motherhood, which may be imputed to the Court, is consistent with the idea of "mother" that, as a general matter in health, we tend to hold—and hold our mothers to.[75] Both mother and child, throughout their lives, tend to have a unitary concept of "mother" and her obligations and responsibilities to her offspring that resists disaggregation. Even when stripped of many of the accretions of what used to be called "middle-class momism," this unitary concept assures a fundamental responsibility for offspring and a realistic expectation in the child that such responsibility will be forthcoming. To explore this, resorting to the descriptions of Winnicott and other psychoanalysts will again be of aid.

This fullness of natural motherhood includes the generative power of begetting. The exercise of that power is fueled by human procreative instinctuality, and preceded by preconceptive fantasies of her baby that find deep roots in many women's unconscious. The intimacy of intercourse points to another intimacy of begetting: an identification of her body, including its genes, with her fetus, flesh of my flesh. This fusion of intercourse, including its attendant fantasies, helps prepare the way for symbiotic fusion with offspring. There is another psychological solidarity as well—with one's parents, physically through the continuity of germ plasm from generation to generation, and psychically through the identification with them that the act of conceiving further completes.[76]

The fullness of motherhood includes bearing the fetus, at one with the future child inside, in a unique relationship that is available to no other. The physical evolution of pregnancy points the way toward further intimacy with the infant to be: the tender soreness of breasts, enlarging for suckling; the body's broadening, suggesting the offspring's passage through to the outside world; the butterfly flutterings of the newly quickened fetus, drawing inner designs that only the woman knows. In being at one, the woman may identify the fetus with herself and her own inner world of thoughts and feelings, and ultimately with the mothering she received as an infant.[77]

The fullness of motherhood then involves the difficult and potentially dangerous struggle of physical separation at birth. But the emotional fusion of pregnancy continues thereafter, with this difference: the mother must now most actively choose to surrender herself to a symbiotic attachment with her infant. The woman's experience of pregnancy and anticipation of motherhood in the last trimester, as well as hormonal changes, have typically led to a deep self-absorption that she can make available to her newborn. Through this powerful identification with the fetus within and then with the infant who "at first seems like a part of herself,"[78] women in health achieve a very powerful sense "for what the infant needs."[79] This "primary maternal preoccupation"[80] forms her predisposition for symbiotic attachment. Nursing, if chosen, affords a special opportunity for infant health and ongoing interpersonal and bodily involvement; in its course, hormones help induce a calm peacefulness that further supports symbiotic fusion with her child.

Finally, the fullness of motherhood includes the storms of all the subsequent separations and growing individuation of the child in the coming years. Whether to allow this potential relation in all its ramifications to unfold, always with the possibility that the unfolding will fail with devastating results—this is the procreative choice that the law may protect.[81]

Appeal to the individual pregnant woman to choose adoption over abortion by persons prepared to promise her a continuity of committed care for her infant honors the pregnant woman's centrally important role in procreation. In preferring adoption to abortion, she sponsors the fetus-infant and clothes it with rights that we must honor. By contrast, honoring the wishes of potential caregiving substitutes, over and against the pregnant woman's choice, accepts the use of state coercion in sundering the dyad.

The adopting parent demonstrates and symbolizes the generosity of love superseding the narcissistic component of genetic parenthood,[82] and the protection of new human life whatever its source. A humane and adaptive cultural response to the many orphans produced by family catastrophe, poverty, overpopulation, the uprooting of peoples, and war would encourage the emphasis upon adoptive parenting which is today in evidence.

But a state regime of adoption as the coerced substitute for abortion makes rending of the dyad a baseline norm. Rescue of the orphan by the love and generosity of the adoptive parents becomes not the exception but the law's answer to the unwillingly pregnant woman: every child, a would-be orphan. Based as it is on the required involvement with her fetus growing within,[83] and then the destruction of that involvement at birth, a mandatory policy of adoption in lieu of abortion is premised on the dissolution of this unity of motherhood after the entire course of pregnancy. That state policy would now arise within a cultural logic of relationship that is premised on separation and not attachment, and would depend on the alienation of a woman from her generative body, of her self from the offspring she brings into being.[84] The lifelong searching by some women for the children they have borne and given up and the searching by some adopted children for their biological parents testify to the deep constitutive element that biological parenthood, including the parental intentions that led to procreation, can have for both mother and child.[85] The drama *Oedipus Rex* models the drivenness of that search and how fateful are our origins for our selves.

But perhaps the reasons for respecting the privileged position of the pregnant woman as against most adoptive parents justify extending a similarly privileged status to the biological father as well. Where the woman has formed a family with a man, through marriage or common law ties, then perhaps she has chosen to share her office as dyadic representative with him. This intimacy should lead to consensual decisions on matters of procreation. But when she wants to abort her pregnancy but he does not, and the disagreement becomes so irreconcilable as to lead to legal dispute, then their procreative family has failed. Does such joint dyadic responsibility as may potentially have existed then fall away from the man or survive in each? Were they both to continue to enjoy this privileged status separately, then might the state forbid abortion when, against her wishes, he demands to reconstitute the dyad at birth by undertaking the office of dyadic mother? Certainly alone among alternative caregivers he shares with the woman not only genetic parenthood and the intimacies of intercourse but also deep cultural support for commitment to the dyad. If a father's claim to reconstitute the dyad were to be accepted as sometimes valid, it would nonetheless be unavailable to the genetic father who fails initially to participate jointly with the woman in a procreative community supporting the dyad's development (as to him the dyadic office was never shared); and it would equally be unavailable to the father who joins in support of the dyad but wishes not to assume the dyadic office but only to coerce the woman into undertaking it. Neither of these men has begun to share in the meanings to the woman of begetting, bearing, and rearing.

But is such a paternal claim ever valid? Again, to the extent that her claims relating to health and bodily autonomy give her a stake in the abortion decision superior to others, they would similarly afford her an interest that is superior to the father's and defeat his claim to reconstitute the dyad. But it may also be that the woman is more suitably prepared for the identificatory office of dyadic mother and has a greater stake in the constitutive decision of procreation than the man by virtue of impregnation, pregnancy, and birth, in all of their multiple biological and psychological dimensions, as reinforced by her own relationship with her mother and interpreted by cultural meanings and myths.[86] Certainly the data showing that women typically continue to provide primary care for infants and that fathers who are not part of ongoing family units often default on their paternal responsibilities are not to the contrary.[87] Although the father who is opposed to an abortion and prepared to undertake full responsibility for the care of his offspring presents the most difficult case for a relational approach, it appears that the nature of the symbiotic unit may still afford the woman a preeminent status as the dyad's representative.

According motherhood a privileged status neither idealizes motherhood—it is exceedingly hard and often unrewarding work—nor diminishes the importance and fullness of fatherhood, for men play a central role in supporting the dyad and helping children as they individuate. At the very beginning, the father can protect, support, and tend to the mother sufficiently so that she can fully devote herself to a successful symbiotic relationship with her fetus-infant. But by virtue of her pregnancy, birth experiences, and nursing (if undertaken), his early involvement with the fetus and neonate often first develops through the mother's greater symbiotic attachment.[88] After the earliest period, the child equally needs direct paternal as well as maternal care. Where men do provide primary infant care, it is often as part of a procreative unit with a woman; then the intimacy of procreative partners helps prepare both for symbiotic involvement. And where, because of some catastrophe, the mother is absent after birth, a father can assume a maternal dyadic role, albeit without the cultural, psychological, and biological preparation. Thus the fullness of fatherhood has many of the same attributes as motherhood except, typically, for the symbiotic stage of pregnancy and early infancy. But this may tend always to give a different quality to fatherhood.[89]

· · ·

It will not surprise those who criticize psychoanalysis as a patriarchal enterprise that this essay's illustrative use of analytic theory leads to a claim for motherhood's privileged status. Why resort, they may ask, to a supplementary justification of the abortion liberty when a woman's claims to bodily autonomy and health can do the same work? Indeed, those claims have the advantage of depending on interests that coincide precisely with pregnancy. That is a significant advantage over the complications of a relational approach that spills over into infancy and beyond. But in addition to the limitations identified in chapters 1 and 2, such arguments from bodily autonomy and health must undertake the task of distinguishing the burdens of pregnancy on women from the burdens of war on men, and from other burdens to which all in society are subject.[90] By contrast, affording the woman a superior status as dyadic representative can adequately, and perhaps convincingly, be defended by focusing on the unique meanings of impregnation, pregnancy, birth, and infant care, and by recognizing the woman's privileged position with respect to these meanings. Whether such meanings are biological, psychological, or cultural in origin, and whether they are natural or imposed, they appear to exist.[91] Our society, for the social end of reproduction, reinforces and exploits—and therefore ought to respect—these meanings.[92]

Why Not Infanticide?

If the onset of individuality occurs through symbiosis at some time after birth, may not the mother abrogate her symbiotic relationship through infanticide?[93]

She may not because of the law's function in containing human ambivalence. Human relationships and human choice, including the choice of parenthood, are characterized by a pervading ambivalence. Culture and its ideologies serve a major function in setting the limits that human beings require to contain their conflicting impulses and to direct them in a constructive course; or, as Freudian instinct theory put it, to enable Eros to harness aggression in its service; or, as Erikson describes the process, to establish those rituals which discipline and release human energy in productive fashion and limit the human capacity for destruction.[94] In our largely secular and atomistic culture, which depends so significantly on rational authority, this function falls in too significant a degree to law.

Some make the instrumental argument that abortion must be prohibited to tame such ambivalence, because a slippery slope leads from abortion to infanticide. In dealing with maternal ambivalence they would adopt the tactic of trying to repress it altogether. A few would even deny its existence with an exaggerated emphasis upon the positive; as a theologian has written:

If it were to become an accepted principle of moral teaching on motherhood to permit a mother whose life was endangered simply to "sacrifice" the life of her child in order to save her own, motherhood would no longer mean absolute dedication to each and every child.[95]

Giving keen expression to a worry that may underlie this argument, Surgeon General Koop queries, "I wonder how many of us would be here today if someone had the option of not feeding us as newborns?"[96] But there does not appear to be a substantial basis for crediting the anxiety that maternal hostility is so uncontrolled and so without affirmative and counterbalancing love as to require the most rigid repression. The regulator's slippery-slope argument is, at best, speculative and unsupported by cross-cultural comparisons with societies that have for decades allowed legal access to abortion.[97]

Instead, it would appear that the law may acknowledge maternal ambivalence and protect dyadic autonomy by affording only a circumscribed period of choice. The nature of ambivalence favors such a reasonable but firm period. For resolving ambivalence requires limits, not more time, despite what some individuals faced with decision believe; indeed, delay in choosing may only serve to express the hostile component of the ambivalence.[98]

Moreoever, good reasons may be found within the symbiotic relationship for so limiting elective abortion. As her maternal identity develops with birth's approach, the woman who is committed to birth increasingly readies herself to experience the fetus-infant as a special kind of other—a constituent part of a symbiotic unit, requiring an active adaptation and extraordinary maternal activity. For after the umbilical connection has been severed, the woman must continually choose to give herself over to infantile need and sensitivity. By prohibiting abortion at some appropriate point in gestation, the law may protect the next generation and extend dignified respect and support to the woman's own experience of coming to value the symbiotic relationship to which she, by choice or indecision, has obligated herself.[99]

In determining at what point to support a woman's commitment by forbidding elective abortion, the reasonable period of approximately six months, which women presently require to make a dyadic choice, should as a practical matter govern. But it is also appropriate to consider when in a developing pregnancy an elective abortion prohibition makes sense with respect to a woman's psychological commitment to the dyad.[100] Here the concepts of personhood discussed in chapter 1 are relevant. The period of four to six months marks a time in pregnancy when differences between fetus and neonate begin to diminish substantially—associated as it is with quickening and the greater involvement that it brings, sentience, and the later development of higher brain capacity and mature organ systems. Besides the woman's knowledge of internal fetal development is the increasing social visibility of pregnancy after the first trimester, which this same fetal growth usually produces. Both the inner and outer dimensions intensify for many women the growing reality of impending birth and their need to prepare for the symbiotic activity it entails. The period identified as reasonable therefore makes sense as a time of development in her pregnancy after which a woman can typically be said to have chosen the affirmative side of the ambivalence and after which the law is justified in trying to support this choice with firm limits. If the developmental stages of the typical pregnancy suggest a somewhat shorter period of choice, perhaps between three to four months, than that required by the contexts of decision actually faced by certain groups, then the former should yield in a legal scheme to what pregnant women actually and reasonably require. But this disjuncture ought to serve as an incentive for the social and technological developments that may eventually shorten the time women reasonably need for making their dyadic choice.

The law may thus effectively provide both for the woman's rejection of mothering and for the opposite of the ambivalence: the wish for a child, the longing for fusion, the generative desire, the urge to parent. That blend consists of a real opportunity to avoid maternity with a firm limit after which one's forthcoming motherhood is confirmed. This confirmation is appropriate not because abortion is located on a particularly slippery slope toward infanticide, but because confirmation is essential to all significant human endeavor.[101] Through such confirmation, human ambivalence, though it remains, is contained and transmuted.

Why Is the Woman the Appropriate Decision Maker?

Assuming the pregnant woman's best intentions, some will still wonder whether a decision about the future of the dyadic unit should be subject to the incompetence of her "mere unaided virtue"?[102] Given the irrational, narcissistic, and self-destructive potential in human decision making and the depths of meaning that are associated with procreation, why, they may ask, should trust be placed in the mother-love of each woman? Can she be expected to make a reasonable decision on behalf of the dyad and, indeed, to make any decision on its behalf rather than solely on her own behalf?

Attachments: Willing and Accepting. A more abstract question preliminary to these others is this: If the basic category of analysis is a dyadic community, is its existence something about which the pregnant woman may make a decision at all?

Activists on both sides of the abortion debate, as the sociologist Kristin Luker has shown, hold deeply divergent beliefs about the capacity of persons to choose their reproductive fates and to direct the procreative lot that is theirs, with deregulators emphasizing the human potential for rational control over nature within and without, and regulators emphasizing the importance of accepting "natural" processes and yielding to the necessity that arises from our bodily existence.

The climax of labor, which takes hold and grips woman and fetus alike until it releases both, may provide some regulators with a model for the entirety of pregnancy: an unfolding natural event that can most successfully be borne by an active surrender. If there are times in life when being most oneself requires yielding to destiny's dictates and accepting more than willing, times when honesty requires rejecting the pretense that she has chosen that to which she accommodates, for some regulators procreation is one of those times. For among the events that seize a person and carry her beyond herself, that demand and obtain an enlarging response and a transcending of previously known capacities, pregnancy must certainly be counted. Although they may not deny the autonomy of women to control reproduction through contraception (or chastity), these regulators hold that if persons are ever to be bound and defined not by a contractualism that honors only autonomous choice but by a felt necessity arising from given relationships and communal norms, such necessity must include a pregnancy already commenced.[103]

From such a vantage, it must seem an unlikely strategy to argue, as I do, for abortion-choice with an account that places human attachment, and not solely human autonomy, at its center. One who would not only proceed in this manner but also use the language of psychoanalysis and the encouragement of advocates of a more relational ethos must acknowledge an apparent ambiguity here respecting whether a right to choose our associations extends to those most fundamental biological relationships that help constitute the choosing self.

Psychoanalysis, admittedly, has faced in two directions: toward a freed if chastened autonomy of the human subject; and toward a determined and caused human object of impersonal forces, and procreative ones at that. While the latter perspective may characterize Freud's major theoretical efforts, the former characterizes the therapeutic core of his theory. Yet even the psychotherapy he inspired partakes of both perspectives, the autonomous subject and constrained object. It asserts not only that "where id was there ego shall be" but also that "where ego is, there id shall come into being again."[104] It subjects to criticism the self's narcissistic tendency to believe in its own capacity for entirely unencumbered and rationally calculating choice, and to deny that it is irrevocably attached to and defined and driven by a body that was once a part of a woman, that is a vessel and sometimes vehicle of the germ plasm of forefathers and foremothers, and that will die while others live on. It demonstrates that persons in health accept (and indeed surrender to) communal obligation, biology, and instinct. Freud's aphorism captures the ambiguity of freedom within an interpersonal necessity: ". . . in the last resort we must begin to love in order not to fall ill."[105] Yet, for all this, it also demonstrates that the patient's coming through self-reflection to exercise free choice in accepting in her own unique way—as distinguished from compliantly submitting to—the constraints of inner and outer reality is essential to health, not only her own but her family's. Indeed, the self's capacity to integrate a complex inner reality as it adjusts actively to the demands of an outer reality is one of the main objects of psychoanalytic study.[106] Thus, analysts make much of the difference between a body's dead compliance and a person's creative initiative in meeting life's givens, and of the fateful consequences for all when a mother does not meet her offspring with a vital response.

A more relational perspective in political theory appears to involve a similar ambiguity in the scope it would afford a person's autonomous will in choosing her constitutive relationships. As it encourages us to find our truer selves in communal participation, to complete those parts of our selves that only the institutions of politics and family and religion can engage, and as it offers prescriptions for a way out of the particular isolating effects of our present individualistic culture, this perspective ambiguously risks either affirming as ultimate the very individualism it criticizes or alternatively justifying substantial incursions on freedom. For if individuals can simply self-will a solidarity with others they presently want, then their community expresses not a transcendent given and constitutive part of themselves but only transient individual preferences amassed; and contemplating our attachments and our community's norms we may without detriment to our selves accept or reject them as they suit each of us.[107] Alternatively, if we cannot act against communal norms and attachments without alienating or denying essential parts of our selves, we are bound, our autonomy truncated with respect to the most vital aspects of social life. As a relational vision empirically criticizes a liberal description of the autonomous subject by showing how given and defined he actually is and must be by his social past and communal present (as Freud demonstrated with respect to his personal past), it risks prescriptively subordinating individual autonomy and initiative to the preservation of a particular, and not necessarily just, social ordering.

One recent proponent of a more relational perspective in political theory, Michael Sandel, navigates this dilemma, as he pursues his critique of the liberal philosopher John Rawls' theory of justice, by focusing on the distinction between the self that chooses its ends and the self that discovers its ends by reflection. As a choosing subject, he argues, the self of deontological liberalism can, with supreme indifference to particular circumstances and goals in the original contracting position imagined by Rawls, agree upon the principles of justice that govern a plurality of individuals as they pursue a plurality of individual ends. Justice secures freedom for those who exist prior to the ends they choose by establishing limiting rules that are not rooted in any particular vision of the common good; such *a priori* rules prevent society's pursuit of its ends (including the regulation of "morals" and mores) at the expense of the rights of the individual. But, argues Sandel, liberalism's vision of the self undercuts its own claim for the primacy of justice as the first virtue of social institutions. Standing in precarious relationship to the ends it chooses, this choosing self risks either evaporating because it cannot be defined apart from whatever changing preferences it may from moment to moment have; or of choosing its ends arbitrarily and capriciously, of being merely willful, because it is defined entirely apart from and without reference to its chosen ends. Either possibility results, suggests Sandel, from liberalism's imagining a self whose very capacity to choose is detached from and prior to the deeper character that comes from already having constituent attachments in a particular family and community of determinate form that afford motives and reasons for choosing ends to be pursued. This *a priori* self is sufficiently thin and its relationship to the ends it chooses—they are mere preferences which cannot be judged by an appeal to any hierarchy of goods in or outside the self—sufficiently arbitrary that, finally, it is not clear to some critics why the protection of its autonomy through rights is all that important.

The point of Sandel's critique is not, I think, to strengthen the state's claim for imposing a particular vision of the good on the uncomprehending or resisting citizen, although the liberal critic understandably views this as the chief risk of a more communal ethos. Rather, it would appear on one "liberal" reading, that Sandel seeks primarily to provide the citizen with a more accurate self-description that he may deepen his self-comprehension and thereby make possible an enlargement and fulfillment of his identity through greater participation with others in a common community. As Sandel writes:

"[C]ommunity" and "participation" may describe a form of life in which the members find themselves commonly situated "to begin with," their commonality consisting less in relationships they have entered than in attachments they have found.[108]

The method of this comprehension involves both self-reflection and dialogue with fellow friends, who, because they understand the nature of their self-defining membership in a joint community, can know each other and help each other come to understand their common path to a fuller self-realization.

What has this to do with a woman's abortion-choice? In contrast to a contractarian model of community, the example of the family is often offered as a community in which our most fundamental relationships are given to us, not chosen, and for which not justice but benevolence and duty most enhance a shared life.

But the view of the family as given more than chosen primarily adopts the perspective of offspring; it does not convey that choice and necessity are more complexly and dialectically distributed between parents and children. Parents choose to cause their children: they cause them to be born. This is the most basic and natural inequality of all. Abortion-choice may highlight this lack of equality but does not enlarge it; nor would the elimination of such choice diminish inequality. The fate that children bewail may be the fate of having been born to particular parents in particular circumstances, as if the child could have it otherwise, as if the wailing self would exist apart from its only parents. Yet once parents have made the extraordinary choice to cause the birth of a child, it is the child who is the new beginning, striving toward sufficient autonomy and freedom from his family to achieve adulthood, while his parents are forever redefined, caught in their appointed task of fostering that freedom before their death.

From the liberal perspective, there is no just warrant for imposing on the unwilling woman an unchosen end such as motherhood; and, assuming that the fetus is not a person with interests, there is no basis in justice for prohibiting abortion. But if the woman of liberal theory stands in relationship to her purposes in a somewhat arbitrary manner, as Sandel implies, her ends reduced to mere preferences that cannot be evaluated in relationship to her self, then perhaps the choice of abortion over motherhood would appear to some as arbitrary, merely a matter of convenience. But a woman of character, a thickly conceived self, has substantial reasons for choosing whether to parent, reasons that relate deeply to her core self-in-relation and her generative purposes, to her attachments and the procreative community of which she may already be a part—as well as reasons that relate deeply to the potential person that would develop out of a constitutive attachment with her. While subject to a plurality of complex conscious and unconscious motivations, the thickly conceived self that psychoanalysis describes (and that we know from our own experience of ourselves and others) has the capacity to integrate those motivations, a capacity that in health it must use. The reasonable period of choice affords women a time of integration, an opportunity not always afforded by the abundance and drivenness and capriciousness of male and female sexuality.

Psychoanalysis moves in the direction of freedom through a self-reflection that comprehends the attachments of life. As presently practiced, it would not deny to persons the important choices that they make but instead would have the choosing subject appreciate the nature of her character and how it is shaped, indeed partly constituted, by the body she inhabits and the community of which she is a part. The question, then, is not whether the pregnant woman can choose respecting the dyad, but rather how she may come to reflect upon the nature of her procreative intentions and her capacity to constitute the dyad with her mother-love.

The Woman and Her Doctor: An Interpersonal Process. Expanding upon the therapeutic model of self-reflection within a noncoercive dialogue, Robert Burt of the Yale Law School has urged, with respect to significant medical decisions which determine life and death or fix identities, that the law should maximize participation, consultation, and engagement, in short, equality, between physician and patient. Through such a process, he believes, destructive irrationality can be tamed and truth emerge. Relying on some of the same psychoanalytic themes described here, Burt argues that our identities as separate beings are precarious achievements maintained by cultural convention, personal effort, and interpersonal struggle with and against others, all in defense against an internal psychic world of primary processes that does not recognize distinctions of self-other, subject-object, or wish-reality.

Burt asserts that the exclusive allocation of decision making in mundane affairs to either the doctor or the patient works because the assumption that we are separate beings with fixed identities works. But in the extremity of medical decisions that affect life or identity, mundane assumptions fail; for neither patient nor physician has a fixed identity in their relationship apart from the other that could provide an archimedean reference for decision respecting such fundamental treatment choices. When these assumptions fail, so does the exclusive allocation of power to doctor or patient. Such an exclusive alloca-

tion elicits the experience of omnipotence in one and helplessness in the other that undermines in each the shaky identity of
separateness. When the illusion of omnipotence and attendant
anxiety confront the reality of life-and-death choices, there
comes the risk of increasingly frantic efforts to maintain this unrealistic and rigid conception of oneself as utterly in control (or
utterly helpless); this in turn may lead to a destructive disengagement by doctor and patient from the struggle of our interpersonal world that provides the basis for realistic decision
making. Moreover, when his identity appears vulnerable because of mental infirmity or death's approach, the patient's very
existence may threaten the physician's own sense of psychic integrity and can elicit a physician's wish to eliminate this threat:
"taking care" of a patient can degenerate into its sinister opposite. Protection does not come from shifting decisional power
to the dependent patient, for the fantasy of omnipotence is if
anything less capable of realization in the patient, who still
remains emotionally vulnerable, indeed permeable, to the destructive wishes of his caregiver. Patient protection and reasonable medical judgments may emerge instead from mutual participation in an ongoing dialogue or dispute. The law's task is to
assure such a dialogue.[109]

In that portion of his argument that is most closely analogous to the abortion setting, Burt seeks to assure "conversations
with silent patients," such as the comatose and the profoundly
retarded, to protect the process of medical decision making concerning them. He rejects proposals that choose an "exclusive
choice maker for an utterly choiceless other":

[T]o legalize and regularize death's dispensation, to identify some
among us—diseased person, doctor, judge—as ultimate and exclusive
decision maker, aborts the very process of communal collaboration by
which each of us sustains our individual identity.[110]

Through a process of consultation with interested persons, Burt
argues that the silent patient will find presence in "the cacophony of voices consulted," a presence which will lead others to engage with him as a real interpersonal force.[111]

If this interpersonal procedural model is applicable to the
abortion decision, it would seem that it would reject either the
woman or physician as an exclusive decision maker. It would

also reject any claim that gives the fetus omnipotent control over the woman and physician, and allows it, by its very existence, to veto her choice. Such fetal power would merely replicate the infant's primary process "belief" in its omnipotence, which the mother nurtures for the infant's psychological and physical benefit. Any such exclusive allocation of power to the fetus by absolutely prohibiting abortion would be doomed to frustration were it motivated by the omnipotent fantasy that a woman can be coerced into loving the fetus and newborn as it wants and needs, and by the unrealistic wish that she is sufficiently bountiful to nurture and contain all that men may spawn.[112] For with or without a legally recognized right to procreative choice, women uncommitted to motherhood have an autonomous subjectivity apart from their children: they may secretly abort, as they have for millenia; they may neglect prenatal care and precautions against miscarriage and, indeed, may unconsciously induce psychogenic miscarriage; and they may implement maternal ambivalence after birth by abuse, neglect, hostility, and indifference.[113]

Roe may be understood as rejecting such exclusive power allocations and instead as creating an interpersonal process of decision making. It explicitly prohibited a state from allocating exclusive power to itself or a corporate board of physicians. Equally, it permitted states to deny to the woman exclusive decision-making power as well. Instead, *Roe* assumed (without requiring) that all states would subject the woman's wishes to interpersonal testing within a clinical relationship, by treating abortion as a medical procedure.

Some read *Roe* as naively and mistakenly assuming that physicians would perpetuate the strict therapeutic model that had governed previously and refuse abortions to most women.[114] But a more plausible interpretation is that the justices of the Court expected only that the woman's abortion decision would be subject not to a physician's veto but to the testing of an interpersonal dialogue. A medical decision, at its best, is made between a patient and a doctor who acts pursuant to professional values, ones developed out of clinical encounters and subjected to peer criticism within a regime of professional education, research, and ethical study. As such, the interpersonal abortion decision includes a medical response that is influenced by the accumulated experience of physicians with women patients, fetuses, and newborns. To appreciate the significance of such response, imagine abortion services provided instead by non-physicians lacking a professional identification and association and having no experience of a variety of life-saving and health-enhancing activities. Then self-interest alone in the marketplace rather than commitment to patient health would explicitly govern the exchange.

This interpersonal dialogue has in fact shaped and limited the decisions of pregnant women and physicians. For example, from this process a consensus favoring first trimester abortions has emerged. Second trimester abortions are not readily available; and in obtaining them, women must confront and persuade physicians, who also must confront fetal remains, nurses, and their professional colleagues.[115]

Furthermore, counseling is a part of the interpersonal abortion process, a counseling that is guided by the significant medical and legal literature on informed consent. Information about fetal growth and the symbiotic relationship may be imparted and the feelings, beliefs, capacities, and commitments of the woman explored. The availabilility of alternative caregivers may also be discussed.

In support of this interpersonal process, the Court has allowed state regulation of abortion that imposes general principles of informed consent and requires evidence of the woman's consent, in order to assure that it is "freely given and is not the result of coercion" and is informed by "full knowledge" of the nature and consequences of an abortion. But the Court has insisted that such regulation not be so burdensome as to restrict the availability of abortion services to nonwealthy women (a concern that explains much of the Court's work on abortion); nor may such regulation interfere with the privacy of the doctor-patient relationship, either by so rigidly specifying the content and method of disclosures as to limit the physician's capacity to individualize the woman's treatment or by mandating in all cases particular disclosures that are intended to dissuade her from aborting.[116] Whatever may be the best mix of general principles and specific rules in governing the informed consent dialogue, there is some data supporting the belief that the Court's primary reliance on the general legal obligation of health care professionals to obtain informed consent, rather than on detailed state regulation of what must be disclosed and how, enhances the quality of interpersonal dialogue in the generality of cases.[117]

With respect to abortions sought by pregnant minors, the Court has enabled the state to structure an additional dialogue with their parents, among the most implicated and knowledgeable potential participants. The state may mandate parental involvement prior to a nonemergency abortion by requiring that a physician use reasonable efforts, where feasible and expeditious, to obtain the consent of parents or at least to afford them notice. Lest such parental participation turn into a *de facto* power to veto their child's choice, the state must provide an alternative confidential and swift judicial or administrative consent procedure by which a minor can avoid parental involvement, when it is not in her best interest or she is sufficiently mature to do without it. Because it cannot give parents an exclusive and absolute veto over the abortion decisions of pregnant minors, the state can only create a setting in which dialogue tends to replace fiat.[118]

Concerning adult women, the goal of fostering a useful dialogue prior to the abortion decision might suggest also providing paternal notice in those cases where the father has demonstrated by his actions a willingness to maintain a family with her and to continue to know her and the dyad. However, problems of administration, the likelihood of counterproductive effects, and inequalities in power between men and pregnant women are very powerful countervailing reasons that should at present prevail against requiring notice and attempting to compel an inclusiveness that does not spring naturally from their relationship.[119] While the Court has denied the husband a veto over a woman's abortion decision, it has yet to review lower court decisions holding unconstitutional such notice requirements.[120] Were it, despite the countervailing reasons, to permit states to require notice, the interpersonal dialogue of woman and physician would expand to include the male. He would have substantial influence, to the extent that the woman wished to maintain a family unit with him. Were she to abort in disregard of his firm opposition, the woman and physician would appear to have exclusive control and the male none, although he may well have helped clarify the decision. But in such circumstance, their procreative relationship would have failed. Then the male would no longer have a useful role because his interest in the dialogue, given the woman's privileged status, arises within his participation in their procreative community.

Thus, the procedure of choice involves the woman in an interpersonal dialogue with physicians and counselors, with her family (or judge) if she is a minor, and potentially with her mate. As such, the woman must express and assert her intentions and reasons to another: to that extent her private feelings are subjected to the interpersonal discipline of a legally mandated process. The simple requirement that one who decides must express his reasons is one of the primary judicial techniques for self-discipline and for review of governmental action, even when a court otherwise lacks substantive criteria with which to review a decision and its justification. In the privacy of an informal informed-consent process, it may help here as well.

If this seems to some a pale image of the kind of self-reflection discussed earlier, by which constitutive attachments may be discovered, it must be recognized that the law can do only so much in furthering that goal. The *Roe* Court implicitly concluded—accurately it seems to me—that in our culture no more populated, public, or formal process[121] than this could hope to foster a dyadic choice and elicit a reliable decision as to whether the woman is committed to her symbiotic unit and judges herself then ready to become (or again become) a mother. To permit strangers (who lack committed involvement with the woman and her dyad and therefore lack knowledge of them and of the woman's other generative commitments) to act as impersonal representatives of the fetus would fundamentally alter the interpersonal process *Roe* created. Indeed, any increased formality, imposition of substantive criteria, and greater representation than that afforded by a dialogue with a physician or health-care counselor, schooled in privacy, commitment to patient well-being, and the enhancement of health, could risk producing a less accurate self-reflective process and a woman's less than whole-hearted compliance with the procedure's outcome. After all, who better than the woman is able to know whether she is prepared to be committed to her fetus-infant?

The Woman's Internal Dialogue. It may be claimed that the foregoing greatly overstates and idealizes the interpersonal aspect of abortion-choice and that physicians, as they have organized the delivery of abortion services, have created a regime in which the woman is the *de facto* exclusive, private, and solitary decision maker.

The Court in *Roe* appears to have assumed that a decision would be made with a woman's own trusted physician whom she has known and consulted for some extended period of time. But that is not the way many receive medical services, especially those who are young, less well-to-do, and geographically mobile. This is especially the case with abortion services, which physicians have provided in substantial degree since *Roe* through clinics devoted primarily to abortion and contraceptive services. Indeed, the Court itself has adamantly protected this form of service delivery from state efforts to limit it, in order to protect choice by nonwealthy women.[122]

In some locales, custom may have produced a condition in which the woman's choice is implemented with only minimal dialogue, the anonymity of the urban clinic and lapses in the application of the informed consent doctrine[123] making her decision truly a private choice. If such is the case, the interpersonal prescriptions discussed in the foregoing may still not be offended, to the extent that the abortion decision simply lies outside the compass of Burt's analysis. For abortion addresses a symbiotic unit characterized by a degree of dependence that may qualitatively distinguish it from cases that involve at least a pretense of separate and individuated persons. The fetal portion of the dyad has never had the interpersonal or social existence that contributes so substantially, according to Burt, to individual identity, and thus it lacks even the minimal identity that Burt ascribes to his silent patients. Moreover, the caregiving required of the pregnant woman is of an entirely different magnitude from the physician's responsibilities that he discusses.

But before concluding that abortion-choice has become truly private in the sense of being both completely internal and self-regarding, it should be noted that it would be a mistake to look only to the woman's individual act and fail to see that a broad social debate has determined the availability and kinds of abortion services, social attitudes toward those services, and the language with which we think about abortion. A woman who seeks an abortion confronts the impact of this societal dialogue in attenuated form in her physician and the clinic.

Moreover, and far more important, it is in the nature of mothering that the pregnant woman herself, in health, assumes an empathic identificatory office in which it is a part of her creative power to act on behalf of the dyadic unit. In preparation for this responsibility of motherhood, the boundaries of her identity loosen and expand. Studies of abortion decision making suggest that women can and do assume this office and engage in an inner dialogue in which they examine what is best for the unit.[124] The woman may clarify her self-definition by examining the good of the dyad, and evaluate her potential relationship with her offspring by appraising her own present capacities for symbiotic participation.

Furthermore, some evidence also exists that women can accommodate to this office without suffering from the irrationalities and rigidities Burt at times seems to associate with the exclusive allocation of decisional power. The view that the woman's decision to abort can have self-destructive meaning[125] is more than counterbalanced by evidence that the decision (itself, and by comparison with the alternative of choosing to give birth) is not destructively traumatic as it has been made in a regime of legality. Relief is often the dominant feeling, although normal grieving may follow, especially at anniversaries of the abortion or during subsequent pregnancies that go to term.[126] Nor is an abortion likely to produce long-term psychiatric sequelae except among women who, pressured by others, abort despite substantial ambivalence; or who, avoiding such experience of destruction and loss as may be theirs from the abortion, fail to mourn the dyad's passing; or who already evidence a pattern of conflicted intimate relationships and of psychopathology which could make them just as vulnerable to childbirth, if not more so.[127] For many, abortion appears to be an event that does not significantly injure self-esteem; and for some it can mark a turning point, or psychological crisis, that leads to greater maturity.[128] For as Carol Gilligan has shown, abortion can be an act of taking responsibility for self and other.

Representatives of the Silent Fetus. Even an ideal realization of an interpersonal decision-making process would presumably leave regulators discontent with the dialogue that they imagine within the woman and between the woman and her physician. They believe, surely, that among the "cacophony of voices" to which Burt refers the silent fetus is missing.

Because *Roe* structured an interpersonal process, because many hospitals and physicians have been reluctant to perform abortions, and because women have sought abortion in substantial numbers, specialized abortion clinics have developed.[129] As a result, antiabortion groups have been able to force themselves into that process directly by addressing pregnant women as they approach the clinic door. Sometimes carrying pictures of fetuses, they try to enter this dialogue in two ways: by seeking to represent the fetus to the woman, and by encouraging the woman's generative potential.

Some try to recreate a direct conversation with the silent fetus. Attempting to reason about abortion by appeal to the golden rule, they ask the woman, for example: "Would you have wanted your mother to abort you?"[130]

This question asks those who possess an independent identity and individuated self to cross over a great epistemic divide in human consciousness. In most situations, an adult who has successfully traversed this monumental divide may have conscious difficulty retracing his steps. After all, he must return to that condition in which he was carried before he enjoyed independent locomotion, when his needs were met without words, which he lacked, and when his self was recognized by others before it existed. Indeed, if a dialogue between oneself as a fetus and one's mother seems impossible to imagine, a futile exercise, it constitutes good evidence that the effort discussed in chapter 1 to ascribe an individuated personhood to the fetus is mistaken.[131] Perhaps this very question reflects an adult conceit, an attempt to maintain the mature fiction of being an independent and autonomous self-made being, even back then in retrospect, and of never having been a fused and "identity-less" creature utterly dependent on a woman.

Even allowing the attempt by those who are strangers to the pregnant woman, utterly ignorant of her and her dyad, to engage her in this imagined dialogue, the results are inconclusive. For it is in the nature of the sounds of silence that people hear different voices: where some hear screams, others hear softer sounds.[132]

The opening query of this dialogue—"Would you have wanted your mother to abort you?"—comes to this: What claims do you, imagining yourself a fetus, feel you could have made, with the law's coercion, against your own Mother? That question leads to others. By what entitlement would you claim a right to her love and efforts on your behalf? What sacrifice would you have coerced? What loss of freedom would you have imposed on her? What pain would you have inflicted? Would you have wanted her prosecuted for feticide? In later years, how much would you sacrifice for your Mother in restitution for the choice you would deny her?

Some, with much anger for wrongs done or imagined, may answer these questions extravagantly. Others may be unable to respond, having trouble imagining their mothers with goals and wishes separate from her children. Yet others may feel a Prufrockian ontological doubt about imagining claims from the womb against parents who are shouldering their adult duty of self-responsibility.[133] No single description can possibly characterize the claims that each person would make on his own mother, imagining her pregnant with the fetus that, after individuation, became himself.

The intervenor's effort to structure the dialogue around the sounds of fetal silence does not work: we lack the epistemological ground for reconstructing a conversation, and the multitude of imagined responses precludes generalization. If at all, such an imagined dialogue begins with the woman who carries and nurtures the fetus and enjoys the potential of helping to constitute its infantile self by becoming its mother. Reflecting upon her self and her inner world of procreative purposes, she begins to have a basis for knowing her offspring. Only she may be in a position to interpret the meaning of this silence.[134]

There is a different conversation that the woman can have, within herself, with her physician and family, and with those who insist upon intervening at the clinic door. It involves the question of what she intends to do with her loving and generative potential, whether that includes begetting, bearing, and rearing her own children, and in addition or as an alternative, caring for others, for communities, and for ideas.

Outside abortion clinics, antiabortion groups seek to persuade women to use their generative potential to carry through each and every pregnancy; and some engage to support them in this latter choice throughout gestation. The question of how persons use their generative potential is an ethical one that broadens the focus from any one pregnancy to a way of living in a particular community. Within this context, the miracle of reproduction, the uses of sexuality, and the protection of family life may be understood; and the character of the participants in this dialogue, how they care for their loved ones, their work, and their community, may be evaluated. The focus of this inquiry avoids the failing effort to represent a fetus in the abstract, and instead may engage adults in coequal dialogue about how all participants will actualize their generative potential in our society. It is also a question that can equally be addressed to men.

4

Coda: Communal Attachments

HERE THEN IS ONE RELATIONAL ACCOUNT. NO SUCH ACCOUNT WILL altogether supplant the categories reviewed in chapter 1. Those categories, rooted as they are in some of our experience, are too fundamental to the way we think to be abandoned, too essential generally to the mutual respect we call rights and to the freedom and autonomy our culture protects. Nor will the demands of female equality permit them to be completely supplanted in this of all subjects. For the woman who declines to enter the dyad and remains in or returns to a nondyadic state, the concepts of chapter 1 do well enough for the law's rough requirements, although they may not afford her a language with which to account to herself for her range of feeling.

But during her pregnancy and at the point of choice those categories do not suffice and ought not be the exclusive ones of the debate: they neither fully capture the reality of procreation nor how people conceive this reality, including those who define the legal status of the fetus. I have accordingly attempted to offer a supplementary account to enlarge the description of this period and to comprehend the present law of procreative choice.

The language of the dyad is not the only possible one for this task, as chapter 2 showed, and for describing what lies behind the concept of procreational privacy. But more than others available to me, it serves to break through the abstract universalism of the language of rights to the particularity of this woman-with-fetus, involving as it does not only an autonomous subject but dependent and constitutive attachments. This language may be used to reject the claim that the fetus can be described adequately with terms that are roughly appropriate for the individual adult, even as it attempts to avoid the underdescribing and undervaluing of the procreative process characteristic of some accounts discussed in chapter 1. Growing as it does out of a clinical tradition, moreover, this dyadic language suggests that the fetus may not in any direct way be the object of representation by strangers who are uninvolved with its care. Finally, its description of the mother-infant relationship challenges the assumption that a woman's love is justly ripe for exploitation.

The psychoanalytic tradition also offers a sufficiently complex account of sexual procreation as to begin to accord with common experience. Such experience suggests that women need and take a period of time after fertilization and before birth to make a dyadic decision. This leads to the standard of a reasonable period of choice for defining the time during which an elective abortion may be appropriate. Society may shorten this period by creating the social, economic, and technological conditions for making a prompt decision, just as it may eventually shorten the period of choice presently defined by the fetal-viability standard by devoting resources to neonatology. But a resulting change in the age of viability reduces the period of choice without changing the contexts of procreative decision that actually confront women. By contrast, the reasonable period of choice focuses social policy directly on those factors, such as education and medical care, that encourage a more enlightened and prompt dyadic responsibility. Finally, unlike the viability standard, the reasonable period of choice does not adhere to the logic of separateness.

It may also be noted that the relational description offered here confounds the constellations of values that the sociologist Kristen Luker has identified as distinguishing antiabortion activists (who value motherhood, and sexual and family values they associate with it) from prochoice activists (who value autonomy, rationality, and self-control). Such constellations are logically far from inevitable. Thus, the dyadic perspective justifies with the same reasons both abortion-choice for a reasonable period of time and the protection that tort and criminal law afford the fetus. And it explains to us why our society and our physicians may be equally and simultaneously committed, at the request of mothers, to the heroic treatment of their fetuses and at-risk newborns and to the performance of abortion. Although not addressed here, the dyadic perspective can also be used to emphasize the special status of women during pregnancy and the months after birth, a focus that favors greater support for mothering than our society presently provides; and it can support preferential treatment for the dyadic representative with respect to, for example, employment benefits, for in that capacity women are not similarly situated to men.[1] Accordingly, the dyadic perspective may evoke more fully than one that focuses exclusively on individual autonomy the nature of procreation and the choices it involves.

Finally, as compared with some other relational accounts noted in chapter 2, the dyadic approach has the advantage of not requiring a radical and general reevaluation of the language of rights and individualism in all spheres in order to apply to procreation, for it may be understood as confining the period of fusion and symbiosis to a limited period of time in each person's prehistory. As such, the account offered here does not implicate certain broader political principles of equal rights under law and a free individualism that some regulators mistakenly assert a regime of abortion-choice dangerously jeopardizes.

On that subject, accusations of historical crimes of the gravest magnitude have been made in a recent volume attributed to Ronald Reagan, president of the United States. Because this invites reaction, I shall in conclusion, rather than summarize this essay further, briefly and very suggestively risk enlarging its themes of dependence and independence, attachment and isolation, and fusion and individuality, as they relate to the nature of a social order that permits abortion-choice.

The title of that volume, *Abortion and the Conscience of the Nation*,[2] seems to imply in context that antiabortionists claim to speak not only for the silent fetus but also for an injured community, whose female members in exercising their self-regarding interest violate the nation's conscience, those enduring natural sentiments[3] and norms that are an essential part of a community's solidarity. Thus that volume would at first seem to share the perspective of those noted at the beginning of chapter 2 who argue, against the position of this essay, that a more relational and communal perspective is inconsistent with a regime of abortion-choice.[4]

But the implication of the title is at odds with the core of that book, which consists of two historical analogies that are common to the arguments of regulators and that imply that a regime of abortion-choice suffers most from its failure to respect individual rights. The volume's essay attributed to the President likens *Roe v. Wade* to *Dred Scott v. Sanford*, in which the antebellum Supreme Court read in the Constitution an intention to exclude slaves and their free descendants from membership in the community of the United States; and it likens the antiabortionists to the abolitionists, calling upon their country's conscience to recognize the "value of certain human lives" that the legal system denies. In the volume's companion essays, C. Everett Koop, surgeon general of the United States, and Malcolm Muggeridge, the writer, take the very much more extreme position of likening abortion to totalitarian oppression and more specifically to the Nazi Holocaust. But a consideration of these analogies suggests again that an exclusively individualistic perspective turns excessive for comprehending procreation.

SPEAKING FOR THE FETUS: THE ABOLITIONIST ANALOGY

In seeking to represent the silent fetus, some invoke the fourteenth amendment, as if the fetus were a member of what, in modern constitutional theory, is described as a discrete and insular minority. Because such minorities are subject to discriminatory prejudice by the majority and because the political process often fails to take into account their interests, the judiciary, this theory posits, has a heightened obligation to afford them and their rights protection under the equal protection clause of the fourteenth amendment. Until the Court or the people overturn *Roe* and the law comes to extend to the fetus the special solicitude they believe is its due under this theory, regulators insist that they themselves must continue to intervene in court and in front of clinics to try to represent it.[5]

But if one were to bear witness to his political commitment to the oppressed fetus by asserting that slogan of solidarity, "I am a fetus; we are all fetuses," he would immediately cast grave doubt on his claim for its special status as a member of a minority, requiring protection from the majoritarian political processes. For the fetus is not a distant creature, an "other," with whom many of us in the majority, the dominant "we" class, have no direct contact and no concern, and toward whom the majority may have only prejudice. We have all been fetuses. Many, including women who have had abortions, are intimately associated with pregnancies that go to term, with the beloved infants that issue from those pregnancies, and with the adults who grow from these issue. Yet the experience that all have of being a fetus, and the intimacy that most have with wanted pregnancy and children, do not dissuade some from believing that the fetus belongs to a specially victimized class that requires representation in each abortion decision by someone other than the woman who presently carries and sustains it.[6] As previously suggested, the claim by strangers to represent the fetus and to interpret its sounds of silence is particularly problematic because it is only through participation that the new generation comes into being. Representation (of abstract rights) without involvement (with persons) within a common community risks unexpected and unwanted results, as is shown by the analogy likening antiabortionists to abolitionists.

The opposition of abolitionists toward the system of slavery is clear. The attitudes and feelings of abolitionists and those in the Republican party of Lincoln toward slaves and former slaves is more complex. Not all of them wished for a world of mutual engagement with former slaves as constituent members of a greater community. At least some spoke from a vision of social relations based only on juridical equality and strict independence in a society governed by contract.[7]

This often meant economic independence. For the free-labor tradition in the Republican party saw both the system of slave labor and the system of wage labor as dangers, for each threatened independent white farmers and artisans with an economic dependence on others which seemed to them like slavery. It is hardly pushing the limits of our understanding to see in the image of the plantation a symbol of dependence that was regressive in its pull, as the supporters of Lincoln faced the rigors of free-market competition in a world increasingly dominated by wage labor.

The triumph of the Republicans helped secure the vision of independent and self-made autonomous man, his self-responsibility assured by the discipline of the free market. At its core this vision resists all dependencies, treats jural persons as free agents who are unencumbered with obligations and without claim on others. Banished was an alternative paternalistic system of dependence and restriction.[8] The adoption of the thirteenth and fourteenth amendments furthered this liberating project of extending freedom and equality of rights before the law regardless of a person's previous condition of servitude or dependence.

But the law, so envisioned, evinced difficulty in dealing with the special needs of the vulnerable class of former slaves in moving from the dependence of slavery and its abolition to independence. Having recognized that the Constitution affords formal juridical equality, the Supreme Court in case after case devastated the special efforts of the Congress to undo the institution of slavery.[9] When it enforced the political compromise of 1877 in the *Civil Rights Cases* by interpreting the fourteenth amendment in a manner that rendered unconstitutional important congressional civil rights legislation, the Supreme Court not surprisingly made the struggle against dependency the heart of its rhetorical case. Giving sadistic expression to the feeling of autonomous self-made men toward those who are vulnerable and in need, Justice Bradley taunted the former slave by suggesting that he was less than an independent man:

When a man has emerged from slavery, and by the aid of beneficent legislation has shaken off the inseparable concomitants of that state, there must be some stage in the progress of his elevation when he takes the rank of a mere citizen, and ceases to be the special favorite of the laws.[10]

Even at the turn of this century, constitutional doctrine remained distant from the modern theory of the fourteenth amendment; and the Supreme Court continued to evince hostility to claims of dependence, as it repeatedly held that state social-welfare legislation violated the fourteenth amendment. Preferring its picture of independent, autonomous, and equal men confronting one another at arm's length in the market to the legislature's picture of men made vulnerable by impersonal market forces and in need of protection from others with superior bargaining power, the Court repeatedly held that social-welfare legislation impermissibly interfered with the liberty of contract that, abstractly, employer and employee equally enjoyed. In striking down New York legislation that limited the work week of bakery employees to sixty hours, the Court wrote, in *Lochner v. New York*, that statutes "limiting the hours in which grown and intelligent men may labor to earn their living, are mere meddlesome interferences with the rights of the individual."[11] In a dissent, upon which modern constitutional critics of *Roe* rely,[12] Justice Holmes accused his brethren of using judicial review to impose their own personal beliefs on the majority of citizens who had embodied their view in state legislative enactments.

Regulators invoke the fourteenth amendment, and its ambivalent history, not on behalf of former slaves who, as "grown and intelligent men" (to quote *Lochner*), needed only (but could not obtain) the removal of the badges and incidents of slavery; but rather on behalf of a being that is only and utterly dependent and who becomes grown and intelligent through first being the "special favorite" (to quote the *Civil Rights Cases*) of an adult who lovingly accepts that dependence. The lessons of this history should caution those who would speak for the fetus only by insisting on abstract negative rights and jural equality from afar.[13]

THE TOTALITARIAN ANALOGY

Surgeon General Koop suggests that abortion is but the entering wedge here for society's radical devaluation of the individual and the sanctity of his or her life, which has already once found ultimate expression elsewhere in faceless fascist slaughter. Abortion seems to threaten the triumph of the total state, in which a mass psychology of the living joins with the mass graves of the dead to obliterate the individual, his and her worth, and his and her conscience. Koop quotes another physician to the effect that:

If there are those in society who think this step [abortion] would be good, let them work for a totalitarian form of government where beginning with the infirm and incompetent and ending with the intellectually dissident, non-persons are disposed of day and night by those in power.[14]

At a time when differences between authoritarian and totalitarian regimes are said to be fundamental in nature, it is surprising to find those who, in suggesting the analogy, are unable to make the far more obvious and essential distinction between private choice and state coercion. They also neglect the distinction between the (often racist) destruction of whole communities and ways of life and the self-governing decisions of individuals and families respecting their reproduction. Although the analogy ignores evidence and abandons any pretense of historical accuracy to a deeply shocking extent[15] and should be dismissed, perhaps reference to competing interpretations of totalitarianism may be instructive in thinking about what, if any, lessons can be drawn from the comparison.

Koop implies that abortion weakens respect for the individual, which in turn weakens the moral restraints that protect a society against totalitarian oppression. And Noonan, as noted at the outset, equates the refusal to define fetuses as persons with a totalitarian exercise of ruthless state power to pick and choose among human beings those who are more and less worthy of state recognition and protection. Such claims bear at least a distant resemblance to one interpretation that totalitarianism develops when the rule of law breaks down; and that, further, the only firm rule of law is one that insists upon an abstract universalism and a pure formal equality among all that is inconsistent with the particularity of judgments about groups and individuals made by the modern regulatory state. Any other understanding of law would, it is said, leave the individual at enormous risk of oppression, of being used as a means to the ends of the group, and the majority weakened in its commitment to individual rights and vulnerable to "totalitarian temptations." From such a perspective, a relational approach which would call into question the absolute separateness and individuality of adults may itself be far down the totalitarian path. But as already noted, the dyadic concept offered here does not derogate from the recognition of adult individuality and separateness.

Nonetheless, for those making the comparison, abortion-choice seems to threaten a breakdown in the protection of each person that the rule of law should afford by opposing the woman's particularistic claims to exercise a self-interested power with universal claims on behalf of the fetus as a creature with at least potential rights. But that suggestion confronts the different understanding that the totalitarian propensities of industrial society are instead, as Sandel puts it, nurtured by the dislocations of attachment and the anonymity of selves in a modern society governed only distantly by abstract rules and without multiple strong, mediating participatory institutions.[16]

From this latter perspective it should be important that *Roe* reduced state authority by recognizing the exercise of procreative power as an act of dyadic autonomy beyond government domination or the demands of organized groups. Contrary to Noonan's interpretation of it as a positivist and totalitarian approach to legal personhood, in which an all-powerful state controls the concept of personhood and can invidiously withdraw its protection from some, the law's privacy doctrine instead treats certain relationships as substantially beyond the limited powers of government. This doctrine may be understood as acknowledging one of the deepest of human bonds, mother-love, and as recognizing that the beginnings of personhood are found beyond governmental regulation in the privacy of the fetus-infant's intense relationship with its mother. At first essential to survival, that relationship, when later conjoined with the wider communal supports of family and school and city, begins to protect offspring against the disorders of isolation and non-attachment.[17]

Moreover, the privacy doctrine has its origins in the protection of family relationships, not individual autonomy. It may be understood as recognizing the family as an institution that pre-dates the state and has an autonomy apart from it, even as the family, the seedbed of society's bonds, contributes crucially to social solidarity.[18] As interpreted here, the law of abortion-choice resists the denigration of attachment and the specter of state-parenting that is found in the logic of separateness, which sees in the potential of new technology a resolution of the abortion dispute.

Finally, it may be noted that the law of abortion-choice recognizes the medical profession as a mediating institution for resolving the complexities of abortion.[19] It has accorded some legal deference to this ancient profession of clinical arts and its capacity, apart from the dictates of the positive state, to develop sustaining values respecting life's preservation, death's dispensation, and the well-being of health, which at its best it can foster in its practitioners.

In *The Origins of Totalitarianism*, Hannah Arendt chronicles the way in which she believes rootless mass men and women, cut loose from the moorings of older institutions and professions, may come to support totalitarian regimes.[20] She concludes this way:

What prepares men for totalitarian domination in the non-totalitarian world is the fact that loneliness, once a borderline experience usually suffered in certain marginal social conditions like old age, has become an everyday experience of the evergrowing masses of our century. . . . The "ice-cold reasoning" and the "mighty tentacle" of dialectics which "seizes you as in a vise" appears like a last support in a world where nobody is reliable and nothing can be relied upon.

But concluding on a note of hope, Arendt writes that all historical ends also mark a new beginning:

"[T]hat a beginning be made man was created" said Augustine. This beginning is guaranteed by each new birth; it is indeed every man.[21]

It may be added that a beginning begins with a mother, and a good beginning with her committed to the new birth. This is the first community. Perhaps by being reliably committed through choice and by intermingling herself with them, she may do her part to protect, though only the community can try to vouch-

safe, the new woman and new man against the lonely root-
lessness of which Arendt warns.

■ ■ ■

Quite apart from their historical subject, these competing interpretations of totalitarianism relate to competing visions of a
good and cohering society, which for many is presently wanting.
But the relationship of these two interpretations to our present
complex reality is problematic at best. As such they have nothing
simple and consistent to teach those of differing views about the
appropriate uses (and appropriate limits) of state power to re-
gain such coherence. With the subject of abortion as with so
much else, one's beginning partially determines one's end.

But it will not do to rest satisfied with one's initial perspective on the subject. For abortion, pertaining so centrally as it
does to the heart of procreation, may be more satisfactorily
understood with an enlarged and relational view of our origins
and an appreciation of the meaning of the pregnant woman's
choice whether to undertake a constitutive relationship.

I began with the hope that by focusing on the centrality to
ourselves of our deepest relationships, a reclamation of shared
understandings might afford some common ground to ongoing
disputants. Even if such territory exists and supports greater
dialogue, it may still be, regrettably, that no ready peace in the
abortion debate will be forthcoming, for as we have seen even
common concepts are the subject of disputed meaning. Yet perhaps such territory can at least provide a locus of agreement
favoring other essential social policies from which the divisive
but fundamental abortion debate diverts our politics. May we
not, for example, reach a consensus, so sadly wanting, that support for the chosen dyad and the family that nurtures it should
be the subject of our most intense and common concern?

Notes

1. The Supreme Court cases extending the abortion liberty against state regulation are: Roe v. Wade, 410 U.S. 113 (1973); Doe v. Bolton, 410 U.S. 179 (1973); Planned Parenthood of Mo. v. Danforth, 428 U.S. 52 (1976); Colautti v. Franklin, 439 U.S. 379 (1979); Bellotti v. Baird (II), 443 U.S. 622 (1979); Akron v. Akron Center for Reproductive Health, 462 U.S. 416 (1983); Planned Parenthood Ass'n v. Ashcroft, 462 U.S. 476 (1983); Thornburgh v. American College of Obst. & Gyn., 106 S. Ct. 2169 (1986) (recently reaffirming the commitment of the majority to *Roe*).

Other abortion decisions of the U.S. Supreme Court do not restrict the power of the states with respect to abortion. For example, the government is not required to provide abortion services in public hospitals or fund such services, for example through Medicaid, even when medically necessary for the woman's health. *See* Beal v. Doe, 432 U.S. 438 (1977); Maher v. Roe, 432 U.S. 464 (1977); Poelker v. Doe, 432 U.S. 519 (1977); Harris v. McRae, 448 U.S. 297 (1980); Williams v. Zbaraz, 448 U.S. 358 (1980). Other cases that do not restrict state regulation of abortion include: H. L. v. Matheson, 450 U.S. 398 (1981) (state may sometimes require notice to parents of a minor's intent to abort); Connecticut v. Menillo, 423 U.S. 9 (1975) (state may prohibit nonphysicians from performing abortions); Simopoulos v. Virginia, 462 U.S. 506 (1983) (acceptable regulation of second trimester abortions); Anders v. Floyd, 440 U.S. 445 (1979) (same); Singleton v. Wulff, 428 U.S. 106 (1976) (issue of standing); Bellotti v. Baird (I), 428 U.S. 132 (1976) (abstention).

2. The justices in the majority, who have been committed to *Roe* and successor cases, are (as of this writing) Brennan, age 81, Marshall, 79, Blackmun, 79, and Stevens, 67, plus retired Justice Powell, 80.

Two other justices, White, 70, and Chief Justice Rehnquist, 63, have, in dissent, called for the overruling of *Roe*, so as to permit the legislatures of the fifty states, the thousands of county and municipal governments, and, possibly, the Congress of the United States to choose whether to forbid abortion altogether or to regulate and curtail substantially the medical performance of abortions. Thornburgh v. American College of Obst. & Gyn., 106 S. Ct. at 2192 (White, J., dissenting) (joined by Rehnquist, J.); *cf. id.* at 2190 (Burger, C.J., dissenting) (indicating that he was prepared to entertain a reconsideration of *Roe*).

Justice O'Connor, age 57 and the only woman on the Court, would give states a very much freer rein to regulate the performance of abortions and thereby make it far more difficult, expensive, and burdensome for women to terminate their pregnancies. But she has refrained from indicating whether she would also join an opinion that, by overruling *Roe*, would remove the constitutional constraint that presently prevents the complete prohibition of elective or therapeutic abortion. *See* Akron v. Akron Center for Reproductive Health, 462 U.S. at 452 (O'Connor, J., dissenting); Thornburgh v. American College of Obst. & Gyn., 106 S. Ct. at 2206 (O'Connor, J., dissenting); *see infra* chapter 1 notes 68–69.

Justice Scalia, age 51, recently appointed by President Reagan, is too new on the Court to have been heard on this issue, but it should not be a surprise if he were to join one or the other of these dissenting positions.

3. *See, e.g.,* Laurence Tribe, *God Save this Honorable Court* (New York: Random House, 1985).

4. *See, e.g.,* Kolder, Gallagher & Parsons, "Court-Ordered Obstetrical Interventions," 316 *New Eng. J. Med.* 1192 (1987); Annas, "At Law: Pregnant Women as Fetal Containers," 16(6) *Hastings Center Report* 13 (1986) (reporting prosecution of woman for causing child to be born brain-dead by failing to comply with physician's warning to refrain from sexual intercourse and drug use and to seek immediate medical care in case of certain pregnancy symptoms); Nelson, Beiggy & Weil, "Forced Medical Treatment of Pregnant Women: 'Compelling Each To Live as Seems Good to the Rest,'" 37 *Hastings L.J.* 703 (1986); In the Matter of Baby X, 97 *Mich. App.* 111, 293 N.W.2d 736 (1980); *see also* Lenow, "The Fetus as a Patient: Emerging Rights as a Person?," 9 *Am. J. Law & Med.* 1 (1983).

INTRODUCTION

1. *See* Magda Denes, *In Necessity and Sorrow: Life and Death in an Abortion Hospital* (New York: Basic Books, 1976) (the best of the case studies of the practice of abortion); Linda Bird Francke, *The Ambivalence of Abortion* (New York: Random House, 1978); *see also* Kristin Luker, *Taking Chances: Abortion and the Decision Not To Contracept* (Berkeley, Los Angeles, London: University of California Press, 1975); Bernard Nathanson, *Aborting America* (Garden City, NY: Doubleday & Co., 1979); *cf.* Carol Gilligan, *In A Different Voice: Psychological Theory and Women's Development* (Cambridge, MA: Harvard University Press, 1982) (describing interviews with women who have had abortions).

2. Luker suggests that the conflict over abortion, at least among abortion activists, arises from fundamentally different world views, which are linked to class positions and their attendant life chances. Quieting of the conflict in the foreseeable future is therefore unlikely. Kristin Luker, *Abortion and the Politics of Motherhood* (Berkeley, Los Angeles, London: University of California Press, 1984). For an example of just how far apart the two sides are, *see* Sidney Callahan & Daniel Callahan, eds., *Abortion: Understanding Differences* (New York: Plenum Press, 1984) (containing articles by women on both sides of the debate who, although they have seriously attempted to communicate with each other, still lack a common ground).

The current compromise of a right to choose but of no federal funding of abortions may be a political compromise that is workable (if unsatisfying) for all but the poor. Whether chance political and legal events will permit this working compromise to hold is not yet clear.

3. Since the antiabortion party has joined with political forces that characterize a broad range of issues in terms of market regulation, it may be appropriate in this essay (and more accurate than the phrases "pro life" and "pro abortion") to characterize the contrasting positions on abortion-choice in terms of market regulation. *Cf.* Posner, "The Uncertain Protection of Privacy in the Supreme Court," 1979 *Sup. Ct. Rev.* 173, 196 ("Court has simply deregulated 'the family'").

A free market in abortion services, unregulated and unfunded by the government, in no way guarantees women, even those with sufficient funds, actual choice since abortion service providers face barriers to market entry aside from the law. Among all counties in the United States, 82 percent, containing 30 percent of the women aged 15–44, lacked any "identified abortion service provider" in 1985; and only some of the providers that did exist performed second trimester abortions. Of all nonmetropolitan counties, 91 percent (containing 79 percent of all nonmetropolitan women) lacked any abortion services; and only 2 percent of all abortions were performed in nonmetropolitan areas. Moreover, many of these nonmetropolitan providers were private physicians who may restrict their services to established patients. Even in metropolitan areas, 50 percent of the counties (containing 15 percent of metropolitan women) lacked a provider. Since 1982, the number of abortion service providers has decreased and the number of counties without a provider has increased. *See* Henshaw, Forrest & Van Vort, "Abortion Services in the United States, 1984 and 1985," 19 *Family Planning Perspectives* 63, 64–67 (1987) (discussing disparities in distribution of abortion services and their impact on abortion rates); *see also* Henshaw, Forrest & Blaine, "Abortion Services in the United States, 1981 and 1982," 16 *Family Planning Perspectives* 119, 120 (1984).

4. *See* John Noonan, Jr., *A Private Choice: Abortion in America in the Seventies* (New York: The Free Press, 1979), pp. 3–4; Noonan, "The Root and Branch of *Roe v. Wade*," 63 *Neb. L. Rev.* 668, 678 (1984) (attributing at the theoretical level a positivist and totalitarian position on personhood to Hans Kelsen, *Pure Theory of Law*, trans. Max Knight [Berkeley, Los Angeles, London: University of California Press, 1967]); John Noonan, Jr., *Persons and Masks of the Law* (New York: Farrar, Straus & Giroux, 1976); *cf.* L. W. Sumner, *Abortion and Moral Theory* (Princeton: Princeton University Press, 1981), p. 57, in which the author states: "In feminist treatments of abortion few meaningful steps have been taken toward clarifying the status of the fetus. . . . [T]he fetus has simply been ignored or forgotten."

5. The phrase comes from Alice Balint, "Love for the Mother and Mother-Love," 30 *Int'l J. Psychoanalysis* 251 (1949), *reprinted in* Michael Balint, *Primary Love and Psycho-analytic Technique* (New York: Liveright Publishing Co., 1965).

6. Those familiar with the secular philosophical and legal literature on abortion may wish to skip the beginning of chapter 1 and proceed to the critique of the technological approach that sees in the potential development of artificial placentas an important means of resolving the abortion issue. *See infra* text accompanying chapter 1 notes 70 *et seq.*

1. INDIVIDUAL RIGHTS AND THE LOGIC OF SEPARATENESS

1. For fuller summaries of the philosophical literature, *see, e.g.,* Daniel Callahan, *Abortion: Law, Choice and Morality* (New York: MacMillan, 1970); Baruch Brody, *Abortion and the Sanctity of Human Life* (Cambridge, MA: MIT Press, 1976); Jonathan Glover, *Causing Death and Saving Lives* (Middlesex, England: Penguin Books, Ltd., 1977), p. 149; Joel Feinberg, "Abortion," in *Matters of Life and Death*, ed. Tom Regan (Philadelphia: Temple University Press, 1980), p. 183; L. W. Sumner, *Abortion and Moral Theory* (Princeton: Princeton University Press, 1981); Michael Tooley, *Abortion and Infanticide* (New York: Oxford University Press, 1983); Wertheimer, "Understanding the Abortion Argument," 1 *Phil. & Pub. Aff.* 67 (1971); *see also* Daniel Wikler, "Concepts of Personhood: A Philosophical Perspective," in *Defining Human Life*, ed. Margery Shaw & A. Edward Doudera (Ann Arbor, MI: AUPHA Press, 1983); Bok, "Ethical Problems of Abortion," 2(1) *Hastings Center Studies* 33 (1974).

For anthologies of the philosophical literature, *see, e.g.,* Joel Feinberg, ed., *The Problem of Abortion*, 2d ed. (Belmont, CA: Wadsworth Publishing Co., 1984); Jay Garfield & Patricia Hennessey, eds., *Abortion: Moral and Legal Perspectives* (Amherst: University of Massachusetts Press, 1984); William Bondeson, H. Tristram Engelhardt, Jr., Stuart Spicker & Daniel Winship, eds., *Abortion and the Status of the Fetus* (Dordrecht, Holland: D. Reidel Publishing Co., 1983); Marshall Cohen, Thomas Nagel & Thomas Scanlon, eds., *The Rights and Wrongs of Abortion* (Princeton: Princeton University Press, 1974); John Noonan, Jr., ed., *The Morality of Abortion: Legal and Historical Perspectives* (Cambridge, MA: Harvard University Press, 1970).

The discussion of philosophical arguments in the text that follows does not address instrumentalist arguments for or against abortion regulation. *See* Sumner, *supra*, at 22–25 (identifying as "side issues": psychological hazards of abortion, benefits to the unwanted fetus, the dangers of overpopulation, and the risk of a devaluation of life leading to involuntary euthanasia, abandonment of the aged, and genocide).

2. In the popular debate, regulators unnecessarily argue that the conceptus (zygote at fertilization, morula in the first week, blastocyst in the second, embryo from the third up to the eighth, and fetus until birth) is alive and that it is a form of human life. Ancient assumptions, that for some period of time the fetus is in an inorganic or vegetative state that is wholly unrelated to human life, are not part of the deregulatory position.

Indeed, if all forms of human life enjoyed rights, germ plasm would require protection that it does not now receive. Although our industrial and nuclear society appears to constitute a significant threat to the future of human germ plasm, male bearers of human germ plasm are seldom substantially burdened by the law on its behalf. *Cf.* Williams, "Firing the Woman to Protect the Fetus: The Reconciliation of Fetal Protection with Employment Opportunity Goals Under Title VII," 69 *Geo. L.J.* 641 (1981) (disussing exclusion of women from certain hazardous employment).

Rather than "human life," the concept of "human being" or "person" is required in analyzing the rights at stake in abortion. Those, like Noonan, who emphasize the importance of biological processes and species membership tend to speak of the rights of human beings, whereas those, like Tooley, who emphasize psychological capacities such as self-consciousness, speak of the rights of persons. Sumner prefers to avoid these words and instead refers to those who have "moral standing." *See supra* note 1; *infra* note 8.

In the text, it is assumed for simplicity that the proponents of a criterion of personhood view it as both a necessary and sufficient condition. For example, many would view having its source in human germ plasm as necessary but not sufficient for personhood. As the age of viability decreases, a deregulator who accepts viability as a relevant criterion may come to view it only as a necessary but not sufficient condition. *See* Zaitchik, "Viability and the Morality of Abortion," 10 *Phil. & Pub. Aff.* 18, 22 (1981).

For an analysis and defense of the essentialist position that the question of abortion requires a determination of those deep characteristics that are essential or of the essence of personhood or moral standing, *see* Brody, *supra* note 1, at 100–114; Sumner, *supra* note 1, at 26–33. Requiring a theory to root its claims about rights in the character of the putative rights-holder and to establish general rules of inclusion and exclusion may guard against the prejudicial exclusion of some who appear different and unworthy to adult decision makers.

3. *See* Hare, "Abortion and the Golden Rule," 4 *Phil. & Pub. Aff.* 201,

205–206 (1975); Weiss, "The Perils of Personhood," 89 *Ethics* 66 (1978); Ruth Macklin, "When Human Rights Conflict: Two Persons, One Body," in *Defining Human Life, supra* note 1, at 225. *But see* Sumner, *supra* note 1, at 73–81; Judith Smetana, *Concepts of Self and Morality: Women's Reasoning about Abortion* (New York: Praeger Press, 1982), p. 135 (finding a woman's evaluation of the personhood question central to her decision making on abortion).

4. *See* Tooley, *supra* note 1, at 347–407; Tooley, "Abortion and Infanticide," 2 *Phil. & Pub. Aff.* 37 (1972); *see also* Warren, "On the Moral and Legal Status of Abortion," 57 *Monist* 43 (1973), *reprinted with postscript in The Problem of Abortion, supra* note 1, at 102 (adopting possibly stricter criteria for personhood than Tooley's, but developing independent grounds for opposing infanticide). For criticism, *see* Sumner, *supra* note 1, at 57–64, 137–142; Stevens, "Must the Bearer of a Right Have the Concept of That to Which He Has A Right?," 95 *Ethics* 68 (1984); Bernard Williams, *Ethics and the Limits of Philosophy* (Cambridge, MA: Harvard University Press, 1985), pp. 112–114.

Tooley's position is restrictive from the perspective of human life in that it excludes all fetuses and neonates and may exclude some who are severely mentally handicapped; it is potentially inclusive of nonhuman intelligent life and, possibly, nonliving artificial intelligence.

5. Sumner, *supra* note 1, at 142. Sumner writes:

Leaving my lawn mower out in the rain is bad for the mower . . . and swatting mosquitoes is bad for the mosquitoes; but there are no moral dimensions to any of these acts unless the interests or welfare of some sentient creature is at stake. Morality requires the existence of sentience in order to obtain a purchase on our actions.

Id. at 137. And:

Consciousness is a necessary condition of sentience, for feelings are states of mind of which their owner is aware. . . . If rationality embraces a set of cognitive capacities, then sentience is rooted in a being's affective and conative life. It is in virtue of being sentient that creatures have interests. . . . [M]orality has to do with the protection . . . of interests.

Id. at 142. Sumner's preference for sentience derives, in part, from his utilitarian philosophical position that makes the pleasure-pain system central to human morality.

6. The movie *The Silent Scream* conveyed the impression that a twelve-week-old fetus experiences pain. This appears to be an unwarranted conclusion from the available data. A simple reflex arc between sense receptors on the skin and the central nervous system can produce fetal movement in response to stimulation at eight weeks. Noonan suggests that since we are unable to know whether the fetus in fact feels pain, we should not presume the absence of pain once this biological substrate is present. *See* John Noonan, Jr., "The Experience of Pain by the Unborn," in *Abortion, Medicine and the Law*, ed. J. Douglas Butler & David Walbert (New York: Facts on File Publications, 1986), pp. 360, 364; *cf.* Report of the HEW Ethics Advisory Board, "Protection of Human Subjects," 44 *Fed. Reg.* 35033, 35040 (1979) (noting that some define "primitive sentience" as the capacity not to experience but to respond to certain sensory stimuli, which arises at eight to ten weeks). However, mere responsiveness is not indicative of pain since any living cytoplasm is irritable or responsive.

But these neural connections do not involve the forebrain and what is typically called sentience, which does not seem to occur until after mid-second trimester at the earliest. One commentator has compared mid-second trimester brain development to the brain state of Karen Quinlan. Even at the beginning of the third trimester, a prematurely delivered infant remains in an ambiguous torpor or sleepy state, though, reports Noonan, it may cry. Not until well into the third trimester are there periods of wakeful alertness. In the intervening period there has been, at about thirty weeks, substantial growth in the cerebral cortex with substantial development of synapse connections. *See* Clifford Grobstein, "A Biological Perspective on the Origin of Human Life and Personhood," in *Defining Human Life, supra* note 1, at 8–10; *see also* Sumner, *supra* note 1, at 149; *infra* note 12.

7. Regulators must provide a justification for distinguishing preconception potential infants and human haploid life from post-conception potential infants. For example, they must explain why spermicides are permissible. Writes Sumner:

Liberals have difficulty in establishing birth as a moral threshold, and thus in distinguishing abortion from infanticide. Preserving the significance of birth requires resort to a shallow criterion of moral standing (spatial location, physical connection to another, etc.). A deeper criterion, if it denies moral standing to fetuses, will deny it also to infants. . . . Conservatives have difficulty in establishing conception as a moral threshold, and thus in distinguishing abortion from contraception. Preserving the significance of conception requires resort to a shallow criterion of moral standing (membership in the human species). A deeper criterion, if it awards moral standing to fetuses, will award it also to gametes.

Sumner, *supra* note 1, at 105.

For Sumner's discussion of sentience and viability, *see id.* at 128–154.

8. John Noonan, Jr., "An Almost Absolute Value in History," in *The Morality of Abortion: Legal and Historical Perspectives, supra* note 1, at 54–57. This position rejects the "developmental" approach that the fetus gradually acquires characteristics of personhood through growth; further, it denies that after fertilization there is any point in fetal development after which its subsequent condition sufficiently differs from any prior condition as to permit reasonable line-drawing. *See* Callahan, *supra* note 1, at 384.

It is worth noting that the title of Noonan's article appears to identify "history" primarily with the intellectual work of males who are Western and monastic, and "values" primarily with the written expression of ideas but not also with those practices lived in daily family life by women and men.

For a criticism of the emphasis upon the zygote's unique genetic endowment as underplaying the "environmental" influences of the woman interacting with the fetal genetic program, *see infra* chapter 2 note 9.

9. For a discussion of the importance of twinning, *see, e.g.,* Paul Ramsey, "Reference Points in Deciding About Abortion," in *The Morality of Abortion, supra* note 1, at 66; *cf.* Hellegers, "Fetal Development," 31 *Theological Studies* 4 (1970); James McCartney, "Some Roman Catholic Concepts of Person and Their Implications for the Ontological Status of the Unborn," in *Abortion and the Status of the Fetus, supra* note 1, at 313, 315–318; Grobstein, *supra* note 6, at 4 (studies of other animals suggest that different genotypes can combine to grow into a unique biological organism). *But see* Brody, *supra* note 1, at 91–92 (criticizing stress on twinning).

But while the blastocyst is multicellular, whether it is a mere collection of cells or a unique integral physical unit that is *indivisum in se* is debated. *Compare* Grobstein, *supra* note 6, at 4–5 *with* "Audience Discussion," in *Defining Human Life, supra* note 1, at 25–27.

With respect to the potential of the blastocyst to develop into a cancer or other growth, *see* Report of the HEW Ethics Advisory Board, *supra* note 6, at 35039; *see also* Rebecca Cook, "Legal Abortion: Limits and Contributions to Human Life," in *Abortion: Medical Progress and Social Implications*, Ciba Foundation Symposium 115, ed. Ruth Porter & Maeve O'Connor (London: Pitman, 1985), pp. 211, 212.

10. Of fertilized ova, it is estimated that only 37 percent eventually are born (leaving aside intentional abortions). Embryonic loss is estimated to be 18 percent in the first week after fertilization, and 32 percent in the second. Half of all loss is attributed to chromosomal abnormality. *See* Report of the HEW Ethics Advisory Board, *supra* note 6, at 35034; Cook, *supra* note 9, at 212. *But cf.* Noonan, *supra* note 8, at 55–56 (estimating 80 percent survival rate; relying on high survival rate to distinguish one's obligation to zygotes from one's obligation to the haploid phase of life, thereby impliedly justifying contraception while opposing abortion).

This degree of fetal loss is problematic for a regulator who argues that personhood begins at fertilization and that a good samaritan duty to aid it exists; for then persons might be under an obligation to develop and take special precautions against early miscarriage although such actions would interfere with the natural selection process. *See generally* "Discussion," in *Abortion: Medical Progress and Social Implications, supra* note 9, at 133–134 (arguing that abortion must be understood within the context of substantial fetal wastage, which is part of a natural design for producing healthy infants).

11. *See, e.g.,* Bernard Nathanson, *Aborting America* (Garden City, NY: Doubleday & Co., 1979), pp. 216–217. Implantation was once thought to have the advantageous characteristic of signaling itself to the human world through physical changes in the woman and chemical

signs that pregnancy tests can recognize. As distinguished from prevention of implantation, termination of pregnancy after implantation involved an intention to abort a specific pregnancy or, where pregnancy
was not verified, an avoidance of available knowledge which some
might consider a "reckless disregard" of its possibility. Now sophisticated (but expensive) tests may identify fertilization prior to implantation in at least some cases, although not without many false-negatives.
Increasingly reliable tests might eliminate a distinction between prevention and termination of implantation that is based on available
knowledge and specific intent (although a woman's actual knowledge of
her pregnancy might not occur until much later).

Proposed legislation and constitutional amendments purporting to
forbid abortion by defining human life as arising at conception leave
ambiguous whether fertilization or implantation is intended.

12. For a discussion of histological differentiation, *see* Becker, "Human Being: The Boundaries of A Concept," 4 *Phil. & Pub. Aff.* 334, 344
(1975). The turn of phrase "becoming human" into "human being" is
his.

For the identification of sentience with lower brain-stem development, *see* Sumner, *supra* note 1, at 145–150.

For a discussion of higher brain development, *see* Quinn, "Abortion:
Identity and Loss," 13 *Phil. & Pub. Aff.* 24, 32–33 (1984) (suggesting full
development of the central nervous system in the late fetus as a likely
point for treating the human organism that has been a fetus as now
being or having become a human being); *see also* Blumenfeld, "Abortion
and the Human Brain," 32 *Phil. Studies* 251 (1977).

For a discussion of the relationship of the definitions of personhood
and death, *see* Robert Veatch, "Definitions of Life and Death: Should
There Be Consistency?," in *Defining Human Life, supra* note 1, at 99; *see
also* Callahan, *supra* note 1, at 386–389.

Veatch maps various biological criteria that may mark the beginning of the person against analogous criteria that define a person's
death. If death is defined as the end of organized brain function, then
neither simple electrical activity in the brain, nor a functioning cardiovascular system, nor a simple heartbeat are of social relevance in defining death. Not even a unique genetic makeup is relevant since individual cells with a person's genes may remain alive for days after "death."
If the criteria of "death" define what is essential to personhood, the
fetus achieves that with which a person cannot be deemed dead, writes
Veatch, between twenty weeks and the end of the second trimester (depending on whether only lower brain or, as some including Veatch now
urge, higher cortical functioning is required). But of course, writes
Veatch, the fetus has potential that the dead lack. How society wishes to
treat that potential is another question.

Veatch's advocacy of higher brain function as the definition of death
leads him summarily to dismiss simple electrical waves as irrelevant

and lower brain stem activity as inconclusive. *See also* Tooley, *supra* note 1, at 347–407; Bernat, Culver & Gert, "Defining Death in Theory and Practice," 12(1) *Hastings Center Report* 5 (1982); Rhoden, "The New Neonatal Dilemma: Live Births from Late Abortions," 72 *Geo. L.J.* 1451, 1493 n.335 (1984); Note, "Technological Advances and *Roe v. Wade*: The Need to Rethink Abortion Law," 29 *UCLA L. Rev.* 1194, 1207–1210 (1982) (describing fetal brain development).

By contrast, Brody, reviewing data on the beginning of brain function, concludes that the fetus becomes a person sometime between the second and twelfth week depending on whether a cardiovascular or brain definition of death is used. With respect to the latter, he asserts that the brain commences functioning at six weeks, but does not initiate fetal movement until between nine and twelve weeks. If death were instead the absence of cardiovascular operation, then personhood, Brody believes, would arrive somewhere between two to seven weeks. Brody, *supra* note 1, at 100–111.

13. Concerning quickening and the common law, *see* James Mohr, *Abortion in America: The Origins and Evolution of National Policy, 1800–1900* (New York: Oxford University Press, 1978); *cf.* Gavigan, "The Criminal Sanction as It Relates To Human Reproduction: The Genesis of the Statutory Prohibition of Abortion," 5 *J. Legal History* 20 (1984).

Concerning viability, *see* Zaitchik, *supra* note 2; Tribe, "The Supreme Court-1972 Term, Foreword: Toward a Model of Roles in the Due Process of Life and Law," 87 *Harv. L. Rev.* 1, 27–28 (1973).

Concerning resemblance after middevelopment, *see* Wertheimer, *supra* note 1; Beverly Harrison, *Our Right to Choose* (Boston: Beacon Press, 1983), pp. 220–224; Jane English, "Abortion and the Concept of a Person," *reprinted in The Problem of Abortion, supra* note 1, at 151, 159; *cf.* S. I. Benn, "Abortion, Infanticide, and Respect for Persons," in *The Problem of Abortion, supra* note 1, at 135, 143; Becker, *supra* note 12; Lisa Cahill, "Abortion, Autonomy and Community," in *Abortion: Understanding Differences*, ed. Sidney Callahan & Daniel Callahan (New York: Plenum Press, 1984), p. 270.

Concerning resemblance in the first trimester, *see* Richard Blandau, "The Complexity of Embryonic Development from Fertilization to Implantation," in *Defining Human Life, supra* note 1, at 33, 58. The developing form of the fetus may be observed in the beautiful book, Lennart Nilsson, Mirjam Furuhjelm, Axel Ingelman-Sundberg & Claes Wirsen, *A Child Is Born* (New York: Delacorte Press, 1977); *see also* Marjorie England, *Color Atlas of Life Before Birth: Normal Fetal Development* (Chicago: Year Book Medical Publishers Inc., 1983).

Concerning birth and the fourteenth amendment, *see* Roe v. Wade, 410 U.S. 113, 156–59 (1973). The state may create a right in the fetus not to be aborted after viability, subject to the health interests of the woman carrying it.

Freud provides an explanation for the centrality of birth that relates to a core quality of personhood. For him, it may be argued, birth marked *the* essential intrapsychic and interpersonal psychological event: "By being born we have made the step from an absolutely self-sufficient narcissism to the perception of a changing external world and the beginnings of the discovery of objects." Sigmund Freud, "Group Psychology and the Analysis of the Ego" (1921), in *The Standard Edition of the Complete Psychological Works of Sigmund Freud*, vol. 18, ed. and trans. James Strachey et al. (London: The Hogarth Press, 1953–1974), pp. 65, 130.

14. *See* Sumner, *supra* note 1, at 52–54 ("morally significant relations among right-bearers do not affect the sets of rights they possess"); Brody, *supra* note 1, at 76–79 (rejecting relevance of response to fetus). *But see* Wertheimer, *supra* note 1, at 92 (treating adult's response to fetus as relevant); Ross, "Abortion and the Death of the Fetus," 11 *Phil. & Pub. Aff.* 232 (1982) (arguing that abortion right must be found in the particularity of the love relationship of parents for children).

15. *Cf.* Thomson, "A Defense of Abortion," 1 *Phil. & Pub. Aff.* 47, 58 (1971) ("Opponents of abortion have been so concerned to make out the independence of the fetus, in order to establish that it has a right to life, just as its mother does, that they have tended to overlook the possible support they might gain from making out that the fetus is *dependent* on the mother") (emphasis in original).

Even when the interconnection is noted, the woman is sometimes thought of as if she were merely a machine of advanced medicine to which a critically dependent patient is attached. But this analogy not only suppresses the woman's existence and autonomy, it misses the human offspring's indebtedness to and involvement with progenitors, an indebtedness not experienced toward machines.

16. If the fetus is not a person, it is a potential person. The claim on behalf of potential persons succeeds at best, it appears, in requiring that their future interests not be disregarded arbitrarily and capriciously. *See infra* note 43.

17. Thomson, *supra* note 15. Thomson, for the sake of argument, grants that a fetus has a right to life at conception and argues that granting the right to life is insufficient to preclude abortion in all cases, such as rape. This is because, in at least some cases, the fetus lacks welfare rights against the woman to the continued provision of sustenance, and thus may not assert a right that trumps a woman's assertion, through abortion, of her right to her own body. For a partial description of her argument, *see infra* text accompanying notes 23–24.

Thomson's article has its detractors who claim that the personhood question primarily matters. *See, e.g.,* Brody, "Thomson on Abortion," 1 *Phil. & Pub. Aff.* 335 (1972); Philippa Foot, "Killing and Letting Die," in *Abortion: Moral and Legal Perspectives, supra* note 1, at 177, 184 (arguing that if the fetus is a person, abortion is a killing and not a "letting die," because, in cases of "letting die," the one who allows it is not, as is the aborting woman, the initiator of the fatal sequence).

18. Some opinion poll data surprisingly suggest that as many as 18 percent of those surveyed would deny abortion in all circumstances, but other data place this number at 8 percent. *See* Mary Ann Lamanna, "Social Science and Ethical Issues," in *Abortion: Understanding Differences, supra* note 13, at 1, 4–6 & nn.4 & 5.

Of course opinion poll data, even when properly obtained, can constitute only a very small part of any effort to determine people's beliefs. There are particular difficulties in interpreting data on abortion since moral evaluation of one's own actions and those of others may greatly diverge, and beliefs about legal regulation of abortion may diverge substantially from moral evaluation. Whether such divergences appear in opinion poll data depend on the phrasing of the question and the care with which the respondent answers.

Among regulators who would allow abortions to save the woman's life, only some would also permit her to protect her health from serious injury. Survey data differ as to the popular acceptance of a maternal health exception. One study indicates that 52 percent of those sampled accept abortion to protect maternal physical health, while another reported 80 percent acceptance. *Id.* at 5; *see also* "Digest," 16 *Family Planning Perspectives* 233 (1984). It should be noted that the common law recognizes a right to defend oneself from grievous injury as well as death. *See also infra* text accompanying note 21.

19. Some would add that even if the woman is sometimes entitled to protect herself against an innocent "aggressor," a third party is not entitled to prefer one innocent life as against another; therefore no physician may aid the aborting woman. *But see* Regan, "Rewriting *Roe v. Wade*," 77 *Mich. L. Rev.* 1569 (1979) (common law has long recognized the right of third parties to come to the aid of a person lawfully defending herself against an aggressor); Thompson, *supra* note 15; *cf.* Thomson, "The Trolley Problem," 94 *Yale L.J.* 1395 (1985).

20. Of little significance to the Catholic Church's teaching is the distinction between aborting a fetus that would otherwise live and aborting a doomed fetus that, absent an abortion, would still die along with the pregnant woman. The dominant distinction is simply between acting against life or letting die. *Cf.* Callahan, *supra* note 1, at 409–410.

For example, Church teaching has prohibited craniotomy, although without it both woman and fetus might once have died. Craniotomy involves the destruction of the fetus by crushing its head to facilitate delivery for the woman who can neither deliver vaginally, because of fetal size or position, nor risk a caesarian. While once a subject of much dispute, it is not now much relied on as a medical procedure, at least in those parts of the world with good medical treatment.

Presumably the secular state would under any regulatory scheme allow the woman to abort the fetus where both would otherwise die, a circumstance which today is exceedingly rare. In such a circumstance, the common law doctrine of necessity would justify saving one innocent life in preference to saving no life.

For a discussion of life-threatening indications for abortion, *see* George Ryan, "Medical Implications of Bestowing Personhood on the Unborn," in *Defining Human Life, supra* note 1, at 84, 85–86 (discussing ectopic pregnancy, intraabdominal surgery, toxemia and diabetes); *cf.* Robert Messer, "Medical Indications for Pregnancy Interruption," in *Pregnancy Termination: Procedures, Safety, and New Developments,* ed. Gerald Zatuchni, John Sciarra & John Speidel (Hagerstown, MD: Harper & Row, 1979), p. 303 (life threatening medical indications for abortion).

21. *See generally,* Davis, "Abortion and Self-Defense," 13 *Phil & Pub. Aff.* 175 (1984); Regan, *supra* note 19, at 1611–1618; Thomson, *supra* note 15, at 53; Sumner, *supra* note 1, at 106–123. That the law of self-defense sometimes permits defense against innocent but threatening persons may in part be attributable to the need for rules that may be applied quickly in those moments of crisis which preclude more refined reflection. To that extent, a law of self-defense that permits defensive acts against innocent persons may not be applicable to the abortion context, where time for reflection is available.

An absolute prohibition on harming the innocent, however, would pose problems not only for the law of abortion, but for the legal defense of necessity and just-war theory as well, *cf.* Michael Walzer, *Just and Unjust Wars* (New York: Basic Books, 1977).

It may be noted that the technical aggressor theory does not protect the woman's choice in every circumstance in which her life is in jeopardy, nor in every case to which the doctrine of double effect applies. For example, the doctrine of double effect allows the destruction of the fetus in cases where it is not a technical aggressor: it permits cancer treatment of the woman that destroys a fetus that is in no sense the cause of the risk. In other cases that involve not a killing but only a letting die, appeal to either doctrine is unnecessary in order to prefer woman to fetus. For example, in the emergency treatment of a massive hemorrhage during labor, a lone physician's choice to omit aid to the fetus by attending to the woman constitutes a permissible omission which may be justified without recourse to the doctrine of double effect.

22. The self-defense exception may, however, be recast in terms of good samaritan obligations. *See infra* text accompanying note 25. However, some put forward a vision of the woman as so utterly devoted to the fetus that, as an especially good samaritan, she disappears as a person with an autonomous subjectivity of her own; in disappearing, so does her interest in self-defense. *See infra* chapter 3 note 95.

23. For a justification of the rape exception, *see, e.g.,* Coleman, "*Roe v. Wade*: A Retrospective Look at a Judicial Oxymoron," 29 *St. Louis U.L.J.* 7 (1984).

For a discussion of the nonobligation of a woman to aid an *in vitro* zygote, *see* Annas & Elias, "*In Vitro* Fertilization and Embryo Transfer:

Medicolegal Aspects of a New Technique to Create a Family," 17 *Fam. L.Q.* 199, 215 & n.68 (1983). More generally, victims in need have not been able to obtain use of the bodies of those who victimized them.

24. *See* Thomson, *supra* note 15, at 57–58; *id.* at 63–64 ("minimally decent samaritan" obligation may arise as a matter of strict liability); Regan, *supra* note 19. The extent to which a good samaritan obligation may oblige a woman to take steps to avoid miscarriage and to act in other ways that avoid harm to the fetus, such as avoiding smoking, alcohol, drugs, and poor nutrition, is beginning to be discussed. *See supra* Preface note 4; *infra* chapter 3 note 99; *cf. supra* note 10.

25. Girls under the age of consent appear to have accounted for less than 12.5 percent of legal abortions in 1980. *See* Christopher Tietze, *Induced Abortion: A World Review, 1983*, 5th ed. (New York: Population Council, 1983), p. 51 table 7.

26. *See* Adrienne Rich, *Of Woman Born: Motherhood as Experience and Institution* (New York: W. W. Norton & Co., 1976), p. 269 ("In a society where women entered sexual intercourse willingly . . . , where adequate contraception was a genuine social priority, there would be no 'abortion issue'. . . . Abortion is violence: a deep, desperate violence inflicted by a woman upon, first of all, herself. It is the offspring, and will continue to be the accuser, of a more pervasive and prevalent violence, the violence of rapism"); Catharine MacKinnon, "*Roe v. Wade*: A Study in Male Ideology," in *Abortion: Moral and Legal Perspectives, supra* note 1, at 45; *cf.* Olsen, "Statutory Rape: A Feminist Critique of Rights Analysis," 63 *Tex. L. Rev.* 387 (1984).

The plaintiff in *Roe v. Wade* attributed her pregnancy to a drunken gang rape, see Barbara Milbauer, *The Law Giveth* (New York: Atheneum, 1983), p. 7; Fred Friendly & Martha Elliott, *The Constitution: That Delicate Balance* (New York: Random House, 1984), pp. 202–204, Philip Bobbitt, *Constitutional Fate: Theory of the Constitution* (New York: Oxford University Press, 1982), p. 165, but she now denies this.

27. For Thomson's argument, *see* Thomson, *supra* note 15, at 65.

For the claim that Thomson's approach does not justify a postfertilization device, as an IUD or certain birth control pills may be, *see* Blumenfeld, *supra* note 12, at 254.

For evidence on female sexual acculturation, *see, e.g.,* Kristin Luker, *Taking Chances: Abortion and the Decision Not To Contracept* (Berkeley, Los Angeles, London: University of California Press, 1975).

Arguments concerning obligations arising from intercourse may be recast in the language of waiver: by engaging in intercourse, women do not waive their common law right to control their bodies. *See* Holly Smith, "Intercourse and Moral Responsibility for the Fetus," in *Abortion and the Status of the Fetus, supra* note 1, at 229. But that move does not especially clarify matters since the concept of waiver in a legal system has no generally established meaning; and a particular legal scheme of waivers may be criticized from the point of view of human obligations and the nature of human intentions.

28. *See, e.g.,* Guido Calabresi, *Ideals, Beliefs, Attitudes, and the Law: Private Law Perspectives on a Public Law Problem* (Syracuse, NY: Syracuse University Press, 1985), pp. 87, 102–106 (advancing thesis that women may have the same right to "equality of access to sex" unburdened by pregnancy as men do); Sidney Callahan, "Value Choices in Abortion," in *Abortion: Understanding Differences, supra* note 13, at 285 (justifying prohibition on abortion in part on obligations of sexuality); Cahill, *supra* note 13, at 268–272 (same); Thomson, *supra* note 15, at 57–58 (discussing obligations of sexuality); Regan, *supra* note 19, at 1594 (same); *supra* note 26 (feminist theories of sexuality); *cf.* Schneider, "Moral Discourse and the Transformation of American Family Law," 83 *Mich. L. Rev.* 1803 (1985) (implying that developing a theory of sexuality might not be difficult).

Some understand the opposition to abortion as deriving as much from beliefs about sexuality as from beliefs about the fetus. *See, e.g.,* Harrison, *supra* note 13, at 125 (criticizing Noonan for his much relied upon history of the Catholic Church's attitude toward abortion because of his failure to link its position on abortion to attitudes toward contraception and celibacy). For a discussion of sexually punitive motivations in the abortion debate, *see, e.g.,* Frederick Jaffe, Barbara Lindheim & Philip Lee, *Abortion Politics* (New York: McGraw-Hill, 1981), pp. 12–13, 108.

In assessing any theory of sexuality, reference may be made to the case law imposing, as a matter of strict liability, support obligations on men who have used reasonable contraceptive precaution, including reliance on the woman's representations. Reference may also be made to the law's acceptance of wrongful birth actions for negligent acts (by physicians) that interfere with a person's choice respecting impregnation.

29. For an argument that the state ought not adopt one among many views of the fetus that is of a religious origin and nature, *see, e.g.,* Tribe, *supra* note 13, at 21–25; Mary Ann Gardell, "Moral Pluralism in Abortion," in *Abortion and the Status of the Fetus, supra* note 1, at 325; David Richards, *Toleration and the Constitution* (New York: Oxford University Press, 1986), pp. 261–269; *cf.* Roe v. Wade, 410 U.S. at 162 ("we do not agree that, by adopting one theory of life, Texas may override the rights of the pregnant woman").

For rejection of such claims regarding the adoption of religiously based theories, *see* Harris v. McRae, 448 U.S. 297, 318–21 (1980) (rejecting first amendment challenge to denial of Medicaid funding for abortions); Laurence Tribe, *American Constitutional Law* (Mineola, NY: Foundation Press, 1978), p. 928 (retracting his own prior first amendment argument); Greenawalt, "Religious Convictions and Lawmaking," 84 *Mich. L. Rev.* 352, 371–380 (1985); *id.* at 380 ("in respect to abortion, the religious perspective informs a judgment of who counts as a member of the community, a judgment that I claim each citizen must make in a nonrational way").

Whether the state should adopt a controversial position that has its origins and support in a religious tradition or not, that position must be capable of being framed in secular terms. For example, in countering the assertion that the status of the fetus is solely a matter of religiously inspired belief, regulators developed arguments that may be addressed to the state of a pluralist society and that appeal to a variety of traditions. In so doing, they have quite successfully channeled a portion of the abortion debate of the past decade into a secular debate about the dignity owed the fetus.

Religious arguments based on the nature of sexuality can justify a ban on abortion as well as contraception without reaching any conclusion about the moral status of the fetus. For an attempt to frame such an argument in secular terms, see Cahill, supra note 13, at 268–272 (deregulators fail to recognize the role of nature and necessity in human life and suffer the mistaken attitude of the rational mind which tries to avoid the realities of biologic existence).

30. A second argument with these same characteristics claims that a good samaritan duty of nine months duration arises not from intercourse but from the woman's having commenced to render aid to the fetus during implantation. But the fetus (even assuming fetal personhood) has suffered no detrimental reliance as a result of implantation, since no substitute samaritan was available to it and no subjective expectations were raised in it. Nor is it worse off than it would have been had the woman never become pregnant and thereby never put it in a dependent position in the first place. Thus, the fact of implantation does not impose any more of an obligation upon the woman than is imposed by virtue of sexual intercourse. See Regan, supra note 19, at 1598–1601. Were technology to permit early fetal "rescue" by another, with only minimal invasiveness of the woman's body, this argument would require more attention, and the relative importance of the "absence of subjective reliance" and the "no worse off" arguments would have to be evaluated.

By contrast, the parent's good samaritan obligation to a born child is importantly shaped by the fact that as long as the child is in the custody of the parents, other potential samaritans will not interfere. When the parent takes steps to find another caregiver, the parent can avoid his or her obligation.

31. Compare Finnis, "The Rights and Wrongs of Abortion," 2 Phil. & Pub. Aff. 117 (1973) with Thomson, "Rights and Deaths," 2 Phil. & Pub. Aff. 146 (1973). There are of course noninvasive ways of killing, but concentrating on the core of bodily integrity serves to locate at the periphery the difficult cases where act and omission blur. That distinction is important enough in some circumstances to justify distinguishing between halting extraordinary (and even ordinary) medical care and shooting the patient. Whether a woman's nurturance of the fetus is to be analogized to extraordinary or ordinary medical treatment and its cessation treated as an act or an omission are unresolved.

32. *But see* Janet Smith, "Rights-Conflict, Pregnancy, and Abortion," in *Beyond Domination*, ed. Carol Gould (Totowa, NJ: Rowman & Allanheld, 1984), p. 265 (arguing that because of the unique physical nature of pregnancy, the fetal right to life has meaning only as a welfare right; and that such a welfare right is subordinate to a woman's negative right to autonomy).

33. If a method caused direct injury only to the placenta then it might have to be resolved whether that constitutes an invasion of the fetus or of the woman. *See supra* text accompanying note 15.

34. *See* Rhoden, *supra* note 12, at 1458; Noonan, *supra* note 6, at 366 (discussing effect of prostaglandins on heart rate).

35. Because of political, administrative, and economic barriers in this country, antiprogestational pills using an antiprogesterone agent may first appear in Europe.

Such pills could make the practical and legal difficulties of regulating or forbidding abortion enormous. Although medical consultation to assure correct use, monitor side effects, and the like would be advisable, with a home pregnancy kit and a black market antiprogesterone pill, abortion would be in the hands of each woman.

An abortion prohibition would then become a matter of the law of controlled substances and would entail many of the same privacy and surveillance problems that justified striking down a Connecticut statute that forbade married couples from using contraceptives. *See* Griswold v. Connecticut, 381 U.S. 479, 500 (1965) (Harlan, J., concurring) (incorporating his reasoning in Poe v. Ullman, 367 U.S. 497, 550–52 [1961] [Harlan, J., dissenting]). *Roe* would then assume a greater similarity to *Griswold's* theory of privacy which some believe finds greater textual support in the Constitution, as in the fourth amendment's right to be free from unreasonable searches and seizures, than does *Roe's* doctrine of procreational privacy.

For medical discussions of early antiprogesterone methods of separation, *see* Couzinet, Le Strat, Ulmann, Baulieu & Schaison, "Termination of Early Pregnancy By the Progesterone Antagonist RU 486 (Mifepristone)," 315 *New Eng. J. Med.* 1565 (1986) (reporting 85 percent rate of success in terminating pregnancies in 100 women when administered within ten days of missed menses; and speculating that the addition of prostaglandins might increase success rate and reduce the minor side effect of heavy bleeding); Crowley, "Progesterone Antagonism: Science and Society," 315 *New Eng. J. Med.* 1607 (1986); Etienne-Emile Baulieu, "Contragestion by Antiprogestin: A New Approach to Human Fertility Control," in *Abortion: Medical Progress and Social Implications*, *supra* note 9, at 192, 198 (reporting complete abortion in 70 percent of pregnancies of seven or fewer weeks since last menstrual period or "LMP"); Csapo, "Antiprogesterones in Fertility Control," in *Pregnancy Termination, supra* note 20, at 16; Kovacs, Sas, Resch, Ugocsai, Swann, Bygdeman & Rowe, "Termination of Very Early Pregnancy by RU 486—An Anti-Progestational Compound," 29 *Contraception* 399 (1984). It appears that by occupying progesterone receptors, RU 486 acts to block uterine use of progesterone, which helps to maintain a pregnancy. Without progesterone, the womb sheds its decidua and with it the embryo.

For greater effectiveness, an antiprogesterone agent may be combined with prostaglandins which help complete the separation by inducing further uterine contractions. For a general discussion of the use of prostaglandins as an abortifacient, *see* M. Embrey, "New Prostaglandin Delivery Systems," in *Voluntary Termination of Pregnancy*, E. Hafez, ed. (Boston: MTP Press, Ltd., 1984), p. 67; Bygdeman & Green, "Menstrual Regulation—Medical Techniques," in *Pregnancy Termination, supra* note 20, at 69; Craft, Evans, Richfield & Yovich, "Extraamniotic Prostaglandin E$_2$ in Gel for Induced Abortion," in *Pregnancy Termination, supra* note 20, at 241. For problems with prostaglandins, *see* Schulman, "Biologic Obstacles to Abortion," in *Pregnancy Termination, supra* note 20, at 2, 4.

36. *See* Philippa Foot, *supra* note 17, at 105. *But see* Regan, *supra* note 19, at 1574–1575, 1585; *cf.* John Robertson, "Medicolegal Implications of a Human Life Amendment," in *Defining Human Life, supra* note 1, at 161, 165.

37. *See* Thomson, *supra* note 15, at 54–56. Thomson's need at this stage of her argument to justify the woman's assertion of bodily autonomy leads her to insist that abortion is a matter of conflicting rights and to insist on the fundamental importance of body-right. *See also* Regan, *supra* note 19, at 1611–1618; Sumner, *supra* note 1, at 106–123 (treating right of self-defense as sometimes including right to protect autonomy); *cf.* George Fletcher, *Rethinking Criminal Law* (Boston: Little, Brown & Co., 1978), sec. 10.5.3 (discussing general right of autonomy); *infra* note 48; *infra* chapter 3 note 81 (discussing "body-right").

Does the right to repel kidnappers with deadly force derive from the right to preserve one's freedom and way of life from a lawless interference of substantial duration, or from the likelihood that one's life will also soon be at risk? Elective abortion involves this latter risk only to a limited extent.

38. Arguments asserting a fetal right to life tend to ignore the fact that the law has rarely treated abortion as homicide, either in terms of penalties authorized or prosecutions actually commenced. However, it could be argued that a prohibition on abortion was analogous to the crime of manslaughter that at times in the past had been considered to be appropriate for the person who kills in response to an illegal arrest. *See* Coldiron, "Historical Development of Manslaughter," 38 *Ky. L.J.*

527, 544 (1950); *cf.* Regina v. Mawgridge, 84 Eng. Rep. 1107, 1114–15 (Q.B. 1707) (concerning bystander). Thus, the argument could go, abortion has been punished not as murder but only in a manner similar to manslaughter because pregnancy is akin to an unprivileged arrest of the woman. The law of feticide prior to the deregulation of abortion could then be understood as accepting that the woman has no duty to aid the fetus and, accordingly, as not punishing her intentional refusal to aid as murder. But it did treat her as powerless to use self-help to avoid the fetus' unprivileged arrest of her. However, prior to deregulation, the law had failed to afford her the same swift remedy that the unlawfully arrested person has with habeas corpus; for that reason, on this analysis, treating an act of abortion as the privileged use of self-help might have been as appropriate as reducing to manslaughter the charge against the illegally arrested person who uses deadly force.

39. *See, e.g.,* Model Penal Code sec. 230.3 (1962); Doe v. Bolton, 410 U.S. 179, 182 (1973) (Model Penal Code provision serving by 1973 as model for abortion statutes in one-fourth of the states); Harris v. McRae, 448 U.S. 297, 302 (1980) (beginning in 1976, Congress cut off Medicaid funding for abortions with exceptions, in some of the ensuing years, for pregnancies resulting from rape and incest reported to the police within sixty days, pregnancies risking the life of the mother, and pregnancies involving grave fetal disability); Tietze, *supra* note 25, at 7–18; Bernard Dickens, "Comparative Legal Abortion Policies and Attitudes Toward Abortion," in *Defining Human Life, supra* note 1, at 240 (primarily discussing Commonwealth countries); *id.* at 250–251 (India permits abortion *inter alia* in case of contraceptive failure); L. Lynn Hogue, "A Comparative Survey of Abortion Legislation: International Perspective," in *Liberalization of Abortion Laws: Implications,* ed. Abdel Omran (Chapel Hill: Carolina Population Center, University of North Carolina at Chapel Hill, 1976), pp. 183, 187, 192; M. Baylson, "Legal Aspects of Abortion," in *Voluntary Termination of Pregnancy, supra* note 35, at 147, 151–152 (as a matter of physician practice in Britain, abortion provided in cases of risk to family's social position, risk to welfare of family members, risk to woman's mental health, fetal indications, rape and incest, and risk to maternal physical health and life); K. Shiota & H. Nishimura, "Epidemiology of Induced Abortion in Japan," in *Voluntary Termination of Pregnancy, supra* note 35, at 3 (1949 amendment to Japan's abortion act permitted abortion where the "health of the mother may be seriously affected . . . due to . . . economic condition").

40. If one ascribes a right of life to the fetus, and believes intercourse gives rise to a good samaritan obligation, the illegality of incestuous intercourse should be irrelevant. Incest with a minor or an incompetent adult, who is incapable of giving consent, or overtly forcible incestuous rape justify abortion only to the same extent as rape generally justifies an abortion.

41. Sumner treats the fetal indications exception as a matter of euthanasia although the latter is also controversial, accelerates the usual timing of euthanasia, and sets stricter limits than currently exist on abortion following amniocentesis. Sumner, *supra* note 1, at 23–24, 156–157. For arguments against such an exception, *see* chapter 3 note 61.

42. Some might argue that one should distinguish between burdens that are unexpected at the time of intercourse and burdens that are known. Because the risks are known in advance, such an approach would reject the claim that the statistical medical risks of pregnancy turn all abortions into permissible therapeutic ones. *Cf. infra* note 55. This approach might permit abortion in the case of a severely abnormal fetus, except when genetic counseling notified parents of the specific risk. This approach might deny abortion to the functioning, though burdened, family unit, but allow abortion to the pregnant woman whose mate deserts her, on the ground that the desertion is unexpected and the resulting burden is excessive.

One could also distinguish between the severity of burdens. For example, one could distinguish between the extent of burdens a single person might reasonably be expected to incur from those a family of limited size might be expected to incur. Such a rule would help confine infants to functioning families.

43. *See, e.g.,* Quinn, *supra* note 12, at 24; *id.* at 54 ("Even the early fetus is a creature whose status arguably brings it at least within the fringes of the morality of humanity. How powerful its rights there are against other competing moral forces . . . is, as Aristotle would say, what the wise man knows"); *cf.* Tooley, *supra* note 1, at 165–241; Joel Feinberg, "The Rights of Animals and Unborn Generations," in *Rights, Justice and the Bounds of Liberty* (Princeton: Princeton University Press, 1980), pp. 159, 178–180; Joel Feinberg, "Is There a Right to be Born?," in *Rights, Justice and the Bounds of Liberty, supra,* at 207; Joel Feinberg, "Potentiality, Development, and Rights," in *The Problem of Abortion, supra* note 1, at 145; Joel Feinberg, *The Moral Limits of the Criminal Law,* vol. 1, *Harm to Others* (New York: Oxford University Press, 1984), pp. 95–104; Parfit, "Future Generations: Further Problems," 11 *Phil. & Pub. Aff.* 113 (1981).

Hare argues that duties to potential persons run equally to the unconceived and the conceived fetus. Thus a decision not to abort may infringe duties owed to other potential offspring. But because of the greater probability that a fetus will develop into a person who is glad to have been conceived and not aborted, there is a presumption that favors allowing that fetus to come to term rather than aborting it in favor of a subsequent, and therefore less probable, conception. But this presumption in favor of the existing potential person is easily defeated by a woman's good reasons, including the facilitation or rendering "possible or probable the beginning of another more propitious" pregnancy. Hare, *supra* note 3, at 211–214, 221.

44. *See* Nathanson, *supra* note 11, at 230–231; Doe v. Bolton 410

U.S. 179, 221–22 (1973) (White, J., dissenting) (referring to "convenience, whim, or caprice of the putative mother"); Jonathan Imber, *Abortion and the Private Practice of Medicine* (New Haven: Yale University Press, 1986), p. 82 (reporting story of a woman who aborted in order to postpone a desired conception for a few months for apparently inconsequential reasons). *But see* Kristin Luker, *Abortion and the Politics of Motherhood* (Berkeley, Los Angeles, London: University of California Press, 1984), p. 285 note 30 (finding on the basis of interviews with over 600 women who have had abortions that "the decision to seek an abortion has been serious, thoughtful, and carefully considered").

45. For a discussion of some of *Roe*'s less controversial claims, *see*, *e.g.*, Heymann & Barzelay, "The Forest and the Trees: *Roe v. Wade* and Its Critics," 53 *B.U.L. Rev.* 765 (1973) (noting some of these less controversial aspects of *Roe*); *cf.* Tribe, *American Constitutional Law, supra* note 29, sec. 15–10.

With respect to the future of the Court's holding on the fourteenth-amendment personhood of the fetus, *see* Thornburgh v. American College of Obst. & Gyn., 106 S. Ct. 2169, 2188 n.8 (1986) (Stevens, J., concurring) (no Supreme Court justice has ever suggested a fetus is a fourteenth-amendment person). The statutory attempt to adopt a "human life statute" purportedly interpreting the fourteenth amendment as applying to the fetus was generally opposed by constitutional scholars and seems politically as well as constitutionally stymied.

For evidence on the historical argument about the intent of the framers of the fourteenth amendment with respect to abortion, *see* "The Human Life Bill: Hearings on S. 158 Before the Subcommittee on Separation of Powers of the Senate Comm. on the Judiciary," 97th Cong., 1st Sess. 433–442 (1981) (statements of Carl Degler & James Mohr). *But see id.* at 464–490 (statement of Victor Rosenblum); *id.* at 454–463 (statement of William Marshner); Calabresi, *supra* note 28, at 93 (arguing that Court completely ignored the general, but not universal, trend in 1866 towards legislation prohibiting abortion and "the gravitational pull of other areas of the law. Our law has for centuries given a fetus substantial kinds of recognition and protection"); Witherspoon, "Reexamining *Roe*: Nineteenth-Century Abortion Statutes and the Fourteenth Amendment," 17 *St. Mary's L.J.* 29 (1985) (arguing that many of the ratifiers of the fourteenth amendment did not intend to prohibit abortion regulation and, far more problematically, that they intended to include the fetus within the protections afforded by that amendment). *See generally* Roe v. Wade, 410 U.S. 113, 158–59 (1973) (discussing use of the word "person" in the Constitution); Charles Baron, "The Concept of Person in the Law," in *Defining Human Life, supra* note 1, at 121.

For a claim that the Court made a mistake from an institutional point of view in rejecting fetal personhood, *see* Calabresi, *supra* note 28, at 93–98. Calabresi argues that its holding that the fetus is not a person is the most (and at a fundamental level the only) controversial part of *Roe*. He asserts that regulators could have tolerated a decision that a woman's right trumps fetal right but cannot abide having their valuation of the fetus read completely out of our fundamental law. It was not the outcome in *Roe* but the Court's method of excluding the fetus from all constitutional consideration, of saying "*Your* metaphysics are not part of *our* constitution," that was the affront. *Id.* at 95. This position is plausible only insofar as citizens cannot accept the state's agnostic attitude toward certain issues that are placed outside the social compact.

For the claim that an affirmative holding on fetal personhood would have resulted in a variety of difficult legal problems, *see* Robertson, *supra* note 36; David Westfall, "Beyond Abortion: The Potential Reach of a Human Life Amendment," in *Defining Human Life, supra* note 1, at 174 (describing multiple consequences of granting constitutional protection to fetus through a "human life amendment").

For the claim that an affirmative holding on fetal personhood would have required forbidding abortion, *see* David Louisell & John Noonan, Jr., "Constitutional Balance," in *The Morality of Abortion: Legal and Historical Perspectives, supra* note 1, at 220, 244–246; Chermerinsky, "Rationalizing the Abortion Debate," 31 *Buffalo L. Rev.* 107 (1982). But a constitutional amendment that would merely make a fetus a fourteenth-amendment person might not preclude abortion, for the right of the fetus to life would not entitle it to welfare rights *vis-a-vis* the woman, or to special constitutional protection that goes beyond the protection to which adults are generally entitled. However, some proposals make a specific reference to a right to life regardless of conditions of dependency. This might succeed in prohibiting abortion as well as creating a variety of ancillary but very substantial problems of constitutional interpretation.

46. The interest in protecting maternal health offers no justification for regulating early abortion, except for treating it as a medical procedure. This may be put to one side for the present. For further discussion of this interest, *see infra* notes 51–52.

The Court could have considered, but did not, other state interests. For example, a state might have argued to the Court that restricting abortion is the most effective way of controlling extramarital sexuality. Such arguments have been tolerated for centuries, but they have recently fallen into disfavor for the reason, among others, that the law ought not treat children as a curse or use them as a means of deterrence. The Supreme Court has sought in a number of less controversial ways to avoid visiting the sins of the father and mother upon the heads of the daughters and sons. *See, e.g.,* Plyler v. Doe, 457 U.S. 202, 219–20 (1982); Parham v. Hughes, 441 U.S. 347, 352–53 (1979); Trimble v. Gordon, 430 U.S. 762, 769 (1977); Mathews v. Lucas, 427 U.S. 495, 505 (1976); Weber v. Aetna Casualty & Surety Co., 406 U.S. 164 (1972). So too, the Court has discounted the state's use of conception as threat. *See*

Roe v. Wade, 410 U.S. 113, 148 (1973) ("Texas, however, does not advance this justification ["to discourage illicit sexual conduct"] . . . and it appears that no court or commentator has taken the argument seriously"); Carey v. Population Services Int'l, 431 U.S. 678 (1977) (striking down limitation on distribution and advertising of contraceptives); Eisenstadt v. Baird, 405 U.S. 438 (1972) (striking down law prohibiting provision of contraceptives to unmarried persons); Griswold v. Connecticut, 381 U.S. 479 (1965) (striking down law forbidding use of contraceptives by married persons). It has not done so because the utilitarian calculus is entirely wrong—for the possibility of begetting children sometimes dims the passions—but because of the perversity of the result when the threat has failed to deter. *Cf.* "Discussion," in *Abortion: Medical Progress and Social Implications, supra* note 9, at 41, 52 (relationship between abortion laws and sexual activity is complex and far from clearly established). An additional perversity of this argument is that it less strongly justifies regulation of abortion within marriage than outside marriage since traditional, secular sexual moralities are generally tolerant of consensual genital sexuality within marriage. Yet to permit abortion within marriage but not outside marriage is to increase the risks to children of family-less upbringing. Thus *Eisenstadt* followed *Griswold,* and thus *Roe* followed *Eisenstadt.*

The state might also have claimed that abortion undermines families. Such a claim is controversial at best and a hard one to sustain empirically. Prohibiting abortions would no doubt increase marriages among the young of certain classes and cultures—that is, among an age group whose marriages are most likely to end in divorce.

The state could have argued that because fetuses resemble infants abortion undermines respect and concern for infants. This is a highly controversial claim, especially regarding early abortion. *Cf. supra* note 13; *infra* chapter 3 notes 97, 99; *infra* chapter 4 note 3.

A state was foreclosed by the establishment clause of the first amendment from arguing that abortion constitutes a disrespect for divinely inspired beings or interferes with the divine nature of sexuality.

Finally, a state could have asserted a strong interest in "potential life" insofar as it claimed to need more soldiers and workers. *See* Maher v. Roe, 432 U.S. 464, 478 n.11 (1977) ("a State may have legitimate demographic concerns about its rate of population growth. Such concerns are basic to the future of the State and in some circumstances could constitute a substantial reason for departure from a position of neutrality between abortion and childbirth"); *id.* at 489 n.* (Brennan, J., dissenting). While the Court might listen to such arguments in an emergency (although this policy requires far more than a decade to be effective), it is hard to imagine the circumstances within the near future under which the argument would be made.

47. In a dissenting opinion calling for the overruling of *Roe,* Justice White, joined by then Justice Rehnquist, wrote: "I can certainly agree with the proposition—which I deem indisputable—that a woman's ability to choose an abortion is a species of 'liberty' that is subject to the general protections of the Due Process Clause." Thornbugh v. American College of Obst. & Gyn., 106 S. Ct. 2169, 2194 (1986) (White, J., dissenting). While denying that "this liberty is so 'fundamental' that restrictions upon it call into play anything more than the most minimal judicial scrutiny," White nonetheless considered only one countervailing state interest, the protection of fetal life, in criticizing Roe. Id. at 2196–2197.

In this dissent, Justice White was not content to challenge the majority on the appropriate standard of judicial review and the proper methodology of substantive due process, although these points constituted the basis of his dissent. Rather, he also felt compelled to provide his own evaluation of the nature of the fetus:

> However one answers the metaphysical or theological question whether the fetus is a "human being" or the legal question whether it is a "person" as that term is used in the Constitution, one must at least recognize, first, that the fetus is an entity that bears in its cells all the genetic information that characterizes a member of the species *homo sapiens* and distinguishes an individual member of that species from all others, and second, that there is no nonarbitrary line separating a fetus from a child or, indeed, an adult human being.

Id. at 2195. That he could not resist offering his evaluation illustrates how strongly the philosophical questions affect the legal and how powerful the woman's claim to liberty is, for it calls forth unnecessary and controversial counter-assertions about the fetus.

48. Although Roe avoided explicit reliance on a woman's interest in bodily autonomy, the Court since Roe has treated bodily autonomy as an especially significant aspect of liberty. For example, the Court recently imposed on a state an affirmative obligation to train and educate a retarded resident of an institution so that he would not have to be continuously restrained, although the Court has otherwise been quite hostile to any claim that the Constitution creates affirmative welfare rights. Though the facts were unusual, the Court weighed his interest in bodily autonomy to be so fundamental that it was willing to establish a constitutional welfare right that ought not be easily cabined, short of a general right to treatment for the committed mentally ill and retarded. See Youngberg v. Romeo, 457 U.S. 307 (1982); cf. Winston v. Lee, 470 U.S. 753 (1985) (surgical removal of bullet to obtain cumulative evidence violates defendant's fourth amendment right to be secure in his person and intrudes on the "individual's dignitary interests in personal privacy and bodily integrity").

49. For privacy cases preceding Roe, see Meyer v. Nebraska, 262 U.S. 390 (1923) (striking down law forbidding schools from teaching foreign language); Pierce v. Society of Sisters, 268 U.S. 510 (1925) (striking down law requiring only public school education); Skinner v. Oklahoma, 316 U.S. 535 (1942) (striking down a compulsory sterilization law for certain repeat felons); Griswold v. Connecticut, 381 U.S. 479 (1965) (striking down law forbidding use of contraceptives by married couples); Loving v. Virginia, 388 U.S. 1 (1967) (striking down antimiscegenation statute); Eisenstadt v. Baird, 405 U.S. 438 (1972) (striking down law forbidding distribution of contraceptives to unmarried persons). See generally Karst, "The Freedom of Intimate Association," 89 Yale L.J. 624, 664–665 & n.183 (1980).

For criticism by justices of efforts to extend the privacy doctrine, see Bowers v. Hardwick, 106 S. Ct. 2841 (1986) (denying due process challenge to criminal sodomy statute as applied to homosexuals on the ground that Court should hesitate before extending privacy cases to new areas); Thornburgh v. American College of Obst. & Gyn., 106 S. Ct. at 2195 (White, J., dissenting) ("Even if each of . . . [various other privacy cases, including Griswold and Eisenstadt in which White concurred] was correctly decided and could be properly grounded in rights that are 'implicit in the concept of ordered liberty' or 'deeply rooted in this Nation's history and tradition,'" Roe is distinguishable and should be overruled, because the life of the fetus is at stake); cf. Dronenburg v. Zech, 741 F.2d 1388, 1396 n.5 (D.C. Cir. 1984) (Judge Bork) (doubting legitimacy of privacy cases). What vision of the country's future and its dangers would lead a judge, as this country approaches the twenty-first century, to wish to abandon the privacy cases completely is not altogether clear.

50. Roe v. Wade, 410 U.S. at 173 (Rehnquist, J., dissenting).

In Roe, only Justice White did not explicitly express a view of whether a state could prohibit abortion when a woman's life or health is at stake; but he noted that Roe involved only nontherapeutic abortions. Doe v. Bolton, 410 U.S. 179, 221 (1973) (White, J., dissenting). Recently, Justice White implied that, were Roe overrruled, an absolute prohibition on abortion might be constitutional: "If either or both of these facets of Roe v. Wade were rejected, a broad range of limitations on abortion (including outright prohibition) that are now unavailable to the States would again become constitutional possibilities." Thornburgh v. American College of Obst. & Gyn., 106 S. Ct. at 2197 (White, J., dissenting). Since Justice Rehnquist joined in this White dissent, it is unclear whether he has changed his position since Roe or whether White's Thornburgh dissent applies only to elective abortion.

51. See Doe v. Bolton, 410 U.S. at 191–92 ("medical judgment may be exercised in the light of all factors—physical, emotional, psychological, familial, and the woman's age—relevant to the well-being of the patient. . . . This allows the attending physician the room he needs to make his best medical judgment. And it is room that operates for the benefit, not the disadvantage, of the pregnant woman"); id. at 207 (Burger, C.J., concurring) (agreeing that the Constitution protects a woman's right to protect her "health, in its broadest medical context"); cf. U.S. v.

Vuitch, 402 U.S. 62 (1971) (construing the word "health," in a statute regulating abortion, as "broadly conceived" and therefore as including a woman's mental health). *But see* Thornburgh v. American College of Obst. & Gyn., 106 S. Ct. at 2197, 2203–05 (White, J., dissenting) (suggesting that the state, to protect fetal life, may burden a woman's health); *id.* at 2216, (O'Connor, J., dissenting) (refraining from discussing when a regulation imposing a "trade off" of the woman's health for fetal survival would become an undue burden on her and thus trigger strict judicial scrutiny).

For the claim that the health of a person may not be jeopardized on behalf of a non-fourteenth-amendment being, *see, e.g.,* Thornburgh v. American College of Obst. & Gyn. 106 S. Ct. at 2188 (Stevens, J., concurring) (distinguishing between strength of state interest in protecting persons and lesser strength of interest in protecting nonpersons under fourteenth amendment).

52. Roe v. Wade, 410 U.S. at 163; Akron v. Akron Center for Reproductive Health, 462 U.S. 416, 429 n.11, 432 (1983) (despite increasing safety of second trimester abortions, reaffirming the use of the trimester heuristic because second trimester abortions may require more careful state scrutiny to assure safety and because their potential for disturbing a woman's emotional well-being is greater). *See generally* Rhoden, "Trimesters and Technology: Revamping *Roe v. Wade*," 95 *Yale L.J.* 639, 648–655 (1986).

In asserting an interest in regulating the performance of abortions to protect maternal health, states have rebutted this presumption of irrationality in the case of some first trimester requirements. *See* Planned Parenthood of Mo. v. Danforth, 428 U.S. 52, 65–67 (1976) (upholding requirement of written informed consent); *id.* at 79–81 (upholding recordkeeping requirement); Planned Parenthood Ass'n v. Ashcroft, 462 U.S. 476, 486–90 (1983) (upholding requirement of pathology report although it could increase costs of an abortion by $40.00); *cf. id.* at 494–98 & n.4 (Blackmun, J., concurring in part and dissenting in part) (discussing pathology requirement).

Some second trimester regulations have also been found, without the influence of the negative presumption, to be justified because based on a "reasonable medical standard" rationally related to maternal health. *See, e.g.,* Simopoulos v. Virginia, 462 U.S. 506 (1983) (affirming state power to license and regulate facilities performing second trimester abortions). Other second trimester regulations have not and have been struck down. *See* Thornburgh v. American College of Obst. & Gyn., 106 S. Ct. at 2181 (striking down reporting requirement that did not sufficiently preserve privacy of patients); Akron v. Akron Center for Reproductive Health, 462 U.S. at 429 n.11, 434–39 (state cannot confine the performance of D&E abortions in weeks twelve to sixteen of pregnancy to hospitals since such a restriction would impose a "heavy, and unnecessary, burden on . . . access to a relatively inexpensive, otherwise accessible, and safe abortion procedure," *id.* at 438); Planned Parenthood of Mo. v. Danforth, 428 U.S. at 75–79 (striking down prohibition on saline instillation method); *id.* at 81–84 (striking down statutory imposition on aborting physician of a duty of care to nonviable fetus).

For examples of regulation covering both first and second trimesters that did not survive the Court's scrutiny, *see* Doe v. Bolton, 410 U.S. at 193–200 (striking down requirement that abortion be performed only in hospitals accredited by Joint Commission on Accreditation of Hospitals, after approval by both a hospital abortion committee and two physicians other than attending one); *infra* chapter 3 notes 116, 118, 120 (informed consent and parental and spousal consent regulations).

Regulations throughout pregnancy are permissible that treat abortions as a medical procedure, with the result that only physicians may perform them, and then only in accordance with prevailing medical standards. Roe v. Wade, 410 U.S. at 163; Doe v. Bolton, 410 U.S. at 216 (Douglas, J., concurring); Connecticut v. Menillo, 423 U.S. 9, 11 (1975) (per curiam) (upholding requirement that abortion be performed only by licensed physician; and suggesting that *Roe* permits first trimester regulations restricting performance of abortion to "medically competent personnel under conditions insuring maximum safety for the woman").

Some of the Court's holdings have been based on the factual finding that abortions through the first third of the second trimester (up to sixteen weeks) are now so much safer than childbirth that restricting a woman's access to them, for example by requiring that abortions be performed in hospitals, can have a serious negative consequence on her capacity to favor her health. Therefore, only a goal other than protecting maternal health could support regulations that substantially reduce the availability of first trimester and early second trimester abortions performed according to accepted medical practice. *See, e.g.,* Akron v. Akron Center for Reproductive Health, 462 U.S. at 434–37; Grimes, "Second Trimester Abortions in the United States," 16 *Family Planning Perspectives* 260, 262 (1984) (even including late abortions in the data, abortion mortality rate is one-seventeenth that of childbirth; D&E abortions in clinics are as safe as in hospitals); Jerome Legge, *Abortion Policy: An Evaluation of the Consequences for Maternal and Infant Health* (Albany: SUNY Press, 1985), p. 19–30. *But cf.* Akron v. Akron Center for Reproductive Health, 462 U.S. at 453–55 (O'Connor, J., dissenting) (suggesting, without evidence, that the Court's reasoning on maternal health is arbitrary as a substantive matter).

53. *Roe,* in part, treated the question of whether the state has a compelling interest in potential life as a burden of proof problem. It concluded that the state had failed in its burden of showing that it had a compelling interest in protecting the fetus prior to viability. *See* Wertheimer, "Understanding Blackmun's Argument: The Reasoning of *Roe v. Wade,*" in *Abortion: Moral and Legal Perspectives, supra* note 1, at

105. In our secular society, the Court declined to engage in theological and philosophical speculation about the fetus, when the fourteenth amendment provided textual support for choosing birth and when the tangible interests of the woman weighed against the more speculative interests of a fetus prior to birth. *Cf.* Joseph Goldstein, "On Being Adult and Being An Adult in Secular Law," in *Adulthood*, ed. Erik Erikson (New York: W. W. Norton & Co., 1976), p. 249. *But see* Greenawalt, *supra* note 29 (rejecting interpretation of *Roe* that mandates giving priority to secular and rational reasons for protecting women over nonrational reasons for protecting fetus).

54. *See, e.g.,* John Noonan, Jr., *A Private Choice: Abortion in America in the Seventies* (New York: The Free Press, 1979); Ely, "The Wages of Crying Wolf: A Comment on *Roe v. Wade,*" 82 *Yale L.J.* 920 (1973); Epstein, "Substantive Due Process By Any Other Name: The Abortion Cases," 1973 *Sup. Ct. Rev.* 159. For synopses of that criticism and responses, *see* Gerald Gunther, *Constitutional Law,* 11th ed. (Mineola, NY: Foundation Press, 1985), pp. 517–549; William Lockhart, Yale Kamisar, Jesse Choper & Steven Shiffrin, *Constitutional Law* (St. Paul: West Publishing Co., 1986), pp. 483–508.

The constitutional commentary does not often focus on the following other important and controversial doctrines to which *Roe* and its progeny should have given some vitality:

    a. The state must individualize decision making and may not act on the basis of irrebuttable presumptions in certain circumstances involving important rights. *See* Bellotti v. Baird (II), 443 U.S. 622 (1979) (state may not irrebuttably presume that minor is immature or that parents act in her best interest, but must provide a factfinding mechanism with respect to these issues); Akron v. Akron Center for Reproductive Health, 462 U.S. at 439–40 (state may not irrebuttably presume that notice to parents is in minor's best interest).

    b. The Court may encourage a legislature to give a second look to legislation where it had failed to engage in serious balancing of competing interests in the original adoption or after changed circumstances. *See* Roe v. Wade, 410 U.S. at 162–65 (describing abortion statute as overbroad and representing a failure to weigh competing interests); *cf.* Doe v. Bolton, 410 U.S. at 190–92. *See generally* Guido Calabresi, *A Common Law for the Age of Statutes* (Cambridge, MA: Harvard University Press, 1982).

    c. Procedural obstacles to or burdens on the exercise of rights will be carefully scrutinized.

    d. Although it will be wary of imposing an affirmative obligation to fund the exercise of rights, the Court will closely scrutinize regulations that burden or foreclose the exercise of important rights by nonwealthy persons.

    e. The fourteenth amendment prescribes particularly severe discrimination even in the absence of proved discriminatory motive and despite the state's articulation of a nondiscriminatory purpose. *See* Roe

v. Wade, 410 U.S. at 163–64 (arguably finding in favor of woman's claims to equality despite state interest in fetus).

    f. The Court will consider only the purposes a state actually articulates in support of a statute's constitutionality and not other possible justifications. *See Roe v. Wade*, 410 U.S. at 152–56; *cf. supra* note 46 (noting other interests state could have argued in *Roe*).

    55. While less controversial, the balancing that led the Court to the conclusion that the woman's interest in her health includes her mental health and physical sequelae of less than serious consequence might for many also be included as a controversial conclusion of *Roe*. *Cf.* Lamanna, *supra* note 18, at 4–5 (a 1981 opinion poll showed that slightly less than 50 percent of those surveyed believed that a threat to a woman's mental health justifies abortion).

    Roe may be interpreted as justifying elective abortion in the first and part of the second trimesters entirely on medical grounds, on the theory that, whatever good samaritan obligations may arise from intercourse, they do not include the requirement that the woman risk her health. *Cf.* People v. Belous, 71 Cal. 2d 954, 971–73, 458 P.2d 194, 204–05, 80 Cal. Rptr. 354, 364–66 (1969) (holding that an abortion performed because of its greater statistical safety was therapeutic). *But see* Thornburgh v. American College of Obst. & Gyn., 106 S. Ct. at 2204 n.7 (White, J., dissenting) (asserting that this proposition "[s]urely . . . cannot be argued"; mistakenly implying that the period of greater statistical safety for abortion as compared with childbirth includes the third trimester; and mistakenly treating, for the sake of argument, the greater risk of childbirth as making abortion medically "necessary" rather than a matter of choice). *See generally* Rhoden, *supra* note 52, at 642.

    56. Akron v. Akron Center for Reproductive Health, 462 U.S. at 452 (O'Connor, J., dissenting); *see also* Rhoden, *supra* note 52, at 639–655 (discussing O'Connor's *Akron* dissent).

    Justice O'Connor, joined by Justice Rehnquist, in a 1986 dissent reasserted her arguments from *Akron*. *See* Thornburgh v. American College of Obst. & Gyn., 106 S. Ct. at 2206 (O'Connor, J., dissenting). Justice White, joined by Justice Rehnquist, also dissented in *Thornburgh* and called for the overruling of *Roe* on the ground that it lacked constitutional justification. Because that case in part turned on a narrow issue of the appropriate appellate order that may issue in reviewing a denial of a preliminary injunction, and because the broader issues canvassed in the dissents of Justices White and O'Connor focused more on constitutional interpretation and appropriate standards of judicial review of legislative action, that case provides a less useful vehicle than *Akron* for discussing the regime of *Roe*. *Thornburgh* is dealt with, as pertinent, in footnotes. *See infra* notes 68–70 and chapter 3 note 116.

    57. Roe v. Wade, 410 U.S. at 160. Using a forty-week gestational period (as measured from the first day of last menses or "LMP"), the first trimester ends at approximately thirteen weeks, and the second at approximately twenty-seven weeks; using a thirty-eight-week gestation (from fertilization), the trimesters end at a little less than thirteen and a little more than twenty-five weeks.

Complicating a physician's determination of viability is the problem of determining the length of gestation. Women's reports of LMP are not always precise and are sometimes very unreliable. Nor do all women have a regular twenty-eight-day period with ovulation always occurring two weeks after LMP. Accordingly, in performing late abortions, ultrasound measurements of fetal head size are also used to estimate gestational age. But head size varies among fetuses and families; and the initial correlation with age is in part based on women's estimates of LMP. The statistical evidence linking head size, as measured by ultrasound, with age is said to have an error of eleven days within two standard deviations. Accordingly, a fetus estimated to be twenty-three weeks LMP could in fact be well into the twenty-fifth week. As a result, Rhoden argues, physicians shy away from approaching the "true" viability point, by declining to abort a fetus that is estimated to be within two weeks of that point. Therefore, even a small drop in the age of viability can have a significant impact on the actual performance of abortions. *See* Rhoden, *supra* note 52, at 661–662; Stubblefield, "Late Abortion and Technological Advances in Fetal Viability: Some Medical Considerations," 17 *Family Planning Perspectives* 161, 161–162 (1985).

In addition to determining gestational age, a physician must also estimate the likelihood of fetal survival at that age, what length of time should constitute survival after birth, and what risks of injury may be imposed in supporting survival. Medical research suggests that viability should be defined in terms of the probability of one year intact survival; a realistic medical definition of viability should not be so low as to involve merely a short postponement of death or substantial injuries imposed in the course of assuring survival. *See infra* note 58; *cf.* Kitchen, Anne Rickards, Geoffrey Ford, Margaret Ryan & Jean Lissenden, "Live-Born Infants of 24 to 28 Weeks' Gestation: Survival and Sequelae at Two Years of Age," in *Abortion: Medical Progress and Social Implications, supra* note 9, at 122, 127–131 (calling the risk of serious sequelae to very-very-low-birthweight neonates "unacceptably high"). Such a definition would arguably be consistent with the Court's holding that the concept of viability reflects a medical judgment that "there is a reasonable likelihood of the [particular] fetus' sustained survival outside the womb, with or without artificial support." Colautti v. Franklin, 439 U.S. 379, 388 (1979); *see also* Roe v. Wade, 410 U.S. at 160, 163 (defining viability as "meaningful life").

Finally the physician must define what chance of (one year intact) survival constitutes viability. Some assert that the *Roe* Court understood viability as meaning a survival rate of 40 percent to 50 percent. *See* Rhoden, *supra* note 12, at 1500; King, "The Juridical Status of the

Fetus: A Proposal for Legal Protection of the Unborn," 77 *Mich. L. Rev.* 1647, 1679 n.144 (1979) (citing study showing the percent of survivors among those born at twenty-eight weeks to have been 46.2 percent); Richard Behrman & Tove Rosen, "Report on Viability and Nonviability of the Fetus," in National Comm'n for the Protection of Human Subjects of Biomedical and Behavioral Research, *Report and Recommendations: Research on the Fetus* (Bethesda, MD: U.S. Dept. of Health, Education and Welfare, 1975), pp. 12–1, 12–50—12–51 (same). *But cf.* Colautti v. Franklin, 439 U.S. 379, 396 n.15 (1978) (among testifying physicians, one treated a 5 percent, and two treated a 10 percent chance of survival as constituting medical viability).

58. For data on current survival rates for extremely premature neonates, *see* Gerdes, Abbasi, Bhutani & Bowen, "Improved Survival and Short-Term Outcome of Inborn 'Micropremies,'" 25 *Clinical Pediatrics* 391, 392 (1986) (reporting approximate survival rate for neonates born after twenty-four weeks gestation at 20 percent; twenty-five weeks at 40 percent; twenty-six weeks at 58 percent; and twenty-seven weeks at 83 percent); Kitchen, Ford, Doyle, Rickards, Lissenden, Pepperell & Duke, "Cesarean Section or Vaginal Delivery at 24 to 28 Weeks' Gestation: Comparison of Survival and Neonatal and Two Year Morbidity," 66 *Obstet. & Gynecol.* 149, 151 (1985) (reporting survival rate for twenty-four weeks at 7.4 percent; twenty-five weeks at 20.4 percent; twenty-six weeks at 45 percent; and twenty-seven weeks at 70.1 percent); Goldenberg, Nelson, Hale, Wayne, Bartolucci & Koski, "Survival of Infants with Low Birth Weight and Early Gestational Age, 1979 to 1981," 149 *Am. J. Obstet. & Gynecol.* 508, 509 (1984) (reporting survival rate for twenty-third week [twenty-two completed weeks] at 17 percent; twenty-fourth week at 9 percent; twenty-fifth week at 18 percent; twenty-sixth week at 29 percent; twenty-seventh week at 53 percent; twenty-eighth week at 57 percent; and twenty-ninth week at 67 percent); Milligan, Shennan & Hoskins, "Perinatal Intensive Care: Where and How to Draw the Line," 148 *Am. J. Obstet. & Gynecol.* 499, 500 (1984) (using mortality to discharge, uncorrected for congenital anomalies incompatible with life, reporting survival rate for twenty-three weeks at 14.3 percent; twenty-four weeks at 39.1 percent; twenty-five weeks at 63.6 percent; twenty-six weeks at 75.6 percent; twenty-seven weeks at 75 percent; and twenty-eight weeks at 80.7 percent); Yu, Orgill, Bajuk & Astbury, "Survival and 2-Year Outcome of Extremely Preterm Infants," 91 *British J. Obstet. & Gynaecol.* 640, 641 (1984) (reporting survival rate for twenty-four weeks at 36 percent; twenty-five weeks at 32 percent; twenty-six weeks at 57 percent; twenty-seven weeks at 70 percent; and twenty-eight weeks at 74 percent); *id.* at 644 (reporting cumulative survival rate from four published studies for twenty-four weeks at 35 percent; twenty-five weeks at 24 percent; twenty-six weeks at 48 percent; twenty-seven weeks at 62 percent; and twenty-eight weeks at 70 percent); Milner & Beard, "Letter: Limit of

Fetal Viability," 1984 *Lancet* I:1079 (reporting 1982 United Kingdom survival rates for twenty-four weeks at 16 percent; twenty-five weeks at 39 percent; twenty-six weeks at 56 percent; and twenty-seven weeks at 58 percent); *cf.* Verloove-Vanhorick, Verwey, Brand, Gravenhorst, Keirse & Ruys, "Neonatal Mortality Risk in Relation to Gestational Age and Birthweight," 1986 *Lancet* I: 55, 56; Sporken, Boo, Boon & Hein, "Survival Probabilities of Infants Delivered Prior to the 34th Week of Pregnancy as Estimated by Means of a Logistic Model," 19 *Europ. J. Obstet. Gynecol. Reprod. Biol.* 215, 216–217 (1985) (Netherland data suggesting 10 percent survival rate at twenty-five weeks).

On the basis of such data, some qualitative assessments place viability typically at twenty-six weeks, while some seem to place it as early as twenty-four weeks. *See* Altaras, Cohen, Reisner & Aderet, "Neonatal Outcome of Infants Delivered at 26–28 Weeks of Gestation," 20 *Gynecol. Obstet. Invest.* 18, 21 (1985) ("it seems reasonable to perform an aggressive approach for infants of 26 weeks or more"); Eggleston, "Management of Preterm Labor and Delivery," 29 *Clinical Obstet. & Gynecol.* 230, 236 (1986) (while there is "little hope of survival for the fetus less than 26 weeks and 750g.," aggressive treatment is nonetheless provided); Gerdes et al., *supra,* at 393 (calling survival and morbidity rate for twenty-four to twenty-six weeks "a reasonable chance of survival" and advising aggressive perinatal management).

Many studies report viability in terms of birth weight, although some have recently reemphasized the importance of gestational age as compared to weight for predicting mortality. Such studies suggest 500 to 600 gm as the critical point below which intact survival is not now possible. *See* Verloove-Vanhorick et al., *supra,* at 56; Raju, "An Epidemiologic Study of Very Low and Very Very Low Birth Weight Infants," 13 *Clinics in Perinatology* 233, 243–244 (1986) (reporting survival rate for neonates in less than 500 gm range at 0 percent; 500–700 gm range at 9 percent; 701–800 gm range at 37 percent; and 801–900 gm range at 49 percent); Yu, Bajuk, Orgill & Astbury, "Outcome of Extremely-Low-Birthweight Infants," 93 *British J. Obstet. & Gynaecol.* 162, 164 (1986) (reporting one year survival rates for 500–599 gm range at 11 percent; 600–699 gm range at 25 percent; 700–799 gm range at 47 percent; and 800–899 gm range at 58 percent); Tompkins, Alexander, Jackson, Hornung & Altekruse, "The Risk of Low Birth Weight," 122 *Am. J. Epidemiology* 1067, 1069, 1075 (1985) (suggesting that "almost all" reports in its data of neonatal survival below 680 gm were erroneous); Goldenberg, Nelson, Koski, Cutter & Cassady, "Neonatal Mortality In Infants Born Weighing 501 to 1000 Grams," 151 *Am. J. Obstet. & Gynecol.* 608, 610 (1985) (reporting survival rate in 501–700 gm range as increasing from 0 percent in 1974 to 23.5 percent in 1983, and in 701–800 gm range from 0 percent to 66.7 percent); Cohen, Stevenson, Ariagno & Sunshine, "Letter: Survival and Morbidity of Our Smallest Babies: Is There a Limit to Neonatal Care?," 73 *Pediatrics* 415, 416

(1984) (suggesting 600 gm as crucial point for predicting any chance of intact survival); Hirata, Epcar, Walsh, Mednick, Harris, McGinnis, Sehring & Papedo, "Survival and Outcome of Infants 501 to 750 Gm: A Six-Year Experience," 102 *J. Pediatrics* 741, 743, 747 (1983) (reporting survival rate in 501–750 gm range at 0 percent before 1975 and at 50 percent for a six-year period ending in 1980); cf. Ross, "Mortality and Morbidity in Very Low Birthweight Infants," 12 *Pediatric Annals* 32, 38 (1983) (fetus under 700 gm generally not viable).

For data on the youngest and smallest neonates to have ever survived, *see* Vintzileos, Winston, Campbell, Dreiss, Neckles & Nochimson, "Intrapartum Fetal Heart Rate Monitoring of the Extremely Premature Fetus," 151 *Am. J. Obstet. & Gynecol.* 744 (1985) (reporting survival of infant of 630 gm and approximately twenty-three weeks five days, and infant of 640 gm and twenty-three weeks LMP); Milner et al., *supra*, at 1079 (no documented survival below twenty-four weeks LMP, but noting anecdotal reports to the contrary); Dunn & Lashford, "Letter," 1984 *Lancet* I:1079 (reporting survival at twenty-three weeks and 540 gm); Dunn & Stirrat, "Capable of Being Born Alive," 1984 *Lancet* I:553, 554 ("Although only a few infants born at 23 weeks' gestation (500–600g) have as yet survived, their numbers are likely to increase"); Pleasure, Dhand & Kaur, "What is the Lower Limit of Viability? Intact Survival of a 440-g Infant," 138 *Am. J. Diseases of Children* 783, 784 (1984) (reporting survival of a 440 gm infant born at twenty-five and one-half weeks gestation as being at the "frontier of viability"; noting that lay literature had reported only two smaller infants but treating these as undocumented reports and noting medical literature report of one smaller surviving infant); Akron v. Akron Center for Reproductive Health, 462 U.S. 416, 457 n.5 (1983) (O'Connor, J., dissenting) (citing newspaper account of a surviving 484 gm and twenty-two-week-old infant); Rhoden, *supra* note 12, at 1465 n.147 (citing article concerning viable fetus at twenty-two to twenty-three weeks).

For data on injury and sequelae among those few who survive a very premature birth, including cerebral palsy, deafness, blindness, and severe or moderate developmental delay, *see* Yu et al., "Outcome of Extremely-Low-Birthweight Infants," 93 *British J. Obstet. & Gynaecol.*, *supra*, at 165–166 & table 4 (of those studied with birthweight under 1000 gm, 16 percent had cerebral palsy, 3 percent were blind, 3 percent had sensorineural deafness and 14 percent had developmental delay; and among the 500–599 gm group who survived, 33.33 percent had such disabilities); Gerdes et al., *supra*, at 392–393 (15 percent had severe to moderate handicaps or developmental delays, and 39 percent had minor sequelae); Yu et al., "Survival and 2-Year Outcome of Extremely Preterm Infants," 91 *British J. Obstet. & Gynaecol.*, *supra*, at 642 (among surviving infants born between twenty-four and twenty-six weeks LMP, about 25 percent had "significant functional handicaps"); Kitchen, Ford, Orgill, Rickards, Astbury, Lissenden, Bajuk, Yu, Drew &

Campbell, "Outcome in Infants with Birth Weight 500 to 999 gm: A Regional Study of 1979 and 1980 Births," 104 *J. Pediatrics* 921, 926 (1984) (with respect to infants born in hospital two years previously, reporting 48.3 percent with either no disability or a "minimal" disability which might later require intervention; 29.2 percent with moderate to mild functional disability, the impact of which on subsequent functioning could not be predicted; and 22.5 percent with severe functional disability); *id.* (of those born outside a hospital with NICU, only 28 percent were free of functional handicap); Hirata et al., *supra*, at 748 (in 501–750 gm range, 67 percent were normal and 22 percent were "functional" but with neurological and developmental sequelae); William Kitchen, Anne Rickards, Geoffrey Ford, Margaret Ryan & Jean Lissenden, "Live-Born Infants of 24 to 28 Weeks' Gestation: Survival and Sequelae at Two Years of Age," in *Abortion: Medical Progress and Social Implications, supra* note 9, at 122, 130–131 (reporting prevalence of major handicap for infants born in weeks twenty-four to twenty-six to be 27 percent, and for those born in weeks twenty-seven to twenty-eight, to be 8.5 percent; and noting other studies that report rates for major handicap among very-very-low-birthweight infants at 31 percent and 44 percent); Milligan et al., *supra*, at 502 (occurrence of major developmental handicaps at twenty-three weeks is 0 percent; at twenty-four weeks, 14.8 percent; at twenty-five weeks, 9.6 percent; at twenty-six weeks, 8.4 percent; at twenty-seven weeks, 19.3 percent; and at twenty-eight weeks, 18.5 percent); Cohen et al., *supra*, at 415 (21 percent of survivors had severe or moderate handicaps in 751-1000 gm range); Orgill, Astbury, Bajuk & Yu, "Early Development of Infants 1,000 G or Less at Birth," 57 *Arch. Disease in Childhood* 823, 826 (1982) (among surviving infants born at below 1000 gm, over 27 percent were handicapped by the experience, and 20 percent were seriously handicapped); Kraybill, Kennedy, Teplin & Campbell, "Infants with Birth Weights Less Than 1,001 G," 138 *Am. J. Diseases of Children* 837, 840 (1984) (of the twenty-nine of fifty-six infants under 1001 gm in study who survived, four were mildly handicapped and four were moderately to severely handicapped); Rhoden, *supra* note 12, at 1451, 1462–1463 nn.108–131 (same); Rhoden, *supra* note 52, at 664.

Follow-up studies evidence the disabilities resulting from very premature birth and its treatment. *See* Lasky, Tyson, Rosenfeld, Krasinski, Dowling & Gant, "Disappointing Follow-up Findings for Indigent High-Risk Newborns," 141 *Am. J. Diseases of Children* 100 (1987); Rivers, Caron & Hack, "Experience of Families with Very Low Birthweight Children with Neurologic Sequelae," 26 *Clinical Pediatrics* 223 (1987); Eilers, Desai, Wilson & Cunningham, "Classroom Performance and Social Factors of Children with Birth Weights of 1,250 Grams or Less: Follow-up at 5 to 8 Years of Age," 77 *Pediatrics* 203 (1986).

Whether increasing the rate of survival below week twenty-six will also increase morbidity rates is uncertain. *Compare* Kitchen et al.,

"Live-Born Infants of 24 to 28 Weeks' Gestation: Survival and Sequelae at Two Years of Age," *supra*, at 127–131 (noting that as medical skills improve and gestational age decreases, the rate of cerebral palsy appears to increase while deafness and blindness decrease) *and* Ross, *supra*, at 38 (rate of injuries among premature infants increasing as age of viability is lowered) *with* Milligan et al., *supra*, at 502–503 (noting increased vulnerability to morbidity at twenty-seven to twenty-eight weeks and suggesting that insult occurring below twenty-seven weeks leads to increased mortality not morbidity).

The rate of intact survival is calculated by combining mortality and morbidity rates. One recent study indicates that at twenty-four weeks 6.2 percent survive without severe handicap; at twenty-five weeks, 14.3 percent; at twenty-six weeks, 28.6 percent; at twenty-seven weeks, 52 percent; and at twenty-eight weeks, approximately 69.8 percent. If suspected developmental retardation (as evidenced by moderate developmental delay) is added to the morbidity rates and the cases in which no data are available are assumed to be developing intact, successful survival rates drop as follows: at twenty-four weeks, 6.2 percent; at twenty-five weeks, 7.2 percent; at twenty-six weeks, 20.4 percent; at twenty-seven weeks, 37 percent; and at twenty-eight weeks, 52 percent. *See* Kitchen et al., "Live Born Infants of 24 to 28 Weeks Gestation: Survival and Sequelae at Two Years of Age," *supra*, at 130–131; Yu et al., "Outcome of Extremely-Low-Birthweight Infants," 93 *British J. Obstet. & Gynaecol.*, *supra*, at 166 (in last year of study, 51 percent died, 16 percent [or approximately 30 percent of survivors] had a disability, and 33 percent were normal); Milligan et. al., *supra*, at 502 (from a predictive or obstetric point of view, reporting percent of intact survivors at twenty-three weeks as 14 percent; at twenty-four weeks, 24 percent; at twenty-five weeks, 54 percent; at twenty-six weeks, 68 percent; at twenty-seven weeks, 56 percent; and at twenty-eight weeks, 62 percent).

The variability in the data among the aforementioned studies may be attributable to variations in the hospitals and populations studied, whether samples derived from a hospital or from a geographic area, the typically small sample size, inaccuracy in estimating gestational age, and the date of the study. Comparison among studies is also made difficult by differing definitions of the relevant variables, including intact survival and major, moderate, and minor disability. *See, e.g.,* Ross, *supra*, at 39 (noting various standards for defining injury to the neonate). Studies may even fail to indicate whether or not gestational weeks refer to completed weeks, and whether counting began at fertilization or last menstrual period. As an additional example, studies which exclude delivery room deaths decrease the mortality rate, as do those which exclude infants born with defects incompatible with life. *See* Yu et al., "Outcome of Extremely-Low-Birthweight Infants," 93 *British J. Obstet. & Gynaecol.*, *supra*, at 167; Kitchen & Murton, "Survival Rates of Infants With Birth Weights Between 501 and 1,000 G," 139 *Am. J. Diseases of Children* 470, 471 (1985) (over 29 percent of deaths of studied infants born in hospital with NICU occurred in delivery room or shortly after admission to NICU); Cohen et al., *supra*, at 416. A change in weight categories by as little as one gram can also affect mortality rates. *See, e.g.,* Hermansen & Hasan, "Importance of Using Standardized Birth Weight Increments to Report Neonatal Mortality Data," 78 *Pediatrics* 144 (1986); Verloove-Vanhorick, Verwey & Keirse, "Letter: Neonatal Mortality in Very Low Birthweight and Very Preterm Infants," 153 *Am. J. Obstet. & Gynecol.* 929 (1985).

Furthermore, studies which determine mortality rates from deaths occurring only within the first twenty-eight days after birth or only until discharge appear to underestimate the mortality rate of very-low-birthweight infants, for deaths in the entire first year have been attributed to a very early birth. *See* Yu et al., "Outcome of Extremely-Low-Birthweight Infants," 93 *British J. Obstet. & Gynaecol.*, *supra*, at 167 (corrected survival rate of infants born in hospital would have increased from 47 percent to 57 percent if delivery room deaths were excluded, and to 62 percent if postneonatal deaths were excluded); Dujardin, Lagasse, Vandenbussche & Wollast, "Letter," 256 *JAMA* 1140 (1986); Buehler, Hogue & Zaro, "Postponing or Preventing Deaths? Trends In Infant Survival, Georgia, 1974 Through 1981," 253 *JAMA* 3564, 3566–3567 (1985); Yu, Kinlay, Orgill, Bajuk & Astbury, "Outcome of Very Low Birthweight Infants Who Required Prolonged Hospitalization," 20 *Australian Pediatric J.* 293 (1984) (reporting study that found 14 percent of deaths of infants born below 1500 gm occurred in postneonatal period); Hirata et al., *supra*, at 746 (using survival rate at discharge because twenty-eight day survival rates are "probably meaningless" for infants under 751 gm). *But cf.* Yu, Watkins & Bajuk, "Neonatal and Postneonatal Mortality in Very Low Birthweight Infants," 59 *Arch. Disease in Childhood* 987, 988 (1984) (smallest infants in group studied are not more disposed to postneonatal mortality than other low birthweight infants).

For data, now several years old, on the costs, ranging from $25,000 to $100,000 in an uncomplicated case, of neonatal intensive care units, *see* Phibbs, Williams & Phibbs, "Newborn Risk Factors and Costs of Neonatal Intensive Care," 68 *Pediatrics* 313, 315–320 (1981); Pomerance, Ukrainski, Ukra, Henderson, Nash & Meredith, "Cost of Living for Infants Weighing 1000 Grams or Less at Birth," 61 *Pediatrics* 908, 909–910 (1978); Rhoden, *supra* note 12, at 1451, 1464 (average cost for survivor under 1000 gm is $40,287.00; including costs of nonsurvivors, it is $61,641.00); *cf.* Milligan et al., *supra*, at 503 (cost of maintaining a neonate born at twenty-five weeks is twice that of maintaining neonate born at twenty-nine weeks). Some research indicates that a majority of infants born prior to twenty-eight weeks who die will do so in the first day; if so, then aggressive care that leads to survival for more than a day may often eventually lead to survival. Yu et al., "Survival and

2-Year Outcome of Extremely Preterm Infants," 91 *British J. Obstet. & Gynaecol., supra,* at 640, 645.

For another reading of some of these data, *see* Rhoden, *supra* note 52, at 658–662.

59. Akron v. Akron Center for Reproductive Health, 462 U.S. at 457 & n.5 (O'Connor, J., dissenting).

The following review of the articles and evidence that Justice O'Connor cites does not support her claim that viability is descending rapidly or significantly below the period of viability described in *Roe.* She cites one article for the proposition that infants of less than twenty-five weeks and weight between 500 and 1249 gm have a 20 percent survival rate: Philip, Little, Polivy & Lucey, "Neonatal Mortality Risk for the Eighties: The Importance of Birth Weight/Gestational Age Groups," 68 *Pediatrics* 122 (1981). That percent is based on five infants born at or below twenty-five weeks in one hospital; but the article also reports a larger set of data from another hospital which are far less optimistic. On balance, the article states, "it is quite clear that the infant whose gestational age is less than 26 weeks is at a particular disadvantage, with a death rate of 90% or more." *Id.* at 129. The authors conclude: "It is clear that considerable improvement has occurred in the last decade, except for the most immature infants (less than 26 weeks)." *Id.* at 127.

O'Connor cites Kopelman, "The Smallest Preterm Infants: Reasons for Optimism and New Dilemmas," 132 *Am. J. Diseases of Children* 461 (1978), for the proposition that preterms with a weight under 1000 gm have a 42 percent chance of survival. While one cited study supports this claim, the author appears to rely on a 32 percent survival rate, of which 78 percent appear to have escaped disability. The focus is on infants born at or above twenty-eight weeks, although brief mention is made of efforts to maintain alive those older than twenty-four weeks.

Finally, she cites Beddis, Collins, Levy, Godfrey & Silverman, "New Technique for Servo-Control of Arterial Oxygen Tension in Preterm Infants," 54 *Arch. Disease in Childhood* 278 (1979). But that article is not especially pertinent to her argument since it involves a study of twelve preterms with weight ranging from 760 to 2260 gm (mean 1640) and age of twenty-six to thirty-four weeks (mean 31.3).

60. Yu, Bajuk, Orgill & Astbury, "Outcome of Extremely-Low-Birthweight Infants," 93 *British J. Obstet. & Gynaecol.* 162, 168 (1986) (on the basis of a review of a hospital's survival rates from 1977 to 1983, concluding that "the survival and 2-year disability rates have not continued to improve. . . . Further improvements in survival and neuro-developmental outcome for these extremely-low-birthweight infants await better understanding"); Dunn & Stirrat, "Capable of Being Born Alive," 1984 *Lancet* I:553, 554 ("extreme immaturity of the lungs and other vital organs before 22 weeks' gestation makes survival exceed-ingly unlikely now or in the future without recourse to complex technology involving an artificial placenta"); *cf.* "Discussion," in *Abortion: Medical Progress and Social Implications, supra* note 9, at 122, 134 (statement of William Kitchen: "The state of maturity of the lungs . . . is probably what now sets the lower limit. This time is unlikely to be changed much by improvements in the available techniques of ventilation. If there is a major breakthrough, it will surely come from an artificial placenta into which a 22-week or 23-week baby could be plugged"); Hein & Lathrop, "The Changing Pattern of Neonatal Mortality in a Regionalized System of Perinatal Care," 140 *Am. J. Diseases in Childhood* 989, 993 (1986) (referring to "limited ability of current medical technology to impact on future reductions of the neonatal mortality rate").

Whether ethical limitations on human and fetal experimentation may limit the development of artificial placentas requires consideration.

61. *See* Grimes, *supra* note 52, at 264; Henshaw, "Characteristics of U.S. Women Having Abortions, 1982–1983," 19 *Family Planning Perspectives* 5, 6 (1987) (using postoperative assessment, reporting that, in 1983, 60 percent of abortions performed after twenty weeks occurred before week twenty-three, with 100 abortions performed after week twenty-four); *infra* chapter 3 notes 60–61.

62. *See* Colautti v. Franklin 439 U.S. at 388 ("Viability is reached when, in the judgment of the attending physician on the particular facts of the case before him, there is a reasonable likelihood of the fetus' sustained survival outside the womb, with or without artificial support"); Planned Parenthood of Mo. v. Danforth, 428 U.S. at 64 ("it is not the proper function of the legislature or the courts to place viability, which essentially is a medical concept, at a specific point in the gestation period. The time when viability is achieved may vary with each pregnancy, and the determination of whether a particular fetus is viable is, and must be, a matter for the judgment of the responsible attending physician"); *id.* at 81–83; *see also supra* note 57. *But cf.* King, *supra* note 57, at 1679–1685 (recommending setting viability at earliest age of any surviving infant).

63. Akron v. Akron Center for Reproductive Health, 462 U.S. at 458 (O'Connor, J., dissenting); *see also* Rhoden, *supra* note 12, at 1491 (agreeing with O'Connor).

64. The trimester system was a convenient way to think about the outcome of the balance that *Roe* struck; it was not the reason for the balance, except insofar as allowing women choice until viability affords poor women, young women, women carrying a seriously handicapped fetus, women with irregular menses, and women with little knowledge about their own fertility the opportunity to discover their pregnancy and reach a conclusion about what to do. *See infra* text accompanying chapter 3 notes 60–61.

65. Akron v. Akron Center for Reproductive Health, 462 U.S. at 461 (O'Connor, J., dissenting) ("At any stage in pregnancy, there is the *poten-*

tial for human life. . . . The choice of viability as the point at which the state interest in *potential* life becomes compelling is no less arbitrary than choosing any point before viability") (emphasis in original); *cf.* Thornburgh v. American College of Obst. & Gyn., 106 S. Ct. at 2196–97 (White, J., dissenting) ("The substantiality of this [state] interest is in no way dependent on the probability that the fetus may be capable of surviving outside the womb at any given point in its development. . . . The State's interest is in the fetus as an entity in itself, and the character of this entity does not change at the point of viability under conventional medical wisdom"). *But cf.* Thornburgh v. American College of Obst. & Gyn., 106 S. Ct. at 2185, 2188 (Stevens, J., concurring).

The claim that the potential of the zygote is the same as the potential of the viable third trimester fetus, and therefore that the state interest in that potential is the same, ignores, at a minimum, the data on the degree of natural "fetal wastage," especially early in any pregnancy. The chance of a zygote's potential of birth ever being realized is under 40 percent. *See supra* note 10.

66. Thornburgh v. American College of Obst. & Gyn., 106 S. Ct. at 2214 (O'Connor, J., dissenting); Akron v. Akron Center for Reproductive Health, 462 U.S. at 464–65 & n.8 (O'Connor, J., dissenting). For Justice O'Connor, a prohibition on the only abortion procedure actually available would apparently be unduly burdensome, as might an absolute parental veto of a minor's abortion choice. Ignoring how they actually worked in practice, O'Connor asserts that the requirements (which were struck down in *Doe v. Bolton*) of hospitalization, of an abortion committee approval, and of the concurrence of two physicians were not unduly burdensome. *Id.* at 464–473 & n.9; *cf. id.* at 420 n.1 (majority opinion) (indicating that effect of O'Connor's views would be to "drive the performance of many abortions back underground, free of effective regulation and often without the attendance of a physician").

67. With respect to procedural problems in pre-*Roe* regulatory schemes, *see, e.g.,* Doe v. Bolton, 410 U.S. at 207 (Burger, C.J., concurring); *see also* U.S. v. Vuitch, 402 U.S. 62, 96 (1971) (Stewart, J., dissenting in part); *id.* at 74 (Douglas, J., dissenting in part); *cf.* Drinan, 31 *Theological Studies* 149 (1970) (suggesting that deregulation may be preferable to a regulator than allowing the state to review the reasons of women and sanction some of them but not others); Luker, *supra* note 44, at 76–91 (regulatory schemes had been so flawed that it was physicians who led the movement for abortion deregulation in the 1960s).

With respect to wide disparities in the pre-*Roe* availability of abortions, *see id.* at 45–47.

Were *Roe* to be overruled and were a state to decide to implement an alternative to *Roe's* regulatory scheme, it could do so through a criminal prohibition that instructed the individual physician when she may perform an abortion, through a two-physician requirement, through a hospital review committee, or through an administrative or judicial determination. Of these, a simple criminal statute aimed at the individual physician might provide the fairest method of implementing a regulatory scheme consistent with both informational privacy and due process concerns.

For practical reasons, attempts to regulate abortion now would be even harder than before because of the fourteen years experience under *Roe*, and such attempts would thus continue to lead to arbitrary enforcement. Stanley Henshaw of the Alan Guttmacher Institute has estimated that, as of 1987, more than 14.7 million (or 16 percent of) women over age 18 have had a legal abortion, and that, conservatively, 17.6 million (or 19 percent of) women over 18 have had an abortion whether legal or not (personal communication). *See also* Tietze, *supra* note 25, at 62 (estimating that almost 8 million women had a legal abortion by 1980). Thus, a generation of women expects procreative choice now more than before. Moreover, a broad cohort of physicians has been trained to provide them safely. Also, developing technology may permit women, without physician assistance, to induce abortions by themselves with an antiprogesterone agent. *See supra* note 35.

For a discussion of the imposition of tort and criminal good samaritan obligations of substantial proportion on men and women alike to avoid running afoul of principles of equality, in case of a future abortion prohibition, *see generally* Regan, *supra* note 19; *cf.* Karst, "Foreword: Equal Citizenship Under the Fourteenth Amendment," 91 *Harv. L. Rev.* 1 (1977).

68. Akron v. Akron Center for Reproductive Health, 462 U.S. at 459 (O'Connor, J., dissenting). Noting that Pennsylvania, a party to the lawsuit, did not seek to have *Roe* overruled, Justice O'Connor again did not address that issue in *Thornburgh* in 1986. That she did not join the *Thornburgh* dissent of Justices White and Rehnquist calling for the overruling of *Roe* may evidence that she is prepared to accommodate to *Roe* as precedent if the Court were to adopt the less strict standard of judicial review that she has advocated. *See supra* text accompanying notes 65–66.

69. How those who would overrule *Roe* would treat the privacy cases, and, in particular, the cases protecting the right to contraception, is not clear from their dissenting opinions. Justice O'Connor has not discussed whether the state's interest in potential life is confined to its diploid phase or extends to the haploid phase as well, in which case the state could regulate or prohibit the use of prefertilization contraceptives such as spermicides. Of greater practical consequence, she has not indicated whether the compelling state interest, which begins at pregnancy, commences with implantation or fertilization and thus whether it might extend to IUDs, various birth control pills, and other pre-implantation methods of birth control that may affect the zygote. *See* Akron v. Akron Center for Reproductive Health, 462 U.S. at 460–61

(O'Connor, J., dissenting) (discussing compelling state interest in potential life at "any stage in pregnancy"). In contrast, Justice White clearly places the point at which the compelling interest arises at fertilization. *See* Thornburgh v. American College of Obst. & Gyn., 106 S. Ct. at 2197 (White, J., dissenting) (focusing on state interest in diploid "entity" which begins at fertilization); *see also supra* note 49.

70. *See* Planned Parenthood Ass'n v. Ashcroft, 462 U.S. 476, 482–86 (1983) (upholding statutory requirement that, unless a woman's health requires otherwise, a second physician must be present to care for the delivered child in a third trimester abortion). *But cf. id.* at 498–501 (Blackmun, J., concurring in part and dissenting in part) (noting that attending physician might employ a D&E procedure that would eliminate the possibility of a live birth); Thornburgh v. American College of Obst. & Gyn., 106 S. Ct. at 2182–83 (striking down a provision that established a duty of care to postviable fetus, during abortion, that is equivalent to duty owed a nonaborted fetus, and a provision that required use of abortion technique that best assures survival of postviable fetus, because neither provision contained an emergency exception providing for the primacy of the woman's health over fetal survival). The abortion techniques used at the edge of viability that presently increase the chances of fetal survival, such as hysterotomy and to a lesser extent prostaglandin instillation, greatly increase the risks to maternal health as compared with a D&E procedure. Grimes, *supra* note 52, at 264.

71. To avoid this outcome, Justice O'Connor would have to either develop a legal theory of sexuality that would impose a good samaritan obligation on the woman (and this might also allow states to prohibit the IUD and other preimplantation methods of birth control); or reject an entire jurisprudence of rights that requires the state to accommodate significant constitutional rights where less burdensome means are available to it; or deny that the woman has any substantial constitutional claim to procreative liberty. While O'Connor has not foreclosed adopting this last position, *see* Akron v. Akron Center for Reproductive Health, 462 U.S. at 459, this strategy might permit stringent state regulation of contraception and jeopardize a whole line of privacy cases, *see supra* notes 49, 69.

72. Two matters should be noted with respect to separation. If the state were to compel only transfers to other women's wombs but not to artificial placentas in lieu of abortion, then it could be argued that the Huxleyan future pictured in the text would not have occasion to arise. But there would be very difficult allocational choices and troubling questions about the disaggregation of biological motherhood, *see infra* text accompanying chapter 3 notes 72–87. Hard choices would arise because of the probable scarcity of recipients of fetal transfers as compared with women wishing separation. Thus, decisions would have to

be made about which fetuses would be transferred and survive and which would die, or alternatively, which women would be permitted to separate and which ones denied a separation.

Second, even if technology existed that permitted the removal whole of an implanted fetus, the risk of injury to it might well justify the prohibition of such techniques. While that would be appropriate, the risk of injury ought similarly to be factored into assessments of viability. This would lead to a less optimistic reading than Justice O'Connor gave the viability data. *See supra* notes 58–59.

For discussions of the appropriateness of the technological solution of separation, *see* Tribe, "The Abortion Funding Conundrum: Inalienable Rights, Affirmative Duties, and the Dilemma of Dependence," 99 *Harv. L. Rev.* 330, 337 n.30, 341 (1985); Tribe, "Structural Due Process," 10 *Harv. C.R.-C.L. L. Rev.* 269, 297–298 (1975); Tushnet, "An Essay on Rights," 62 *Tex. L. Rev.* 1363 (1984); Rhoden, *supra* note 12; Robertson, *supra* note 36, at 166; Mahowald, "Concepts of Abortion and Their Relevance to the Abortion Debate," 20 *Southern J. Phil.* 195 (1982); *cf.* Thomson, *supra* note 15, at 66 ("[y]ou may detach yourself even if this costs him his life; you have no right to be guaranteed his death, by some other means, if unplugging yourself does not kill him"). Bernard Nathanson also advocates separation as the proper resolution of the conflicting interests of woman and fetus:

> To solve the abortion dilemma—to respect the pregnant woman's right to be rid of an unwanted pregnancy and simultaneously to respect alpha's [Nathanson's designation of the fetus] right to exist—we require . . . an instrument of sufficient delicacy . . . [to] pluck alpha off the wall of the uterus like a helicopter rescuing a stranded mountain climber. . . . Besides transplantation into an artificial womb, the tiny alpha plucked from its implantation site could be transferred directly to another prepared uterus. . . . The abortion of the future, then, will consist simply of early detection of the alpha, removal of alpha from the unwilling mother, and transfer either to a life-support system or re-implantation into a willing and eager recipient. All rights are respected in this situation.

Nathanson, *supra* note 11, at 282–283.

Calabresi writes:

> [I]f one thinks . . . of the possibility that in time early fetuses could be separated simply and safely from women seeking abortions and then be brought to term, even the wishful seems possible. The [*Roe*] opinion as written, instead effectively demeaned the losing values and made such desirable wishful thinking impossible.

Calabresi, *supra* note 28, at 198–199 n.396. He also states:

> One can imagine a time and a technology in which a woman who wished an abortion could have the fetus removed without pain or risk to her and without necessary harm to it. One also can imagine that *willing* volunteers, women who wished to adopt babies, could have that same fetus implanted in them and brought to term. Why should our Constitution prevent states from requiring *this* form of separation (if truly riskless)

rather than another form which entails destruction? What special interest—different from the male interest which has been held by the courts
to be of no weight—would the female have which would give her the
right to destroy her genes or offspring? Why, in other words, under such
a technology, should those who wish to preserve both life values and
equality values not be able to legislate so as to achieve both.
Id. at 113 (emphasis in original).

The constitutional problems of administering state supervised transfers and hatcheries would be substantial. *Cf.* Youngberg v. Romeo, 457
U.S. 307, 317 (1982) ("When a person is institutionalized—and wholly
dependent on the State—it is conceded by petitioners that a duty to
provide certain services and care does exist, although even then a State
necessarily has considerable discretion in determining the nature and
scope of its responsibilities").

2. A SEARCH FOR A LOGIC OF ATTACHMENT

1. For a critique of the individualistic, rights-based language of the
abortion debate, *see* Jean Elshtain, "Reflections on Abortion, Values
and the Family," in *Abortion: Understanding Differences*, ed. Sidney
Callahan & Daniel Callahan (New York: Plenum Press, 1984), pp. 47,
52–61; Theodora Ooms, "A Family Perspective on Abortion," in *Abortion: Understanding Differences, supra*, at 81; Lisa Cahill, "Abortion,
Autonomy, and Community," in *Abortion: Understanding Differences, supra*, at 264–267; *id.* at 268–272 ("we have not grasped the reality of
the moral situation when we define freedom only as 'freedom over' the
body and not also as 'freedom in' or 'freedom through' the body. The
body makes peculiar demands, creates peculiar relationships, and
grounds peculiar obligations. . . . The liberal ethos discourages making
personal sacrifices and encourages at best a minimal appreciation of
the virtue and even the necessity of constructive suffering. . . . We cannot be freed from all infringements on our self-fulfillment"); Churchill
& Simán, "Abortion and the Rhetoric of Individual Rights," 12(1) *Hastings Center Report* 9 (1982). *But cf.* Virginia Abernethy, "Commentary,"
in *Abortion: Understanding Differences, supra*, at 276–283 (employing
communal perspective to account for abortion as a method of increasing the next generation's survival chances).

For a discussion of a duty-based approach to abortion, *see* Weiss,
"The Perils of Personhood," 89 *Ethics* 66, 75 (1978) ("our responsibilities ['duties'] to the fetus arise not out of its rights, but rather out of its
needs and its total dependence on *us*"); *id.* at 74 ("If . . . we approach
the abortion issue from the perspective of duties rather than of rights,
all these questions begin to allow and require reexamination") (minimizing complexity and texture available through the analysis of good
samaritan duties); Finnis, "The Rights and Wrongs of Abortion," 2 *Phil.
& Pub. Aff.* 117 (1973); L. W. Sumner, *Abortion and Moral Theory* (Prince-

ton: Princeton University Press, 1981), pp. 182–187 (describing the conservative position as essentially a duty-based, not rights-based, theory, but one that can be translated directly into rights language).

2. For a brief discussion of the function of rights in our culture, *see, e.g.,* Schoeman, "Rights of Children, Rights of Parents, and the Moral Basis of the Family," 91 *Ethics* 6, 8 (1980) ("the language of rights typically helps us to sharpen our appreciation of the moral boundaries which separate people, emphasizing the appropriateness of seeing other persons as independent and autonomous agents").

For a discussion of the protection that rights afford caretakers, *see, e.g.,* Carol Gilligan, *In a Different Voice: Psychological Theory and Women's Development* (Cambridge, MA: Harvard University Press, 1983).

The philosophical literature on abortion is deeply split over the usefulness of the concept of rights. *Compare* Thomson, "A Defense of Abortion," 1 *Phil. & Pub. Aff.* 47 (1971) *with* Finnis, *supra* note 1, *with* Becker, "Human Being: The Boundaries of a Concept," 4 *Phil. & Pub. Aff.* 334 (1975). While Thomson acknowledges that no adequate philosophical account of rights exists, she also asserts that no adequate account of moral duties can develop without reference to rights. *See* Thomson, *supra,* at 59–62; *cf.* Thomson, "The Trolley Problem," 94 *Yale. LJ.* 1395 (1985); Regan, "Utilitarianism, Vegetarianism and Animal Rights," 9 *Phil. & Pub. Aff.* 305 (1980) (discussing role of rights in affording protection to animals).

3. John Noonan, Jr., *A Private Choice: Abortion in America in the Seventies* (New York: The Free Press, 1979), p. 192; *id.* at 191–192 (blaming the abortion debate for a "sinister and Orwellian reshaping of our language"); John Noonan, Jr., "How to Argue About Abortion," in *Contemporary Issues in Bioethics,* ed. Tom Beauchamp & Leroy Walters (Belmont, CA: Wadsworth Publishing Co., 1982), p. 210 (calling Thomson's violinist analogy to motherhood "grotesque").

4. For Winthrop's sermon, *see* John Winthrop, "A Model of Christian Charity," *quoted in* Robert Bellah, Richard Madsen, William Sullivan, Ann Swidler & Steven Tipton, *Habits of the Heart: Individualism and Commitment in American Life* (Berkeley, Los Angeles, London: University of California Press, 1985), p. 28.

With respect to a definition of citizenship, *see, e.g.,* U.S. Const. amend. XIV, sec. 1 (defining United States citizenship). Citizenship depends on whether one emerges from the womb in the United States, or is "naturalized" in case of a foreign birth. But unlike membership in families, the birth-mother need not be a member of the community, but only a transient, passing through.

5. Michael Sandel, "Introduction," in *Liberalism and its Critics,* ed. Michael Sandel (New York: New York University Press, 1984), pp. 5–6:

> [In modern liberalism, the] priority of the self over its ends means I am never defined by my aims and attachments, but always capable of standing back to survey and assess and possibly to revise them. This is what it

means to be a free and independent self, capable of choice. And this is the vision of the self that finds expression in the ideal of the state as a neutral framework. . . .

Communitarian critics of rights-based liberalism say we cannot conceive ourselves as independent in this way, as bearers of selves wholly detached from our aims and attachments. They say that certain of our roles are partly constitutive of the persons we are. . . . Open-ended though it be, the story of my life is always embedded in the story of those communities from which I derive my identity—whether family or city. . . . On the communitarian view, these stories make a moral difference, not only a psychological one. They situate us in the world, and give our lives their moral particularity.

See also Michael Sandel, *Liberalism and the Limits of Justice* (Cambridge: Cambridge University Press, 1982), p. 179 ("To imagine a person incapable of constitutive attachments . . . is not to conceive an ideally free and rational agent, but to imagine a person wholly without character, without moral depth"); *id.* at 183 ("Once the bounds of the self are no longer fixed, individuated in advance and given prior to experience, there is no saying in principle what sorts of experiences could shape or reshape them"). *But see* Baker, "Essay: Sandel on Rawls," 133 *U. Pa. L. Rev.* 895 (1985) (criticizing Sandel's interpretation of the Rawlsian anthropology, and asserting that a full, "thick" version of the person as constituted by her attachments is consistent with Rawls' work).

For recent work of others evincing communal concerns, *see* Michael Walzer, *Spheres of Justice: A Defense of Pluralism and Equality* (New York: Basic Books, 1983), pp. 31–63; *id.* at 61 ("the distribution of membership is not pervasively subject to the contraints of justice"); Bellah et al., *supra* note 4; Robert Wolf, "There's Nobody Here But Us Persons," in *Women and Philosophy, Toward a Theory of Liberation,* ed. Carol Gould & Mary Wartofsky (New York: Putnam, 1976), pp. 128, 140–141 (a society in which the ideal is "treating all persons as interchangeable public persons . . . toward which we now seem to be moving, would be the perfect, rational realization of the ideals and images of classical liberalism out of which our modern political philosophies have grown. It would also be the ultimate denial of the humanity of man").

6. Schoeman, *supra* note 2, at 8.

Even within the traditional discourse of rights, in social contract theory and the law, the family and children are the occasion for exceptional treatment and an exceptional language of duty and obligation. A critique of rights and individualistic language may proceed here without calling into question the general categories of liberalism and constitutional discourse.

It is worth noting that the peculiar position of the family in liberal political theory and the paucity of political categories for comprehending family relationships in a world of autonomous individuals may account for some of the difficulties the Supreme Court has had in explaining the privacy doctrine, as evidenced by the short time between the contraception cases of Griswold v. Connecticut, 381 U.S. 479 (1965), and Eisenstadt v. Baird, 405 U.S. 438 (1971), but the great distance between their rationales. The former protects the fundamental privacy of the marriage relationship and its precincts in the bedroom, while the latter protects the contraceptive choices of individuals. *See generally* Schneider, "Moral Discourse and the Transformation of American Family Law," 83 *Mich. L. Rev.* 1803, 1855–1859 (1985)(discussing rights rhetoric in family law); Olsen, "The Family and the Market," 96 *Harv. L. Rev.* 1497 (1983).

7. Schoeman, *supra* note 2, at 9, 19. Schoeman would limit the language of rights within families to certain fundamental matters that are destructive of the child's future independence. *See also id.* at 9 (instead of having rights, infants are better "thought of primarily as having needs, the satisfaction of which involves intimate and intense relationships"); *id.* at 8 ("etymology of 'intimate' relates it to a verb meaning 'to bring within'").

For a discussion of the relationship of intimacy to privacy, *see* Robert Gerstein, "Intimacy and Privacy," 89 *Ethics* 76 (1978); *cf.* Charles Fried, *An Anatomy of Values* (Cambridge, MA: Harvard University Press, 1970), pp. 75–86, 137–152; Joseph Goldstein, Anna Freud & Albert Solnit, *Beyond the Best Interests of the Child* (New York: The Free Press, 1979), pp. 3–28, 105–111 (state intervention erodes parental omnipotence that children need).

8. *See, e.g.*, Caroline Whitbeck, "A Different Reality: Feminist Ontology," in *Beyond Domination*, ed. Carol Gould (Totowa, NJ: Rowman & Allanheld, 1984), pp. 64, 77 (advocating a feminist ontology that rejects the dualism and antagonism of self-other, in favor of a relational view of persons: "relationships to other people are fundamental to being a person"); *id.* at 77 ("[a] person is an historical being whose history is fundamentally a history of relationships to other people").

This position is consistent with those who identify one task of feminism as implementing that which is different and unique in women's nature. At the grandest level, this line of thought takes up the critique of western rationality and its project of the domination of nature by man. Rather than trying to join men in this project by triumphing over their own nature, these feminists urge the rediscovery of the creativity that women, as the "progynitors" of the human race, naturally possess. The implications of this perspective with respect to abortion are ambiguous. For some the right to abortion protects female power over her creative potential and is a necessary defense to male sadistic exploitation. *See* Mary Daly, *Gyn/Ecology: The Metaethics of Radical Feminism* (Boston: Beacon Press, 1978). For others, abortion is a betrayal of this nature. Sidney Callahan, "Value Choices in Abortion," in *Abortion: Understanding Differences, supra* note 1, at 285.

A contrasting line of feminist theory argues that the power to have an abortion not only frees women in a practical sense to pursue careers and develop a variety of life plans as men may, but also, at a general level, it is that which lets women escape from the necessity of their biological condition into the realm of freedom and autonomy. Without that power, some believe the structure and prejudices of patriarchy will always exclude women from equality and full-fledged participation in the Western project of rational mastery over nature. *Cf.* Shulamith Firestone, *The Dialectics of Sex* (New York: Morrow, 1970) (arguing that technology can free women from the necessity of nature to realize their species- and gender-being by transferring the labor of pregnancy to advanced machines, operated by and for the community). *See generally* Elshtain, *supra* note 1, at 261.

This ambivalence about the nature of the feminine and nature in the feminine has at times offered those opposed to abortion-choice the opportunity to make the most of an apparent heartlessness in the implication that abortion is an act of reason transcending nature, no matter how compellingly deregulators evoke the pain and oppression of women and the children they bear.

9. *See* Evelyn Keller, *Reflections on Gender and Science* (New Haven: Yae University Press, 1985), 158–176 (discussing work of Barbara McClintock that proceeded on an assumption, which differed from those of leading male biologists, that DNA was not the "master" of cell growth, but functioned in interaction with organism and environment); *id.* at 150–157 (describing Keller's own work rejecting idea that organismic growth depended on a directing "pacemaker" patriarchal cell).

10. Beverly Harrison, *Our Right to Choose* (Boston: Beacon Press, 1983) (quoted *infra* chapter 3 note 53); Nel Noddings, *Caring: A Feminine Approach To Ethics & Moral Education* (Berkeley, Los Angeles, London: University of California Press, 1984) pp. 87–89; Rosalind Petchesky, *Abortion and Woman's Choice: The State, Sexuality, and Reproductive Freedom* (Boston: Northeastern University Press, 1985), pp. 344–345 & n. 59 (sketching an argument suggestive of portions of chapter 3 of this essay and noting relevance of object-relations theory to personhood debate); Caroline Whitbeck, "The Moral Implications of Regarding Women as People: New Perspectives on Pregnancy and Personhood," in *Abortion and the Status of the Fetus,* ed. William Bondeson, H. Engelhardt, Jr., Stuart Spicker & Daniel Winship (Dordrecht, Holland: D. Reidel Publishing Co., 1983), pp. 217, 250; *infra* chapter 3 note 53; *cf.* Ross, "Abortion and the Death of the Fetus," 11 *Phil. & Pub. Aff.* 232 (1982) (while showing no particular feminist influence, basing argument not on abstract universals but on the particularity of the parent-offspring relationship, and thus anticipating arguments in chapter 3).

11. Gilligan, *supra* note 2, at 19. She describes the relationship between the two ethics this way:

> To understand how the tension between responsibilities and rights sustains the dialectic of human development is to see the integrity of two disparate modes of experience that are in the end connected. While

an ethic of justice proceeds from the premise of equality—that everyone
should be treated the same—an ethic of care rests on the premise of nonviolence—that no one should be hurt. . . . This dialogue between fairness and care not only provides a better understanding of relations between the sexes but also gives rise to a more comprehensive portrayal of
adult work and family relationships.

Id. at 174.

Maturation tends to involve different kinds of moral growth for men
and women. For a man, it involves tempering concepts of absolute
rights with the ethics that grow out of particular attachments, and
allowing "the concept of identity [to] expand . . . to include the experience of interconnection." *Id.* at 173; *see also id.* at 166 (noting of one
male subject: "his concern with injustice was complicated by a new
understanding of human attachment"). Epistemologically, for men
growth involves "shifts from the idea of knowledge as a correspondence
between mind and form to the Biblical conception of knowing as a process of human relationship." *Id.*

By contrast, moral growth for a woman involves a recognition of
rights. That growing recognition allows a woman a new respect for her
own self that her ethic of care does not foster: "the language of rights
underlines the importance of including in the network of care not only
the other but also the self." *Id.* at 173.

12. *See* Nancy Chodorow, *The Reproduction of Mothering* (Berkeley,
Los Angeles, London: University of California Press, 1978); Nancy
Chodorow, "Toward a Relational Individualism: The Mediation of Self
Through Psychoanalysis," in *Reconstructing Individualism*, ed. Thomas
Heller, Morton Sosna & David Wellbery (Stanford: Stanford University
Press, 1986), p. 197; Jean Baker Miller, *Toward a New Psychology of
Women* (Boston: Beacon Press, 1976); Gilligan, *supra*, note 2; Carol
Gilligan, "Remapping the Moral Domain: New Images of the Self in Re-
lationship," in *Reconstructing Individualism, supra*, at 237.

13. *See, e.g,* Justin Call, Eleanor Galenson & Robert Tyson, eds.,
Frontiers of Infant Psychiatry, vols. 1, 2 (New York: Basic Books, 1983;
1984); Robert Emde, ed., *Rene A. Spitz: Dialogues from Infancy* (New
York: International Universities Press, 1983); Daniel Stern, *The First Re-
lationship* (Cambridge, MA: Harvard University Press, 1977); Michael
Rutter, *Maternal Deprivation Reassessed* (Middlesex, England: Penguin
Books, Ltd., 1972). *But see* Jerome Kagan, *The Nature of the Child* (New
York: Basic Books, 1984).

14. This approach seeks to avoid the problematic quality of legal
thought identified by the constitutional law professor, Thomas Reed
Powell: "If you can think of something which is inextricably related to
some other thing and not think of the other thing, you have a legal
mind." *Quoted in* Wetzel v. Liberty Mutual Ins. Co., 372 F. Supp. 1146,
1157 (W.D. Pa. 1974) (subsequent history omitted).

3. ABORTION AND SYMBIOTIC ATTACHMENT

1. The phrase is from John Rawls, *A Theory of Justice* (Cambridge, MA: Belknap Press of Harvard University Press, 1973), p. 27.

2. *See* Erik Erikson, *Childhood and Society*, 2d ed. (New York: W. W. Norton & Co., 1963); Erik Erikson, *The Life Cycle Completed* (New York: W. W. Norton & Co., 1982).

3. To further justify reliance on psychoanalysis would require another essay and possibly another author. Those persons may reject this essay's use of psychoanalysis who do not accept that there is evidence supporting fundamental aspects of psychoanalysis, *see, e.g.*, Frederick Crews, *Skeptical Engagements* (New York: Oxford University Press, 1986); *cf.* Morse, "Crazy Behavior, Morals and Science: An Analysis of Mental Health Law," 51 *S. Cal. L. Rev.* 527, 613–615 (1978); who do not accept the distinction between the science of nature and the science of people and culture, *see* Bruno Bettelheim, *Freud and Man's Soul* (New York: Knopf, 1983) (defending the distinction); *see also* Peter Gay, *Freud for Historians* (New York: Oxford University Press, 1985), pp. 42–77; who identify psychological knowledge only with the statements that academic psychology will sanction, based on what it determines can be measured and quantified, *cf.* Jerome Kagan, *The Nature of the Child* (New York: Basic Books, 1984); who do not identify a portion of the truth with actuality, *see* Erik Erikson, *Insight and Responsibility* (New York: W. W. Norton & Co., 1964), p. 161 (defending the distinction); or more generally, who suffer "the human tendency to mistake what can be submitted to established techniques for the true nature of things," Erikson, *The Life Cycle Completed, supra* note 2, at 25.

4. Jeffrey Abramson, *Liberation and Its Limits: The Moral and Political Thought of Freud* (New York: The Free Press, 1984), pp. 2–4; *id.* at 1–2 ("Freud stands against community, in this ["prevailing interpretation"], because he dismissed almost all forms of group allegiance as curious, sometimes dangerous, attempts to console man the infant for the harshness of reality. . . . Freud preferred the psychology of alienation over the loyalties bred by either religion or politics"); *cf.* Paul Roazen, *Freud: Political and Social Thought* (New York: Knopf, 1968). *See generally* Philip Rieff, *Freud: The Mind of the Moralist* (Garden City, NY: Doubleday, 1961). For Freud on the flight from individuality, *see* Sigmund Freud, "Group Psychology and the Analysis of the Ego" (1921), in *The Standard Edition of the Complete Psychological Works of Sigmund Freud*, vol. 18, ed. and trans. James Strachey et al. (London: The Hogarth Press, 1953–1974), p. 65 [hereinafter *Standard Edition*]; Sigmund Freud, "Observations On Transference Love" (1915), in *Standard Edition*, vol. 12, *supra*, at 157.

5. For a discussion of Freud's taking the existence of the self for granted at first, *see* Erikson, *The Life Cycle Completed, supra* note 2, at 86

("the *Ich* . . . this elemental consciousness, to Freud, seems to have been one of those primal human facts which he took for granted . . . and on which, for the moment, he imperiously refused to reflect"); M. Masud Khan, "Introduction," in D. W. Winnicott, *Through Paediatrics to Psycho-Analysis* (New York: Basic Books, 1975), p. xxxvi ("Freud took the entity of the patient as a person for granted"); *cf.* Erikson, *Childhood and Society, supra* note 2, at 279 ("the patient of today suffers most under the problem of what he should believe in and who he should—or, indeed, might—be or become; while the patient of early psychoanalysis suffered most under inhibitions which prevented him from being what and who he thought he knew he was").

6. Sigmund Freud, "Three Essays on the Theory of Sexuality" (1905), in *Standard Edition*, vol. 7, *supra* note 4, at 123, 222.

For a description of the mother-infant relationship in terms of identification and incorporation, *see* Sigmund Freud, "The Ego and the Id" (1923), in *Standard Edition*, vol. 19, *supra* note 4, at 1, 29; Sigmund Freud, "Mourning and Melancholia" (1917), in *Standard Edition*, vol. 14, *supra* note 4, at 237; *see also* Erikson, *Childhood and Society, supra* note 2, at 72–76. While a mother's breast is a prototype and symbol of her love, it is perfectly clear that it is not "essential as a vehicle of mother love." D. W. Winnicott, "Primitive Emotional Development," in *Through Paediatrics to Psycho-Analysis, supra* note 5, at 145, 152.

7. Sigmund Freud, "Instincts and Their Vicissitudes" (1915), in *Standard Edition*, vol. 14, *supra* note 4, at 109, 138.

8. *See, e.g.,* Abramson, *supra* note 4; Nancy Chodorow, "Toward a Relational Individualism," in *Reconstructing Individualism*, ed. Thomas Heller, Morton Sosna & David Wellbery (Stanford: Stanford University Press, 1986), p. 197.

For a history of the development of themes of relatedness and attachment in and after the work of Freud, *see* Harry Guntrip, *Personality Structure and Human Interaction* (New York: International Universities Press, 1961); *see also* Harry Guntrip, *Psychoanalytic Theory, Therapy, and the Self* (New York: Basic Books, 1971).

9. The psychology of the fetus at the end of gestation is addressed in D. W. Winnicott, "Birth Memories, Birth Trauma, and Anxiety," in *Through Paediatrics to Psycho-Analysis, supra* note 5, at 174–193 (discussing birth memories). Winnicott specifically asks the question: "at what age after conception does psychology come in?" He answers:

> [I]f there is an important stage at five to six months there is also an important stage round about birth. My reason for saying this is the great differences that can be noticed if the baby is premature or post-mature. I suggest that at the end of nine months' gestation an infant becomes ripe for emotional development, and that if an infant is post-mature he has reached this stage in the womb, and one is therefore forced to consider his feelings before and during birth. On the other hand a premature infant is not experiencing much that is vital till he has reached the age at which he should have been born, that is to say some weeks after birth.

Winnicott, *supra* note 6, at 148; *see also* Otto Rank, *The Trauma of Birth* (New York: Robert Brunner, 1952); Sigmund Freud, "Inhibitions, Symptoms and Anxiety" (1926), in *Standard Edition*, vol. 20, *supra* note 4, at 75, 127 (describing extreme agoraphobia as a "regression . . . to a time when the subject was in his mother's womb"); *infra* note 30.

10. *See, e.g.,* Therese Benedek, "Parenthood as a Developmental Phase: A Contribution to the Libido Theory," 7 *J. Am. Psychoanalytic Ass'n* 389, 390–392 (1959).

Balint notes a variety of terms describing this condition of fusion with a good enough mother: from Bion, the "container" with the "contained"; from Anna Freud, the "need-satisfying object"; from Hartmann, the "average expectable environment"; from Khan, "the protective shield"; from Mahler, the "extra-uterine matrix"; from Balint, a "primary substance"; and from Winnicott the phrases, the "ordinary devoted mother," "primary maternal preoccupation," "facilitating environment," and maternal "holding function." *See* Michael Balint, *The Basic Fault* (New York: Brunner Mazel, 1969), pp. 167–168; *see also* Rene Spitz, "The Psychogenic Diseases in Infancy: An Attempt at Their Etiologic Classification," 6 *Psychoanalytic Study of the Child* 255, 255– 256 (1951) (the infant ego "would be completely inadequate for self-preservation were it not complemented by an external helper, a substitute ego as it were. . . . A psychiatric investigation of infancy will . . . have to examine the structure of this 'closed system' . . . [which] consists only of two components, the mother and the child"); T. Berry Brazelton, "Pediatrics," in *Rene A. Spitz: Dialogues from Infancy*, ed. Robert Emde (New York: International Universities Press, 1983), pp. 439, 440 ("nurturing adult was necessary to provide a containing envelope for a newborn"); Little, "On Basic Unity," 41 *Int'l J. Psychoanalysis* 377 (1960) (referring to "basic unity" or "absolute identity of mother and infant").

Freud conveyed a similar idea when he said about infant functioning according to the pleasure principle:

> It will rightly be objected that an organization which was a slave to the pleasure principle and neglected the reality of the external world could not maintain itself alive for the shortest time, so that it could not have come into existence at all. The employment of a fiction like this is, however, justified when one considers that the infant—provided one includes with it the care it receives from its mother—does almost realize a psychical system of this kind.

Sigmund Freud, "Formulations on the Two Principles of Mental Functioning" (1911), in *Standard Edition*, vol. 12, *supra* note 4, at 214, 219– 220 n.4.

The writings of the psychoanalytic self-psychologists are, if less felicitous than some others, also clearly relevant and supportive of this description of symbiosis. For example, Kohut writes:

> The child that is to survive psychologically is born into an empathic-responsive human milieu (of self-objects) just as he is born into an atmosphere that contains an optimal amount of oxygen if he is to survive

physically. And his nascent self "expects" . . . an empathic environment to be in tune with his psychological need-wishes with the same unquestioning certitude as the respiratory apparatus of the new born infant may be said to "expect" oxygen to be contained in the surrounding atmosphere. . . . [When the infant needs attention, the mother] establishes tactile and/or vocal contact with the child . . . and thus creates conditions that the child . . . experiences as a merger with the omnipotent self-object [*i.e.*, the mother]. The child's rudimentary psyche participates in the self-object's highly developed psychic organization; the child experiences the feeling states of the self-object—they are transmitted to the child via touch and tone of voice—as if they were his own.
Heinz Kohut, *The Restoration of the Self* (New York: International Universities Press, 1977), pp. 85–86; *see also* Marian Tolpin, "Discussion of Papers by Drs. Stern and Sander," in *Reflections on Self Psychology*, ed. Joseph Lichtenberg & Samuel Kaplan (Hillsdale, NJ: The Analytic Press, 1983), pp. 113, 121–122 ("The starting point of developmental psychology and self psychology is the smallest indivisible psychological unit, the unit of child and expectable parental environment").

11. While she can survive without the fetus, the woman as mother, more than at any other time, exists not so much as an individual but rather in relation to the fetus-infant and in thrall to the procreative process. Physiologically she shares her body during pregnancy, and, to a lesser degree, in nursing. Near pregnancy's end, she becomes more and more predisposed to a full preoccupation with the dyadic unit. After birth, the infant, in its total dependency, demands an absorption which at times seems to her and others as her temporary obliteration as an individual woman. *See* Balint, *supra* note 10, at 163 ("libidinally, the mother is almost to the same extent dependent on her baby as the baby is on her; neither of them may have this particular form of relationship and the particular satisfaction independently from the other"); Alice Balint, "Love for the Mother and Mother-Love," 30 *Int'l J. Psychoanalysis* 251, 256 (1949); Harold Searles, *Collected Papers on Schizophrenia and Related Subjects* (New York: International Universities Press, 1965), p. 539 ("the core of any human being's self esteem is traceable to the healthy infant's experience that he is indeed needed to complete the psychological wholeness of the mothering person; it is there . . . that the core of the *raison d'etre*, for each of us, is to be found").

12. Plato, *The Symposium*, trans. Walter Hamilton (Middlesex, England: Penguin Books, Ltd., 1951), pp. 63–64. Similar myths are found in other traditions.

13. Roe v. Wade, 410 U.S. 113, 162 (1973) (after reviewing the law's treatment of the fetus, concluding that "the unborn have never been recognized in the law as persons in the whole sense"). *But cf.* Ely, "The Wages of Crying Wolf: A Comment on *Roe v. Wade*," 82 *Yale L.J.* 920, 931 (1973) (dismissing this phrase without exploring its meaning).

14. Morris Eagle, *Recent Developments in Psychoanalysis* (New York: McGraw-Hill, 1984), p. 185 (for Mahler the move is from "symbiosis to separation-individuation"; for Kohut from "complete reliance on the self-object for self-definition and self-esteem to self-cohesiveness"; and for Fairbairn from "infantile dependence and primary identification to differentiation and mature dependence"). Of this process Eagle writes, "separation-individuation is a truly universal and inevitable challenge . . . upon which personality most often founders." *Id.* at 25.

For a description of Mahler's position, *see id.* at 20–28, 226; Margaret Mahler, Anni Bergman & Fred Pine, *The Psychological Birth of the Human Infant: Symbiosis and Individuation* (New York: Basic Books, 1975), p. 44 (mother and infant exist within "the symbiotic orbit of the mother-child dual unity"). Mahler has dated this symbiotic period as lasting from two to five months. Prior to that she postulates a period of primary autism in which the neonate, sleeping most of the time if satisfied, remains a closed and, when properly mothered, contented "system." Modifying the classical analytic position in light of her own observations, object-relations theory, and what is being learned about early infant perceptual capacities, Mahler has over time proposed shorter periods of primary autism, so that, in one of her last formulations, she limited this autistic period to only one or two months. Infant research may require complete abandonment of the theory of normal autism and the classical theory of primary narcissism, in favor of an object-related view of the infant. *See* Joseph Lichtenberg, *Psychoanalysis and Infant Research* (Hillsdale, NJ: The Analytic Press, 1983).

15. D. W. Winnicott, "The Theory of the Parent-Infant Relationship," in *The Maturational Processes and the Facilitating Environment* (New York: International Universities Press, 1965), pp. 37, 40 [hereinafter *Maturational Processes*]. Winnicott locates symbiosis earlier than Mahler, from approximately birth to three months.

16. *Id.* at 43 (emphasis omitted); *see also* Mahler et al., *supra* note 14, at 3–4 ("The capacity to hatch out of [normal] autism comes only by way of mothering").

17. D. W. Winnicott, "The Capacity to be Alone," in *Maturational Processes, supra* note 15, at 29.

The young infant experiences "omnipotence" in part because it fails to understand that its survival depends on its mother who is meeting its essential needs and desires. And even the more mature infant, who dimly perceives its caregiver as an object, feels entitled that she conform to its needs and fails to understand that she has a subjective autonomy and interests of her own. *Cf.* Mahler et al., *supra* note 14, at 46 (at five months, infant has a dim awareness that need satisfaction cannot be provided by oneself but comes from somewhere outside the self); Alice Balint, "Love for the Mother and Mother-Love," *supra* note 11, at 251 (discussing infantile attitude toward one's mother that is expressed by a patient's "deep conviction that it belongs to the duties of a loving mother to let herself be killed for the well-being of her children, should an occasion demanding it arise"); *id.* at 251–252 (describing patient who "demanded *absolute unselfishness* from her mother. . . . The ideal mother has no interests of her own"); *id.* at 254 ("For all of us it remains self-evident that the interests of mother and child are identical, and it is the generally acknowledged measure of the goodness or badness of the mother how far she really feels this identity of interests").

Related to the capacity to recognize others as autonomous persons with interests of their own, and thus to the capacity to recognize the limits of oneself, is the capacity to distinguish what is inside from what is outside the self, and to accept one's skin as a rough boundary between me and not-me. Inside and out, me and not-me, these distinctions mark great psychic achievements of the infant and growing child, as they mark dreadful failures of the hallucinating psychotic who does not contain within his skin his own feelings, sensations, and experiences but instead projects them elsewhere. As Winnicott writes:

> [T]here comes into existence what might be called a limiting membrane, which to some extent (in health) is equated with the surface of the skin, and has a position between the infant's 'me' and his 'not-me'. So the infant comes to have an inside and an outside, and a body-scheme. In this way meaning comes to the function of intake and output; moreover, it gradually becomes meaningful to postulate a personal or inner psychic reality for the infant.

Winnicott, *supra* note 15, at 45; *see also* D. W. Winnicott, "The Child in Health and Crisis," in *Maturational Processes, supra* note 15, at 69; D. W. Winnicott, *Playing and Reality* (London: Tavistock Publications, 1971).

18. *See* D. W. Winnicott, "Ego Distortion in Terms of True and False Self," in *Maturational Processes, supra* note 15, at 140, 145–146; Winnicott, *supra* note 15, at 54 ("If maternal care is not good enough then the infant does not really come into existence, since there is no continuity of being; instead the personality becomes built on the basis of reactions to environmental impingement"); D. W. Winnicott, *The Child, the Family, and the Outside World* (Middlesex, England: Penguin Books, Ltd., 1964).

19. It appears that infants vary in their vulnerabilities and that children and adults differ in their capacities to make use of subsequent corrective emotional experiences. *See generally* Michael Rutter, *Maternal Deprivation Reassessed* (Middlesex, England: Penguin Books, Ltd., 1972).

With respect to Spitz, *see* Rene Spitz, "Hospitalism: An Inquiry into the Genesis of Psychiatric Conditions in Early Childhood," 1 *Psychoanalytic Study of the Child* 53 (1945); Rene Spitz, "Hospitalism: A Follow-Up Report," 2 *Psychoanalytic Study of the Child* 113 (1946); Spitz, "Anaclitic Depression: An Inquiry into the Genesis of Psychiatric Conditions in Early Childhood," 2 *Psychoanalytic Study of the Child* 313 (1947); *id.* at n.1 (describing mortality rate of 33 percent among abandoned children in a foundling home as "a major catastrophe"). *Contra* Pinneau, "The Infantile Disorders of Hospitalism and Anaclitic Depression," 52 *Psy-*

chol. Bull. 429 (1955) (criticizing methodology of Spitz); *cf.* Spitz, "Reply to Dr. Pinneau," 52 *Psychol. Bull.* 453 (1955). The higher mortality rates and permanent growth failures associated with maternal deprivation are also reported elsewhere. *See* Eagle, *supra* note 14, at 14.

Institutionalized care can avoid many of the problems found by Spitz by providing personalized care in the event that such resources are available. *See* Brazelton, *supra* note 10, at 439 (attributing improvement in institutional care of infants to Spitz' work).

With respect to Fraiberg, *see Clinical Studies in Infant Mental Health*, ed. Selma Fraiberg (New York: Basic Books, 1980), pp. 103–140, 197–241; *id.* at 104 ("Whether or not the baby will thrive outside of the hospital depends upon the mother's capacity to follow the medically prescribed regime to insure adequacy in caloric intake for her baby and to provide the psychological nutriments for growth and development").

With respect to the disruption of the self's relationship to the external world, *see* Winnicott, *supra* note 15, at 49. Failure of the caretaker to adapt to infantile needs in the earliest phase "does not produce anything but an annihilation of the infant's self." D. W. Winnicott, "Primary Maternal Preoccupation," in *Through Paediatrics to Psycho-Analysis, supra* note 5, at 304. It produces "unthinkable anxiety":

> Unthinkable anxiety has only a few varieties, each being the clue to one aspect of normal growth.
> (1) Going to pieces.
> (2) Falling forever.
> (3) Having no relationship to the body.
> (4) Having no orientation . . . specifically the stuff of the psychotic anxieties . . . [or] schizoid element . . . in an otherwise nonpsychotic personality.

D. W. Winnicott, "Ego Integration in Child Development," in *Maturational Processes, supra* note 15, at 56, 58–59. To the extent that Winnicott was in part describing schizophrenia, that part of his work would be firmly modified or rejected by the current work of psychiatrists who agree that schizophrenia has a substantial biological etiology.

With respect to the disruption of the self's capacities for attachment, *see* Selma Fraiberg, *Every Child's Birthright: In Defense of Mothering* (New York: Basic Books, 1977); *cf.* Christopher Lasch, *The Culture of Narcissism* (New York: W. W. Norton & Co., 1979).

20. Balint, *supra* note 10, at 22, 89.

Others have described the experience of the basic fault this way: from Bion, "nameless dread" and "psychological catastrophe"; from Fordham "nuclear hurt"; from Laing "heartbreak"; from Tustin "psychotic depression," in which loss of another includes the experience of a loss of part of one's body; and from Kohut, a "nameless preverbal depression" and a "sense of deadness" and "apathy." Victoria Hamilton, *Narcissus and Oedipus: The Children of Psychoanalysis* (Boston: Routledge & Kegan Paul, Ltd., 1982), pp. 44–45.

21. Balint, *supra* note 10, at 22, 131, 136, 66. This state of primary love "presupposes an environment that accepts and consents to sustain and carry the patient like the earth or the water sustains and carries a man who entrusts his weight to them." *Id.* at 145.

22. Winnicott, like Balint, also described the therapeutic work of cure through regression to the early mother-infant dyad. He claimed that the therapeutic work had to proceed to a point where the patient would give up a false front or false self. He described this as an organized psychic system that was strikingly different from the traditional analytic notion of rigid defense—different in part because it arose at a time prior to a developed distinction of self and other, inside and out. This false self takes up all relations with the outside world to protect the potential true self that never received the protection and presence of a good enough mother to allow it to thrive. But this internalized, manufactured mother is not good enough to get the patient through life, for it lacks the self's basic vital energy. The patient can give up its response to maternal deprivation or intrusion in the first year of life, and allow the passing away of this crustacean shell of a false self, only when the analytic situation has proved to be a reliable enough environment to permit regression to earliest infancy. Then the patient's hibernating potential for interaction may awake in relationship with a good enough analyst and develop an "I." *See* Winnicott, *supra* note 15, at 54.

Similarly, Harold Searles, an American psychoanalyst, has written that psychotherapy with schizophrenics must proceed in normal fashion to address affect, memory, and defense. But for success, the work must eventually progress to a period in the transference and countertransference (that is, in the affective and fantasy relationship of patient and therapist) when boundaries between the two disappear. Not without such fusion can improvement occur. This period is one of intense rapture, in which a boundless sense of well-being can exist from mere presence with the other, and in which, during the session, all concerns fade away. On the level of play and fantasy, verbal material may appear suggesting an exchange of body parts between the pair (like the placenta), of occupying the innards of the other (as the fetus in the woman), and of a general diminishment of the boundaries that maintain our individuality. In the therapeutic symbiosis, anxiety over separation has been left far behind. *See* Searles, *supra* note 11, at 338–340, 536–537. Indeed anxiety by either party destroys the fusion. *Cf.* Harry Stack Sullivan, *The Interpersonal Theory of Psychiatry,* ed. Helen Swick Perry & Mary Gawel (New York: W. W. Norton & Co., 1953), pp. 41–45 (discussing disorganizing effects of early maternal anxiety).

23. Balint, *supra* note 10, at 112.

24. *Id.* at 145.

For discussion of the analyst's anxiety that precedes full regression, *see, e.g.,* Searles, *supra* note 11, at 533–535; D. W. Winnicott, "Hate in the Countertransference," in *Through Paediatrics to Psycho-Analysis, su-*

pra note 5, at 194; Little, *supra* note 10, at 383 ("the point of unity is also the point of annihilation, it is the point of . . . chaos, or absolute ambivalency. . . . It is not only the analysand who experiences this anxiety; the difficulty is shared by the analyst").

25. Michael Balint, *Primary Love and Psychoanalytic Technique* (New York: Liveright Publishing Corp., 1965), p. 84.

26. D. W. Winnicott, "Further Thoughts on Babies as Persons," in *The Child, the Family, and the Outside World, supra* note 18, at 85; *see also* Winnicott, *supra* note 15, at 39.

27. *See* E. J. Anthony, "Foreword" (quoting statement of Winnicott), in *Frontiers of Infant Psychiatry*, vol. 1, ed. Justin Call, Eleanor Galenson & Robert Tyson (New York: Basic Books, 1983), pp. xvii, xxi.

28. Winnicott, "Further Thoughts on Babies as Persons," *supra* note 26, at 88.

29. Although recent developments in psychoanalysis have had a broad impact within and outside analysis, finding their way into such influential books as Lasch, *The Culture of Narcissism, supra* note 19, and Nancy Chodorow, *The Reproduction of Mothering* (Berkeley, Los Angeles, London: University of California Press, 1978), they cannot claim to provide a generally accepted account of human development; indeed, much of the world has never heard of them. Since this chapter uses an object-relations account, it is appropriate to review briefly the place of object-relations theory in psychoanalysis and criticisms of that theory.

With respect to criticism of the entire psychoanalytic enterprise, *see supra* note 3.

Differences Within the Object-Relations School. For ease of presentation, the description here of analytic theory minimizes differences among analysts who emphasize attachment and fusion. It does so by emphasizing the work of only a few analysts: Winnicott, Balint, Spitz, Fraiberg, and Erikson. Further, it minimizes differences among them and it does not stress differences between these and other analysts with related views. "Interpersonal" might be a better generic label for all of these analysts; but, because of my primary emphasis, I have taken the improper liberty of collecting a broad group of analysts under the label "object-relations school."

The extended group of analysts discussed here includes, of course, the true object-relations theorists—a group of analysts working in England who came to emphasize the crucial importance of early mothering as they worked with schizoid, borderline, and psychotic patients; this group was also influenced by the study of childhood trauma arising from the mother-child separations during the German bombing of London. It also encompasses a more disparate group of clinicians who stress interpersonal relatedness, such as Erikson, and those who specialize, like Spitz and Fraiberg, in infant observation and treatment. Also implicitly referenced are psychoanalytically oriented observers of therapy and self-analytic groups who have stressed themes of fusion, merger, and deindividuation. *See* Philip Slater, *Microcosm: Structural, Psychological and Religious Evolution in Groups* (New York: Wiley, 1966); W. R. Bion, *Experiences in Groups* (New York: Basic Books, 1961). The work of Melanie Klein is not included because of her highly individuated view of the infant. The particular theoretical approach of John Bowlby is not relied on, although his clinical observations on attachment and maternal deprivation are obviously central. *See* John Bowlby, *Attachment and Loss*, vol. 1, *Attachment*; vol. 2, *Separation: Anxiety and Anger*; vol. 3, *Loss: Sadness and Depression* (New York: Basic Books, 1969; 1973; 1980). Self-psychologists, like Kohut, are congruent and supportive of the account offered here to the extent that they stress the infant-parent regulatory unit, although their language is more individualistic than those who speak of symbiosis. *See, e.g., supra* note 10; *Reflections on Self Psychology, supra* note 10, at 37–123.

Criticism From Within Psychoanalysis. While there has been broad agreement throughout psychoanalysis that at the depths of even the healthy adult is a substratum that lacks firm reality-oriented boundaries, confuses what is inside and out, and does not know whether satisfaction must be supplied from others or can be obtained from within, there are, nevertheless, differing views among psychoanalysts regarding infancy: classical analysts stress the narcissistic side, while the object-relations theorists stress the symbiotic. Thus, even within psychoanalysis, there are those who do not accept the object-relations account.

For example, object-relations theory treats infants as intensely related to their caregivers, in contradistinction to the classical analytic understanding that infants are in a state of primary narcissism, completely self-centered and self-interested beings who primarily require physical ministration. Put differently and technically, for object-relations theorists, libido is primarily person-seeking rather than, as Freud believed, pleasure-seeking.

Object-relations theory also differs from classical theory in locating the fundamental crisis of personhood in the infant's disentanglement from a kind of dependence in a two-person relationship best characterized at first by the word "fusion." Classical theorists, in contrast, locate this fundamental crisis in later interactions of individuated children with parents in a three-person relationship.

Finally, for object-relations analysts, the deepest pathologies derive from an environmental failure of the mothering one to provide an average expectable environment; whereas for Freud the central psychological danger comes from within, from instinctual demands and inherent conflictedness. *See* Eagle, *supra* note 14, at 109–111; *id.* at 84 ("for Fairbairn, the starting point for defense is internalizing what was external [namely, introjecting the frustrating and depriving qualities of the mother and environment in an attempt to control them], while for

Freud, defense consists in making external what was internal," namely, projecting a wish or impulse that constitutes a threat and requires defense).

Leaving aside these technical terms and intramural theoretical differences, these disputes reduce in part to the question of whether persons in origin and essence are fundamentally alone, separate, and self-interested, or rather related, interpenetrating, influencing, and involved. *See, e.g.,* Hamilton, *supra* note 20 (arranging psychoanalytic theories of infantile development on a continuum ranging from highly individualistic to symbiotic).

While no empirical test will finally resolve this dispute, clinically the implications of object-relations theory are presently in ascendance in psychotherapy. Its clinical findings and its emphasis upon separation and individuation have become guiding paradigms among a broad range of therapists in their clinical practice and theoretical work. *See* Modell, "The Ego and the Id: 50 Years Later," 56 *Int'l J. Psychoanalysis* 57, 58 (1975) ("if object-relations theory cannot be integrated within *The Ego and the Id,* this latter itself will not survive as the central paradigm of psychoanalysis").

These disputes ought not be prematurely resolved, for psychoanalysis has the distinct theoretical advantage of containing two competing visions of personhood, which jointly serve to keep important issues of self and other in dialectical interaction with each other. Such issues may be lost in more traditional empiricist psychological research.

Criticism From Outside Psychoanalysis. A more serious criticism of the object-relations account may come not from within psychoanalysis, but rather from the recent research of infant psychologists who have in the last decade begun to study the infant's developing self. These studies have led to recent efforts to integrate the psychoanalytic picture of the infant's subjective life with the observational data of developmental psychology. *See, e.g.,* Daniel Stern, *The Interpersonal World of the Infant* (New York: Basic Books, 1985); Stern, "The Early Development of Schemas of Self, Other, and 'Self with Other,'" in *Reflections on Self Psychology, supra* note 10, at 49; Joseph Lichtenberg, *supra* note 14. *See generally* Justin Call, Eleanor Galenson & Robert Tyson, eds., *Frontiers of Infant Psychiatry,* vols. 1, 2 (New York: Basic Books, 1983; 1984).

Some infant psychologists criticize object-relations theory for exaggerating the long-term importance of maternal attachment. *See* Rutter, *supra* note 19, at 53–79; Jerome Kagan, Richard Kearsley & Philip Zelazo, *Infancy: Its Place in Human Development* (Cambridge, MA: Harvard University Press, 1978), pp. 108–109. *See generally* Emde, "Changing Models of Infancy and the Nature of Early Development: Remodeling the Foundation," 29 *J. Am. Psychoanalytic Ass'n* 179 (1981). But even these critics appear to acknowledge an infant's need for a fundamental kind of interaction that parents—and especially mothers—are disposed to give.

Many others regard the observational data of the infant psychologists as largely confirmatory of the object-relations theorists with respect to the relatedness of infants and the appropriateness of treating infant and caretaker as a unit. *See, e.g.,* Louis Sander, "Investigation of the Infant and Its Caregiving Environment as a Biological System," in *The Course of Life: Psychoanalytic Contributions Toward Understanding Personality Development,* vol. 1, *Infancy and Early Childhood,* ed. Stanley Greenspan & George Pollack (Washington, D.C.: National Institute of Mental Health, 1980), pp. 177, 195 [hereinafter *The Course of Life*] (describing infant and caregiver as an interactive regulatory system); Theodore Shapiro & Daniel Stern, "Psychoanalytic Perspectives on the First Year of Life—The Establishment of the Object in an Affective Field," in *The Course of Life, supra,* at 113; Lichtenberg, "Implications for Psychoanalytic Theory of Research on the Neonate," 8 *Int'l Rev. Psycho-Analysis* 35, 45–47 (1981).

While acknowledging the fundamental importance of a primary caretaker for the development of the self and the usefulness of studying the dyad, some of these researchers, like Daniel Stern, believe that the observational data undermine the additional object-relations claims regarding fusion and infantile omnipotence. *See* Stern, *The Interpersonal World of the Infant, supra; see also* Peterfreund, "Some Critical Comments on Psychoanalytic Conceptualizations of Infancy," 59 *Int'l J. Psychoanalysis* 427, 435–436 (1978). However, it appears to this outside reviewer that rejection of the concept of symbiosis would be premature.

A basic theme of the infant psychologists is the "competent infant." They assert that even the young infant has advanced capacities in perception, motility, learning, memory, and control over these capacities which are far beyond what has heretofore been accepted. But such advanced capacities are not inconsistent with the fantasy and affective life described by the object-relations theorists. For example, Winnicott recognizes the infant's capacity to have memories based on perception, but treats this as different from its being personalized in a self. *Cf.* Eagle, *supra* note 14, at 218 n.30 ("One can accept the recent arguments of . . . Stern . . . that some degree of self-other differentiation is already present at birth and continue to maintain that normal psychological development is marked by an *increasing* degree of such differentiation") (emphasis in original).

The apparent conflict may at present grow out of the different sorts of data on which the infant psychologists and object-relations theorists rely, the so-called "crib-couch gap", *see* Gerald Stechler, "Infancy Research: A Contribution to Self Psychology," in *Reflections on Self Psychology, supra* note 10, at 43, 44. No amount of criticism of the evidence of psychoanalytic reconstruction and myth interpretation can avoid the purely observational nature of the infant research data which, especially because infants lack verbal language, also require the most careful inferential use. Nor is the conflict a simple contrast between infant observation versus clinical reconstruction. Winnicott did not base his work exclusively on reconstruction: by 1948 (and he was to work many more years) Winnicott asserts that he had taken 20,000 pediatric histories. *See* D. W. Winnicott, "Pediatrics and Psychiatry," in *Through Paediatrics to Psycho-Analysis, supra* note 5, at 157, 158; *cf.* D. W. Winnicott, "On the Contribution of Direct Child Observation to Psycho-Analysis," in *Maturational Processes, supra* note 15, at 109.

Moreover, some of the claimed conflict is overdrawn. For example, one reviewer asserts that the object-relations theory of symbiosis requires a passive infant—a view contradicted by the observational data that testify to great infant perceptual capacities. *See* Horner, "The Psychic Life of the Young Infant: Review and Critique of the Psychoanalytic Concepts of Symbiosis and Infantile Omnipotence," 55 *Am. J. Orthopsychiatry* 324 (1985). But Horner's claimed contradiction seems unsupported by a reading of object-relations theory. Winnicott, for example, emphasizes the creative nature of the infant even as he maintains its fused state. *See, e.g.,* Winnicott, "Ego Integration in Child Development," *supra* note 19, at 59–60 ("it is not so much a question of giving the baby satisfaction as of letting the baby find and come to terms with the object"); Balint, *supra* note 21, at 108 (speaking of the active not passive infant and noting that the mother is recognized perceptually but her separateness remains uncomprehended); *cf. id.* at 125; Winnicott, "Ego Integration in Child Development," *supra* note 19, at 57 (distinguishing an experience of omnipotence from feeling omnipotent).

Finally, as does the debate within psychoanalysis, the debate between psychoanalysis and the infant psychologists reflects fundamental positions on human relatedness. As Stern cogently acknowledges, differences ultimately arise from beliefs "about whether the essential state of human existence is one of aloneness or togetherness." Stern, *The Interpersonal World of the Infant, supra,* at 240.

It comes to this. Academic psychology does not confirm some claims of object-relations theory. Yet the theory's source of data, use of data, and modes of inference differ sufficiently from academic psychology that claims of contradiction must be asserted with caution. It is far too early, in their science, for infant psychologists to abandon analytic data about affective states of dependence. For in our groping for a description of infants, it is best not to throw away words prematurely lest concepts be lost. *Cf.* Kohut, *supra* note 10, at 77–78, 206 (discussing principle of complementarity according to which, as in physics, the same phenomenon requires two simultaneous explanations).

In contrast with some academic psychology, object-relations theory speaks a language that emphasizes what common sense tells us—that infantile helplessness and dependence is of a different order, requiring special categories to comprehend. Whether or not the particular word "symbiosis" continues to be employed because it so usefully describes the dependence, harmony, synchronicity, and lack of sharp differentiation between mother and infant, it seems clear that there is agreement among many who study infants about the conceptual need for comprehending the infant in relation to its caretaker.

30. *See* Benedek, "The Psychosomatic Implications of the Primary Unit: Mother-Child," 19 *Am. J. Orthopsychiatry* 642, 643–44 (1949) (dating onset of symbiosis at conception when physiological interaction begins).

To the extent that, prior to the end of gestation, the fetus lacks a psychology or a capacity for mental representations, some analysts then may claim that it is a creature beyond analytic ken. While Winnicott believes that the fetus in its very final stages of development has a psychology similar to the neonate, his psychoanalytic use of the dyadic concept probably does not depend on presupposing a fetal or neonatal psychology; for Winnicott treats the dyadic unit as the biological and environmental substrate of an infant's later personal psychology. *See, supra* note 9. For discussions, of very uneven quality, in the psychoanalytic literature concerning the fetus, its capacity for mental representations and a psychology near birth, and its interaction with the pregnant woman, *see, e.g.,* Pirkko Graves, "The Functioning Fetus," in *The Course of Life, supra* note 29, at 235; Balint, *supra* note 10, at 66; Calvin Hall, "Are Prenatal and Birth Experiences Represented in Dreams," 54 *Psychoanalytic Review* 157 (1967) (and articles cited therein); Muncia, "On the Beginning of Mental Life in the Foetus," 62 *Int'l J. Psychoanalysis* 351 (1981); Ployé, "Does Prenatal Mental Life Exist," 54 *Int'l J. Psychoanalysis* 241 (1973); *cf.* Darlington, "The Problem of Pre-Natal Mentation," 32 *Psychoanalytic Review* 319 (1945); Sadger, "Preliminary Study of the Psychic Life of the Fetus and the Primary Germ," 28 *Psychoanalytic Review* 327 (1944); Liley, "The Foetus as a Personality," 6 *Australian & New Zealand J. Psychiatry* 99 (1972); Sontag, "Implications of Fetal Behavior," 134 *Annals New York Academy of Sciences* 782 (1966).

31. There is for the most part no explicit textual basis in their writings to believe that the analysts cited would agree with the uses concerning abortion to which this essay puts their clinical concepts. But the arguments do not purport to be a "psychoanalysis" of abortion decisions but rather to show what a relational account might look like using certain psychoanalytic concepts. To be sure, contrary arguments could have been made with other analytic concepts, claiming, for example, that abortion expresses, individually and culturally, a self-destructive, sadistic, and neurotic choice.

There is little psychoanalytic material directly on the subject of abortion. *See, e.g.,* Pines, "The Relevance of Early Psychic Development to Pregnancy and Abortion," 63 *Int'l J. Psychoanalysis* 311 (1982). In the writing that exists, there is disagreement. Some analysts see abortion-choice as a natural power of women. *See, e.g.,* Alice Balint, *supra* note

11, at 255 (quoted *infra* in note 112); Helene Deutsch, *The Psychology of Women*, vol. 2, *Motherhood* (New York: Grune & Stratton, 1945), p. 179 ("In my view, every woman has the right to achieve motherhood and to renounce motherhood, and every normal woman seems to assume this right emotionally, whether it is legal or not"). *But cf. id.* at 184–185 (discussing a woman's anger at mate after abortion). *See generally* American Psychoanalytic Association, *Position Statement on Abortion* (May 1970) ("Though there are always emotional aspects of each [abortion] . . . , there is no evidence that these are necessarily negative or enduring. . . . [W]e are aware of the existence of many motives behind the pregnancy and its termination and of the presence of psychological conflict which are less effects of the abortion per se than of the underlying difficulty. . . . We support a woman's right to choose whether or not to continue her pregnancy").

Others have seen abortion in some circumstances as the best external alternative among bad internal psychological alternatives. For example, A. A. Brill wrote:

> [A]bortions invariably leave a psychic scar. . . . [N]o woman wishes really to interrupt her pregnancy. . . . Left to herself no woman would think of having an abortion. . . . Abortion belongs to those social problems which cannot possibly be solved at the present time because we do not know enough of its phyletic implications. *Abortions are symptoms of cultural maladjustments.* . . . [T]hey represent a struggle between natural laws and socalled civilization. . . . *[N]ature forces the individual to reproduce himself, and civilization for good reasons of its own strives to stop it, or permit it only under special regulations.* . . . Most of us are still torn by the contending forces [of nature and civilization].

A. A. Brill, "Some Psychiatric Aspects of Abortion Problems," 156 *Medical Record* 409, 412 (1943) (emphasis in original). *Cf.* George Devereux, *A Study of Abortion in Primitive Societies: A typological, distributional, and dynamic analysis of the prevention of birth in 400 preindustrial societies,* rev. ed. (New York: International Universities Press, 1976).

Yet others have seen abortion primarily as a self-destructive act that interferes with a woman's basic instincts and that is often undertaken at the behest of a man who himself fails to achieve the maturity of his gender. *See infra* note 125.

Three comments on the subject of abortion by Freud, Erikson, and Winnicott should be noted, given this essay's use of their work. Freud made the following comment on abortion in describing a woman's dream in which she wished her seventeen-year-old daughter dead:

> The child was the fruit of an unhappy marriage which was soon dissolved. Once, while she still bore her daughter in her womb, in a fit of rage after a violent scene with her husband she had beaten with her fists on her body in order to kill the child inside it. How many mothers, who love their children tenderly, perhaps over-tenderly, today, conceived them unwillingly and wished at that time that the living thing within them might not develop further! They may even have expressed that

wish in various, fortunately harmless, actions. Thus their death-wish against someone they love, which is later so mysterious, originates from the earliest days of their relationship to that person.

Sigmund Freud, "Introductory Lectures on Psycho-analysis" (1916), in *Standard Edition*, vol. 15, *supra* note 4, at 202.

Erik Erikson has written:

[T]he children to be born from here on will have every right to ask why they were chosen to be born by free agreement if, indeed, the responsible adults do not know or care what ideals they [the parents] can personify for them, or what choices they can give them. . . .

The choice to procreate or not, however, remains a free choice only if we cease to deny the psychobiological fact that matured sexuality is part of generativity. Mankind can play with any and all drives and use them for the glory of being alive, of being together, and of being creative; and yet, in the long run, it will have to account for them. To know that adulthood is generative, does not necessarily mean that one must produce children. But it means to know what one does if one does not. And it means that one participates otherwise in the establishment, the guidance, and the enrichment of the living generation and the world it inherits. The right (or the obligation) to have fewer children (or none) can only be a liberated one if it means a greater personal and communal responsibility for all those born, and the application of parental concerns to the preservation of what enhances the whole cycle of life.

Erikson, *Dimensions of a New Identity: The 1973 Jefferson Lectures in the Humanities, supra* note 31, at 122–123.

In an essay apparently triggered by a letter to *The Times* from the Archbishop of Canterbury concerning abortion and when a fetus becomes a person, Winnicott wrote:

[T]here is very rapid growth at the inception of the changes which lead to there being a brain [at two to three months gestation]. It is a very different matter to think of a child as a human being before there is a brain and to think of the child as a human being once a brain has become anatomically established. These arguments will not of course affect those who have a tremendous emotional bias towards the idea that the human being starts at the time of the fertilization. . . . A consideration of this stage carries with it a discussion as to whether a child who is born anencephalic is a human being, and there is infinite room for disagreement in regard to the status of children with the various degrees of mental defect. . . . [W]e may find degrees of backwardness which makes us want to have a category of backwardness that puts a child outside classification as human. Tremendous emotions must be roused in any discussion on either the existence of such a borderline, or the placing of children relative to it.

D. W. Winnicott, "The Beginning of the Individual," in *Babies and Their Mothers*, ed. Clare Winnicott, Ray Shepherd & Madeleine Davis (Reading, MA: Addison-Wesley Publishing Co., Inc., 1987), pp. 51, 52–53. In addition to other important developmental stages, ranging from preconceptive fantasies of having children through the process of separation and individuation, he notes that "to anatomy and physiology becomes added psychology" sometime before birth; this along with the "immense change that takes place in the attitude of the parents" and the recognition "by all the world" of the "infant as an individual" makes the period around birth an important event for the abortion debate. *Id.* at 54–55.

32. Toth v. Goree, 65 Mich. App. 296, 303–04, 237 N.W.2d 297, 301 (1975).

For other cases evidencing a sense of contradiction between *Roe* and the tort protection afforded the fetus, *see* Wallace v. Wallace, 120 N.H. 675, 679, 421 A.2d 134, 137 (1980) ("it would be incongruous for a mother to have a federal constitutional right to deliberately destroy a non-viable fetus . . . and at the same time for a third person to be subject to liability to the fetus for his unintended but merely negligent acts"); *cf.* Justis v. Atchison, 19 Cal. 3d 564, 139 Cal. Rptr. 97, 565 P.2d 122 (1977) (fetus not a person for purposes of a wrongful death statute).

In criminal cases, courts, sometimes relying on *Roe*, have also refused to treat a fetus as a person, declining to find acts such as beating a pregnant woman or drunken driving resulting in fetal death as homicide. *See* People v. Smith, 59 Cal. App. 3d 751, 129 Cal. Rptr. 498 (1976); Larkin v. Cahalan, 389 Mich. 533, 208 N.W.2d 176 (1973); *see also* Guido Calabresi, *Ideals, Beliefs, Attitudes, and the Law* (Syracuse, NY: Syracuse University Press, 1985), p. 188 n.350 (and cases cited therein). The property cases recognizing bequests to those conceived prior to a testator's death are not especially relevant, since they merely reflect the law's purposes of realizing the testator's presumed intent and providing financial care for children who are born.

Among commentators who see a contradiction, David Louisell and John Noonan have argued that the legalization of abortion, while purporting to constitutionalize a basic common law liberty, is utterly at odds with the common law's progressive development of the last thirty years. David Louisell & John Noonan, Jr., "Constitutional Balance," in *The Morality of Abortion: Legal and Historical Perspectives,* ed. John Noonan (Cambridge, MA: Harvard University Press, 1970), pp. 220, 226–230, 246; *id.* at 258 (abortion "is a loveless act offensive to the conscience of our common law tradition"); *see also* Calabresi, *supra,* at 93–94 (accusing *Roe* of ignoring and of "undercut[ting]" tort cases that protect the fetus); Walker & Puzder, "State Protection of the Unborn After *Roe v. Wade*: A Legislative Proposal," 13 *Stetson L. Rev.* 237, 239 (1984) (claiming that *Roe* and legislative and common law protection for the fetus create a potentially untenable dilemma); Note, "The Law and the Unborn Child: The Legal and Logical Inconsistencies," 46 *Notre Dame Law.* 349, 350 (1971). This rarefied issue even made its way into the 1980 presidential debates, when Ronald Reagan queried how an assault on a woman which injured her fetus could be criminal when that same woman could abort.

Roe's analytic framework provides one answer to this supposed quandary: the state may protect the nonviable fetus against the tort-feasor or criminal assailant because, unlike the pregnant woman, he has no superior right that precludes the state from protecting an as-yet not compelling interest in potential life. *Cf.* Kader, "The Law of Tortious Prenatal Death Since *Roe v. Wade*," 45 *Mo. L. Rev.* 639, 664–665 (1980).

Yet, Louisell's, Noonan's, and Reagan's complaint seems to stem from a deeper sense of contradiction in the law's development. This disjuncture disappears if it is recognized that what the law has come to protect over the past generation is the dyad. Further study of damages actually awarded in cases claiming to protect the fetus would be useful to understand how they correspond to the interests of the dyadic couple: emotional pain and suffering of the adult constituent with respect to the unit; extraordinary costs including medical costs of maintaining the unit; and the later extraordinary costs of supporting the individuated child.

For general discussions of the status of the fetus in tort and criminal law, *see* Kader, *supra;* Robertson, "Toward Rational Boundaries of Tort Liability for Injury to the Unborn: Prenatal Injuries, Preconception Injuries and Wrongful Life," 1978 *Duke L.J.* 1401; Morrison, "Torts Involving the Unborn—A Limited Cosmology," 31 *Baylor L. Rev.* 131 (1979); *see generally,* King, "The Juridical Status of the Fetus: A Proposal for Legal Protection of the Unborn," 77 *Mich. L. Rev.* 1647 (1979).

33. The term wrongful birth, as used here, includes the torts that various courts have named wrongful conception (e.g., negligent sterilization or provision of birth control), wrongful pregnancy (e.g., failed abortion or failure to diagnose a pregnancy in time for a first or possibly second trimester abortion), and wrongful birth (e.g., negligent provision of information concerning potential genetic or teratogenic defects of child, where lack of such information forestalls abortion). The damages sought in wrongful birth actions are the costs of pregnancy and damages for the associated emotional burdens, the extraordinary costs of raising a handicapped child, and, possibly, the ordinary costs of raising a healthy but unwanted child. *See, e.g.,* Smith v. Cote, 513 A.2d 341, 348–49 (N.H. 1986); "Special Project: Legal Rights and Issues Surrounding Conception, Pregnancy, and Birth," 39 *Vand. L. Rev.* 597, 724–750 (1986).

For a discussion of the conflicting ways courts have treated a duty to mitigate damages through abortion in wrongful birth claims, *see, e.g., id.* at 738–739 & nn.823–825, 736 & n.799; Note, "Wrongful Birth: The Avoidance of Consequences Doctrine in Mitigation of Damages," 53 *Fordham L. Rev.* 1107 (1985). Courts have not insisted that the woman sunder the dyad by placing the child for adoption, although that too would mitigate the damages of raising the child.

34. In wrongful life actions, the offspring may try to claim general damages such as pain and suffering for violation of a right not to be alive, in addition to those special damages for medical costs and care that the parents may typically recover in a wrongful birth action. For the most part, courts have uneasily responded to wrongful life suits by holding that one's own life is never an injury. *See* Smith v. Cote, 513 A.2d at 351–55. *But see* Turpin v. Sortini, 31 Cal. 3d 220, 643 P.2d 954, 182 Cal. Rptr. 337 (1982) (limiting recovery to special damages); Procanik v. Cillo, 97 N.J. 339, 478 A.2d 755 (1984) (same); Harbeson v. Parke-Davis, Inc., 98 Wash. 2d 460, 656 P.2d 483 (1983). *See generally* Robertson, *supra* note 32; Rogers, "Wrongful Life and Wrongful Birth: Medical Malpractice in Genetic Counseling and Prenatal Testing," 33 *S.C.L. Rev.* 713 (1982); Kashi, "The Case of the Unwanted Blessing: Wrongful Life," 31 *U. Miami L. Rev.* 1409 (1977); Tedeschi, "On Tort Liability for 'Wrongful Life,'" 1 *Israel L. Rev.* 513 (1966).

For cases raising the possibility of wrongful life suits by children against parents, *see* Grodin v. Grodin, 102 Mich. App. 396, 301 N.W.2d 869 (1980); Curlender v. Bio-Science Labs & Automated Lab Sciences, 106 Cal. App. 3d 811, 829, 165 Cal. Rptr. 477, 488 (1980) ("we see no sound public policy which should protect those parents [who "made a conscious choice to proceed with a pregnancy, with full knowledge that a seriously impaired infant would be born"] from being answerable for the pain, suffering and misery which they have wrought upon their offspring"). The California legislature has since precluded such suits against parents by statute. Cal. Civ. Code sec. 43.6 (Deering Supp. 1987).

35. *See generally* Report of the HEW Ethics Advisory Board, "Protection of Human Subjects," 44 *Fed. Reg.* 35033, 35036, 35045, 35057 (1979) (recommending that only reimplantation into donor be permitted in *in vitro* fertilization research receiving federal support); *see also* Note, "Frozen Embryos: The Constitution on Ice," 19 *Loyola L.A.L. Rev.* 267 (1985); *cf.* Mary Shelley, *Frankenstein* (London: Dutton, 1960) (maternal-sponsorship absent).

For alternative proposals for regulating the dispostion of orphan zygotes, *compare* Ill. Rev. Stat. ch. 38, sec. 81–26(7) (1981) (anyone who intentionally "causes fertilization of ovum extra utero shall have care and custody of the human being thereby produced") *with* American Fertility Society, "Ethical Statement on In Vitro Fertilization," in American Society of Law & Medicine, *What About the Children? An International Conference on the Legal, Social and Ethical Implications of New Prenatal Technologies* (Cambridge, MA: Oct. 29–30, 1984), p. 390 pars. 4–7 (conceptus is property of gamete donors; unused, frozen concepti are to be destroyed at end of female donor's reproductive life, but donor may transfer them to other infertile couple) *with* "Report of the Committee of Inquiry into Human Fertilization and Embryology," in American Society of Law & Medicine, *supra*, at 7, 8 par. 10.12 ("When one of a couple dies the right to use or dispose of any embryo stored by that couple should pass to the survivor. If both die that right should pass to the storage authority").

The problem of orphan zygotes does not arise solely from their multiple creation in *in vitro* fertilization. Even when only one ovum is fertilized and frozen for implantation at the appropriate time, the intervening death of the prospective parents, as has happened, creates the problem of zygote disposition. *See* Capron, "The New Reproductive Possibilities: Seeking A Moral Basis for Concerted Action in a Pluralistic Society," 12 *Law, Medicine & Health Care* 192, 195–196 (1984). Interest in human embryos may also lead to the creation and sustenance of zygotes solely for research purposes. *See generally* Report of the HEW Ethics Advisory Board, *supra*, at 35039–35042.

For a discussion of potential conflicts between parents over the disposition of a frozen zygote, *see infra* note 86.

36. Eisenstadt v. Baird, 405 U.S. 438, 453 (1972).

37. For example, subject to rebuttal by proof of parental abuse or neglect, the presumption that parents act in their child's best interest justifies a very substantial reduction in the formality of the hearing required prior to a psychiatric hospital admission of a child pursuant to his parent's consent. Parham v. J.R., 442 U.S. 584 (1979). In that case the Court noted, "our jurisprudence historically has reflected Western civilization concepts of the family as a unit with broad parental authority over minor children." *Id.* at 602. Similarly, Justice Stewart wrote: "For centuries it has been a canon of the common law that parents speak for their minor children. So deeply imbedded in our traditions is this principle of law that the Constitution itself may compel a State to respect it. *Id.* at 621 (Stewart, J., concurring) (footnote omitted); *see also infra* note 118.

38. For other descriptions of the woman as the best decision maker, *see* Tribe, "The Supreme Court 1972 Term—Foreword: Toward a Model of Roles in the Due Process of Life and Law," 87 *Harv. L. Rev.* 1 (1973) (explaining *Roe* as a case involving the allocation of decision-making power to the pregnant woman as the best decision maker); Tribe, "Structural Due Process," 10 *Harv. C.R.-C.L. L. Rev.* 269 (1975). For a description of the woman-fetus relationship as something like a unit, *see* George Williams, "The Sacred Condominium," in *The Morality of Abortion: Legal and Historical Perspectives, supra* note 32, at 146.

39. The dyadic concept would not absolutely preclude regulation of the behavior of the dyadic representative who chooses to give birth. *Cf. supra* Preface note 4; Note, "The Creation of Fetal Rights: Conflicts with Women's Constitutional Rights to Liberty, Privacy and Equal Protection," 95 *Yale L.J.* 599 (1986).

40. Charles Taylor, "Atomism," in *Powers, Possessions, and Freedom: Essays in Honour of C. B. Macpherson*, ed. Alkis Kontos (Toronto: University of Toronto Press, 1979), p. 39. Taylor writes:

> For if atomism means that man is self-sufficient alone, then surely it is a very questionable thesis.
>
> What then does it mean to say that men are self-sufficient alone? That they would survive outside of society? Clearly, lots of men would not.

And the best and luckiest would survive only in the most austere sense that they would not succumb. It would not be living as we know it. Surely proponents of the primacy of rights don't have to deny these brute facts. Just because one would fail a survival course and not live for a week if dropped north of Great Slave Lake with only a hatchet and a box of (waterproof) matches, does one have to stop writing books arguing for the minimal state on the basis of the inviolable rights of the individual?

Id. at 41–42.

41. *See* Epstein, "Substantive Due Process by Any Other Name: The Abortion Cases," 1973 *Sup. Ct. Rev.* 159, 168–173; *see also* L. W. Sumner, *Abortion and Moral Theory* (Princeton: Princeton University Press, 1981), p. 16 (identifying the deregulatory position with a Millian claim that abortion is private, and thus beyond state power, because the fetus lacks all moral standing); *id.* at 152 ("if it violates no one's rights, early abortion (like contraception) is a private act").

42. Philip Bobbitt, *Constitutional Fate: Theory of the Constitution* (New York: Oxford University Press, 1982), pp. 160–161; *see also id.* at 159 (referring to power to coerce "intimate acts").

43. Karst, "The Freedom of Intimate Association," 89 *Yale L.J.* 624, 641 (1980). By intimate association, Karst means a relationship significantly "comparable to a marriage or family relationship." *Id.* at 629; *see also id.* at 638, 640.

Karst links the intimate association right to a first-amendment right of association and individual self-expression. But he recognizes that an association takes on an existence independent of its individual members and accordingly may shape the identities of its members and the values they express. *See id.* at 629 ("An intimate association, like any group, is more than the sum of its members; it is a new being, a collective individuality with a life of its own"); *cf.* Laurence Tribe, *American Constitutional Law* (Mineola, NY: Foundation Press, 1978), p. 989; Pollak, "Thomas I. Emerson, Lawyer and Scholar: *Ipse Custodiet Custodes*," 84 *Yale L.J.* 638, 650–653 (1975) ("in due course, we will see Griswold as a reaffirmation of the Court's continuing obligation to test the justifications offered by the state for state-imposed constraints which significantly hamper those modes of individual fulfillment which are at the heart of a free society").

Among the Justices writing in *Roe*, Justice Stewart most explicitly referred to these associational interests:

Certainly the interests of a woman in giving of her physical and emotional self during pregnancy and the interests that will be affected throughout her life by the birth and raising of a child are of a far greater degree of significance and personal intimacy than [are found in other prior privacy cases].

Roe v. Wade, 410 U.S. 113, 170 (1973) (quoting Abele v. Markle, 351 F. Supp. 224, 227 [D. Conn. 1972]).

The Supreme Court implicitly rejected Karst's broadest statement of the right of intimate association in Bowers v. Hardwick, 106 S. Ct. 2841, 2846 (1986) (denying due process challenge to statute criminalizing sodomy as applied to homosexual acts); *cf. id.* at 2848 (Blackmun, J., dissenting) (referring to freedom of intimate association and Karst's article). While there are good reasons for believing that *Hardwick* may be limited to homosexual acts, *see, e.g., id.* at 2847 (Burger, C.J., concurring) (long-standing social opprobrium justifies denying due process protection for homosexual acts), the Court's opinion evidences substantial concern over the privacy doctrine, and impliedly the doctrine of intimate association, because of the absence of a specific textual basis for it in the Constitution. Justice White's majority opinion in *Hardwick* and his dissent in *Thornburgh, see supra* chapter 1 notes 49, 56, 69, are two expressions of the same position with respect to the privacy doctrine; and *Hardwick* helps set the doctrinal stage for a retrenchment of the constitutional right of abortion-choice should a majority coalesce for that end.

Justice Powell's swing vote in these two five-to-four cases made the difference: in *Hardwick* against extending the privacy doctrine and in *Thornburgh* for strongly reaffirming *Roe* and its progeny. In fact, *Hardwick* and *Thornburgh* may coexist in the canons of privacy cases and their holdings rationalized. *Hardwick* implies that the constitutional right of privacy does not depend on recognizing the essential role of sexuality in identity and self-expression; or, alternatively, that the state may limit sexual activity to certain approved modes, even at the expense of self-expression. But *Griswold, Eisenstadt, Carey,* and *Roe* may be understood as involving not solely the expression of personal sexual freedom and association, but the right of procreative nonassociation, and the protection of the autonomy of adults in determining whether to enter into the dyad, which after all may not be dissolved after birth as easily as associations between consenting adults.

44. Karst, *supra* note 43, at 626; *see also id.* at 635–637, 655–659.

45. In modern interpretation, the thirteenth, fourteenth, and first amendments amount to prohibitions on many forms of coercion that fundamentally and unalterably determine human identity. The military draft is one exception to such prohibitions, but, in peacetime, the draft usually impinges only for a brief period in young adulthood, whereas parenthood can affect all but the preadolescent stages of life, *see* David Scharff, *The Sexual Relationship: An Object Relations View of Sex and the Family* (Boston: Routledge & Kegan Paul, 1982), p. 170 ("The decision or lack of one around conception represents one of the major turning points of adult life").

46. *See supra* note 24.

47. *See* Charles Fried, *Contract As Promise: A Theory of Contractual Obligation* (Cambridge MA: Harvard University Press, 1981), p. 90; *see also id.* ("Between the adult or near-adult [teenage] members of the family the sharing must come freely. Where the will to share is lacking, then in due course the sounder, healthier instinct dictates that the unit be dissolved"); Burt, "Constitutional Law and the Teaching of the Parables," 93 *Yale L.J.* 455, 486 (1984) (the parables of Jesus "teach that communal membership cannot be commanded by any force, no matter how divine or seemingly omnipotent. Forced love is a contradiction in terms, a reign of terror"); Ross, "Abortion and the Death of the Fetus," 11 *Phil. & Pub. Aff.* 232, 242 (1982) ("We can be obligated to do only that which we could conceivably be made to do. . . . This [loving a child] is not something we can be made to do, not because it is in some sense outside our competence to love in response to force (as it is outside our competence to fly in response to force) but because what can be done in response to force cannot be love. It cannot be a genuine response of *ours*. . . . [I]t is in the deepest sense of the term self-expressive. It is entirely the subject's to give or withhold"); Karst, *supra* note 43, at 633 ("while it is undoubtedly possible to have a sense of commitment to an association one has not chosen, surely that sense is heightened when there is a measure of real choice whether to maintain the association") (footnote omitted); *id.* at 637–638.

48. Erikson, *Childhood and Society, supra* note 2.

49. Feminist critics of contractarian theories of rights assert that women have hitherto lacked the power to choose whether to enter into association with others, having often had their associational ties dictated by their biology. *See* Zillah Eisenstein, *The Radical Future of Liberal Feminism* (New York: Longman, 1981), *quoted in* Beverly Harrison, *Our Right to Choose* (Boston: Beacon Press, 1983), p. 51.

For a discussion of the prevalence of abortion from one who does not seem to view the practice of abortion as increasing the freedom of women, *see* Devereux, *supra* note 31.

50. Maher v. Roe, 432 U.S. 464, 475–76 (1977) (footnote omitted) (holding that state may implement its interest in potential life by funding medical services for childbirth but not abortion).

51. Compelled association may produce favorable results under certain circumstances. *See* Brown v. Board of Education, 347 U.S. 483 (1954); Gordon Allport, *The Nature of Prejudice* (Cambridge, MA: Addison-Wesley Publishing Co., 1954), pp. 261–281 (social-psychological research demonstrates that social stereotypes may be diminished through proximity). But the clinical literature is equally clear that proximity among family members does not regularly reduce destructive stereotypes or eliminate hate that has its source intrapsychically or interpersonally.

52. Thornburgh v. American College of Obst. & Gyn., 106 S. Ct. at 2196 (White, J., dissenting). For a discussion of the way the debate has limited the potential state interests to the protection of potential life, *see supra* chapter 1 note 46. For a discussion of adoption as a means of furthering this state interest, *see infra* text accompanying note 67 *et seq.* For a discussion of the consequences of uncommitted caretakers, *see supra* text accompanying notes 18–19.

53. A feminist theologian writes:

> Those who are born in the absence of such an act of human covenant by already living persons . . . frequently do not really live at all. Our acknowledgment of each other in relation is not an optional addition to life, an afterthought; it is constitutive of life itself. For a vital human life to be born, a woman must say yes in a strong and active way and enter positively into a life-bearing . . . process. Freedom to say yes, which, of course, also means the freedom to say no, is constitutive of the sacred covenant of life itself.

Harrison, *supra* note 49, at 256; *see also* Caroline Whitbeck, "The Moral Implications of Regarding Women as People: New Perspectives on Pregnancy and Personhood," in *Abortion and the Status of the Fetus*, ed. William Bondeson, H. Tristram Engelhardt, Jr., Stuart Spicker & Daniel Winship (Dordrecht, Holland: D. Reidel Publishing Co., 1983), pp. 247, 250–251 ("the relationships between the parties are those which are central and indeed necessary in order for one of the parties ever to become a moral agent").

54. The evidence concerning the offspring of women who seek but are denied abortion is very limited and grows out of particular sociocultural and historical settings. The main study followed children born in one Swedish city between 1939 and 1942 after the refusal of a therapeutic abortion pursuant to a 1939 abortion law that allowed abortion on several grounds, including the mother's life and health, rape, incest, genetic defect, and the like. The study followed 120 such children for approximately 35 years and compared them against controls, born at the same time in the same hospitals, with respect to objective data concerning schooling, crime and delinquency, reliance on public assistance, alcoholism, marriage and divorce, and psychiatric consultation and hospitalization. The study found that the group born to mothers who sought but were denied abortion had more frequent social and psychiatric disabilities than the control group. But these comparative disabilities manifested themselves most strongly in childhood and, although present, diminished once the group had grown to adulthood. While the differences on each variable were consistently in the direction of social and psychological pathology for the studied group, some of these differences were never statistically significant, and some ceased to be significant after the cohort reached adulthood. *See* Forssman & Thuwe, "Continued Follow-Up Study of 120 Persons Born After Refusal of Application for Therapeutic Abortion," 64 *Acta psychiatrica scandinavica* 142 (1981). The authors attribute the difficulties not to maternal ambivalence per se but to the worse circumstances into which those in the studied group were born, such as unstable families and single parent homes, which themselves led to the request for abortion. *See*

Forssman & Thuwe, "One Hundred and Twenty Children Born After Application for Therapeutic Abortion Refused," 42 *Acta psychiatrica scandinavica* 71 (1966); *see also* Z. Matějček, Z. Dytrych & V. Schüller, "Follow-Up Study of Children Born to Women Denied Abortion," in *Abortion: Medical Progress and Social Implications*, Ciba Foundation Symposium 115, ed. Ruth Porter & Maeve O'Connor (London: Pitman, 1985), p. 136 (similar study in Czechoslovakia finding consistent but not dramatic differences between a group of 220 children and controls, but finding that the differences *increased* through adolescence); David & Matějček, "Children Born to Women Denied Abortion: An Update," 13 *Family Planning Perspectives* 32, 33 (1981); *cf.* Feder, "Preconceptive Ambivalence and External Reality," 61 *Int'l J. Psychoanalysis* 161 (1980); Caplan, "The Disturbance of the Mother-Child Relationship by Unsuccessful Attempts at Abortion," 38 *Mental Hygiene* 67, 68 (1954) (attributing disturbance of mother-child relationship to frustration of intention to abort). *See generally* Malcolm Potts, Peter Diggory & John Peel, *Abortion* (Cambridge: Cambridge University Press, 1977), pp. 505–524.

55. Psychotherapists who wish to treat an infant treat the parent. It is understood that they must recognize and control their own impulses to rescue their young patients from very distressing circumstances (impulses that are technically referred to as "omnipotent rescue fantasies"). For unless the therapist or someone else is ready to take over the full-time task of mothering, there is no aid that he or she can render except by helping the parent and trusting that the aided parent will support the healthy growth of the infant. *See, e.g.,* Fraiberg, *supra* note 19.

56. The argument put forth here differs from the criticized claim that persons have value only because they are wanted by another. *See* Daniel Callahan, *Abortion: Law, Choice and Morality* (New York: Mac-Millan, 1970), pp. 457–460. Nor is this argument burdened by the problem, which Callahan raises against this other theory, of the pregnant woman who dies though her infant survives.

By not having aborted previously, it may be said that the woman clothes the infant in the mantle of a right to life that survives her: for are we not bound to respect the worth of each being once sponsored by a mother?

57. *See* "U.S. Birthrate, Annual Number of Births Fell Between 1982 and 1983," 16 *Family Planning Perspectives* 236 (1984).

58. In 1985, 1,588,600 abortions were performed. Twenty-five percent of all pregnancies were terminated through intentional abortion. This amounted to 298 abortions per 1000 (or 30 percent of) pregnancies not ending in miscarriage or stillbirth. Almost 3 percent of all women of childbearing age had an abortion in 1985.

Despite some fluctuation, the number of abortions has remained fairly stable since 1981 when the number was 1,577,300; the abortion rate has also been fairly stable since 1979. *See* Henshaw, Forrest & Van Vort, "Abortion Services in the United States, 1984 and 1985," 19 *Family*

Planning Perspectives 63, 64 & table 1 (1987) (providing estimates of Alan Guttmacher Institute which because it uses more intensive survey methods yields a greater annual number of abortions than do those of the Center for Disease Control); *see also* Henshaw, Forrest & Blaine, "Abortion Services in the United States, 1981 and 1982," 16 *Family Planning Perspectives* 119, 121 (1984).

In understanding this data, the following contexts are relevant:

a. Expert estimates of the total number of illegal pre-*Roe* abortions ranged from 200,000 to 1.2 million in the early 1960s; and some suggest that approximately one-half of the legal abortions performed in the wake of *Roe* would have been performed as illegal ones prior to *Roe*. *See* Christopher Tietze, *Induced Abortion, A World Review, 1983*, 5th ed. (New York: Population Council, 1983), p. 21; *see also* Ryan, "Medical Implications of Bestowing Personhood on the Unborn," in *Defining Human Life*, ed. Margery Shaw & A. Edward Doudera (Ann Arbor, MI: AUPHA Press, 1983), pp. 84, 87–88. *But see* Louisell et al., *supra* note 32, at 220, 241–243 (noting estimates of the total number of illegal abortions ranging between 50,000 and 1.2 million).

b. Worldwide, the number of legal abortions performed is estimated to be as high as 50 million. *See* Tietze, *supra*, at 19.

c. The ratio of abortions to live births is not substantially different from the estimates of midnineteenth century physicians that 20 percent to 33 percent of all pregnancies ended in abortion. To what extent these nineteenth century estimates may be credited is uncertain. *See* Kristin Luker, *Abortion and the Politics of Motherhood* (Berkeley, Los Angeles, London: University of California Press, 1984), pp. 19–20, 48–50.

d. A vast increase in female procreative *capacity* has occurred in the Western world in this century. The enormous increase in the number of times a woman ovulates during her life is due not only to reductions in the number of her pregnancies and length of time she nurses, but also to advances in nutrition, public health, and medicine, all of which have led to an earlier onset of her menarche, an increase in the length of time that she remains fertile, and an increase in the regularity of her ovulations. One study estimates that a rural woman of one African tribe ovulates approximately 48 times in her life, compared to over 420 times for a Western middle-class woman. *See* Carl Djerassi, *The Politics of Contraception* (New York: W. W. Norton & Co., 1979), p. 13 (reporting study by R. V. Short).

59. *See* Grimes, "Second-Trimester Abortions in the United States," 16 *Family Planning Perspectives* 260, 262 (1984). Ninety-one percent of all abortions occur prior to the thirteenth week after the woman's last menstrual period [hereinafter "LMP"]. The speed with which many women procure an abortion is evident from the further statistic that 51 percent of all abortions occur within the first eight weeks LMP, the first two of which are prior to fertilization, and the first three to four of which precede the availability of cheap and accurate tests to identify pregnancy. *See* Henshaw, Binkin, Blaine & Smith, "A Portrait of American Women Who Obtain Abortions," 17 *Family Planning Perspectives* 90

(1985); *see also* Henry David, "Post-Abortion and Post-Partum Psychiatric Hospitalization," in *Abortion: Medical Progress and Social Implications, supra* note 54, at 150, 159 (quoting study that found 75 percent of aborting women decided to abort within one week of learning of pregnancy).

60. Between 8 to 9 percent of women make an abortion choice during the first two months of the second trimester, with less than 1 percent of all abortions occurring after twenty weeks. Henshaw et al., *supra* note 59, at 90.

For the reasons that women have abortions in the second trimester, *see* "Digest: Late Abortions Linked to Education, Age and Irregular Periods," 13 *Family Planning Perspectives* 86 (1981); Grimes, *supra* note 59, at 262 (irregularity of menses is one of the two most important factors associated with second trimester abortion; other associated factors include attitudes toward abortion, whether the woman talked with others about her suspicion that she was pregnant, awareness of legality of abortion, use of contraceptives, and length of time with partner; but most variation remained unexplained by these multiple factors); "Discussion," *Abortion: Medical Progress and Social Implications, supra* note 54, at 14, 99–100 (30 percent of second trimester abortions in English study were due to failure by doctor and patient together to diagnose pregnancy; lack of money and problems in scheduling abortions also caused delay, with the National Health Service requiring an average of 3.9 weeks to schedule an abortion); Ketting, "Second-Trimester Abortion as a Social Problem: Delay in Abortion Seeking Behaviour and Its Causes," in *Second Trimester Pregnancy Termination*, ed. Marc Keirse, Jack Gravenhorst, Dirk Van Lith & Mostyn Embrey (The Hague: Leiden University Press, 1982), p. 12 (providing Western European data); Brewer, "Induced Abortion After Feeling Fetal Movements: Its Causes and Emotional Consequences," 10 *J. Biosoc. Sci.* 203 (1978) (of forty women—45 percent of whom were sixteen or less—having abortions in weeks twenty to twenty-four, eleven had menstrual irregularity as defined by having been at least one month overdue; five had first been medically diagnosed as not pregnant; at least one had been told she was probably infertile; and fourteen were labeled "wishful thinkers"); *id.* (estimating that, in the sample, 25 percent identified their pregnancy in the second month, 37 percent in the third month, 10 percent in the sixth month, and 7.5 percent did not know they were pregnant until they consulted a physician for other reasons).

Especially where a woman delays identifying or acknowledging a pregnancy, the male's desertion, if it occurs, may be delayed into the second trimester.

61. While 75,000 women have amniocentesis each year in the United States, only 1500 to 3750 of them, or 2 percent to 5 percent, go on to have legal abortions. The number of abortions for fetal defect is approximately this number, or at most, it appears, approximately 0.25 percent of all abortions. *See* Grimes, *supra* note 59, at 261; *cf.* Barron, "Some Aspects of Late Abortion for Congenital Abnormality," in *Abortion: Medical Progress and Social Implications, supra* note 54, at 102, 103–104 (somewhat similar percentages for Great Britain). *See generally* Milunsky, "Fetal Abnormalities: Detection, Counseling, and Dilemmas," in *Defining Human Life, supra* note 58, at 62; Rosenberg, "Toward an Even Newer Genetics," in *Defining Human Life, supra* note 58, at 303.

Another genetic test, chorionic villi testing, is available earlier than amniocentesis, but at present involves greater risks to the embryo or fetus and fails to identify certain defects. *See* Rhoden, "Trimesters and Technology: Revamping *Roe v. Wade*," 95 *Yale L.J.* 639, 681–683 (1986); Rhoden, "The New Neonatal Dilemma: Live Births From Late Abortions," 72 *Geo. L.J.* 1451, 1490 n.314, 1505 n.389 (1984). Sonography and fetal blood tests are also used for identifying abnormalities.

Even among those who may favor deregulation generally, some nonetheless oppose abortion in cases of severe fetal abnormality, distinguishing the decision not to become a mother from the decision not to mother a particular fetus. Some who draw this distinction seek to avoid discrimination against the moderately handicapped, against males or females, and against fetuses of particular racial or ethnic paternity. *See, e.g.,* Delgado & Keyes, "Parental Preferences and Selective Abortion: A Commentary on *Roe v. Wade, Doe v. Bolton* and the Shape of Things to Come," 1974 *Wash. U.L.Q.* 203; *see also* Elshtain, "Review, A Feminist Agenda on Reproductive Technology," 12(1) *Hastings Center Report* 40 (1982). It should be noted that some chromosomal abnormalities are sex linked, that information about sex identity may be essential for a physician advising about the risk of genetic abnormality, and that this may lead to abortion rates that differ according to sex. Tietze, *supra* note 58, at 66. But physicians, who have indicated their policy at the commencement of the doctor-patient relationship, may refrain from disclosing the gender of a fetus to the parents and from condoning a parent's unwillingness to commit to the dyad solely on account of gender.

Tests for fetal abnormality increase reproduction in at least some cases by encouraging at-risk parents to conceive. *See, e.g.,* Rebecca Cook, "Legal Abortion: Limits and Contributions to Human Life," in *Abortion: Medical Progress and Social Implications, supra* note 54, at 211, 216.

62. A greater availability of abortion services would probably reduce the percentage of second trimester abortions, since second trimester abortions are associated with areas in which few abortions are performed. *See* Grimes, *supra* note 59, at 261; *cf.* Ketting, *supra* note 60. In Sweden, possibly with a greater availability of abortion services, the percentage of second trimester abortions has remained at about 4 to 6 percent. Shulman, "Second Trimester Abortion: Techniques and Complications," in *Gynecology and Obstetrics*, ed. John Sciarra (Hagerstown, MD: Harper & Row, 1982), p. 1; Tongplaew Singnomklao, "Abortion in Thailand and Sweden: Health Services and Short-Term Consequences," in *Abortion· Medical Progress and Social Implications, supra* note 54, at 54, 61–62.

63. *Roe* generally does not protect the choice of women whose reasons for wanting to abort in the third trimester are similar to the reasons of women for aborting in the second trimester, such as a serious genetic abnormality discovered very late due to a flawed amniocentesis procedure, or a very young adolescent pregnancy that has escaped detection, or a third trimester dissolution of the procreative unit through the death or desertion of the male. Such women, in their third trimester, would be denied abortion both under *Roe* and the standard of a "reasonable period of choice" discussed here, unless their reasons were so to affect their psychosomatic health as to justify a therapeutic abortion. The law's need for clear rules and its capacity to aid a woman's choice by establishing firm limits for the containment of maternal ambivalence, *see infra* text accompanying notes 92–100, may justify denying abortion in the third trimester to that occasional woman whose reasons do not meet either the reasonable period of choice or the therapeutic abortion standard.

These issues now arise only very infrequently. One study found that lawful third trimester abortions occur at the rate of 4 per 100,000 abortions, with most alleged cases consisting of removal of fetuses that had died spontaneously *in utero*. Of these rare abortions, only a few produce live births. *See* Grimes, *supra* note 59, at 264; *see also* Rhoden, "The New Neonatal Dilemma: Live Births From Late Abortions," *supra* note 61; *cf.* Planned Parenthood Ass'n v. Ashcroft, 462 U.S. 476, 486 n.9 (1983). It may be assumed that in a third trimester therapeutic abortion, the woman (except, for example, in cases affecting her mental health) would typically desire a live birth when it can be effected safely for her and the fetus.

64. Near the edge of the viability line there is a very small statistical chance of a live birth resulting from the abortion of a previable fetus. This is because a physician's conclusion that a fetus is not viable is a prognosis subject to some error and because nonviable fetuses may be born alive only to die soon thereafter.

Late second trimester abortions of nonviable fetuses are not necessarily performed in a manner that results in an occasional live birth. The Court has held unconstitutional a state's attempt to prohibit one method of second trimester abortion (saline instillation) that is less likely than the prostaglandin instillation method to result in the live birth of a nonviable fetus. The Court reasoned that the state's prohibition substantially reduced access to abortion procedures (the prostaglandin technique being largely unavailable then) without otherwise enhancing the woman's interest in her life and health. *See* Planned

Parenthood of Mo. V. Danforth, 428 U.S. 52, 75–79 (1976). Given the greater safety for the woman of a D&E procedure over instillation methods, and the increasing use of the D&E procedure later and later in the second trimester, the possibility of a live birth following an abortion is decreasing. The Court, according to the reasoning of *Danforth*, should not sanction a state's attempt to increase the small chance of a live birth of a previable fetus by forbidding a D&E near viability.

But if an abortion procedure were developed that would increase the chance of a live birth and be as safe for the woman as a D&E and equally available (or substantially so), a state would be justified, according to a logic of separation, in requiring the use of that method. *See, e.g.*, Rhoden, "The New Neonatal Dilemma: Live Births from Late Abortions," *supra* note 61, at 1506 (noting that as the age of viability is reduced, D&Es will eliminate the chance of a live birth of a previable fetus); *cf.* Ross, *supra* note 47 (discussing whether there is duty to try to save an aborted fetus); Wikler, "Ought We to Try to Save Aborted Fetuses?" 90 *Ethics* 58 (1979) (same).

65. Should viability drop substantially into the second trimester, some states might consider a statutory scheme that would limit procreational choice to the first and early second trimesters, unless the dyadic representative were first able to bring herself within one of the special classes identified in the text as requiring additional time.

Such a regulatory approach, while plausible, would have serious problems. In allocating to some other decision maker the determination of whether a woman falls within an exceptional class, this approach would suffer from at least some of the problems of pre-*Roe* regulatory schemes. *See supra* text accompanying chapter 1 note 67. It would also have the negative effect of delaying what would already be a late and therefore less safe abortion. It would single out for a substantial additional burden many of those women and girls who were already having especial difficulty in exercising their dyadic responsibilities. Finally, it would be based on the assumption that the reasons for second trimester abortions are so rare and dubious as to justify an intrusive regulatory procedure, assumptions which appear unwarranted given the obvious natural preference of most women who terminate their pregnancies for an early abortion. *See supra* notes 59–60.

However, if social development were to permit a shortening of the period of reasonable choice, a specific exception for women who, after the close of this period, were found to be carrying a severely abnormal fetus would be less problematic. This is because the inquiry as to whether a woman falls in this category may be treated as a technical medical question that is relatively clearcut, although further clarification of what constitutes "a risk of severe abnormality" would be required. *See, e.g.*, Rhoden, "The New Neonatal Dilemma: Live Births from Late Abortions," *supra* note 61, at 1503–1508 (proposing special exception to permit abortion of severely abnormal fetus should viability occur prior to twenty weeks).

66. A judicial reinterpretation of *Roe* could rely on equal protection arguments. *See* Regan, "Rewriting *Roe v. Wade*," 77 *Mich. L. Rev.* 1569 (1979); Calabresi, *supra* note 32; Ginsberg, "Some Thoughts on Autonomy and Equality in Relation to *Roe v. Wade*," 63 *N.C.L. Rev.* 375 (1985). Nancy Rhoden has advocated a reinterpretation of "viability" which focuses, she asserts, not on its medical but its social meanings. *See* Rhoden, "Trimesters and Technology: Revamping *Roe v. Wade*," *supra* note 61, at 673–691.

67. *See, e.g.*, Herbenick, "Remarks on Abortion, Abandonment and Adoption Opportunities," 5 *Phil. & Pub. Aff.* 98 (1975) (arguing that principles of equal citizenship require that married couples who are naturally childless be afforded equal opportunity for parenthood by forbidding abortion and providing social inducements to put unwanted children up for adoption). For a discussion of the demand for adoption by such couples, *see infra* note 68. Whether or not such an argument has merit, it should not apply in favor of the many couples who are voluntarily surgically sterile for contraceptive reasons and who later change their minds.

68. Some make optimistic predictions that, were elective abortion prohibited, enough adoptive parents would become available to provide satisfactory care for those who will be born. This claim lacks support in part because data on adoption in this country are quite limited, as are informed inferences in the literature from such data concerning the pool of potential adoptive parents. A scarcity of data makes optimism hazardous.

The absence of much literature by those with training in this subject makes it necessary for me to attempt to develop, in a suggestive and exploratory manner, inferences from such data as I have found to criticize the optimistic prediction and to support the contrary claim made in text. That contrary claim is: no state that prohibited abortion could in good faith promise to arrange anything like maternal care for the number of infants who now would be born if not earlier aborted—unless it is also assumed that most women would keep their children if forbidden to abort or that abortions would continue to be performed illegally and substantially unabated.

Two approaches may be taken to the data. The first examines actual adoption statistics and notes the enormous disparity between actual adoptions and the number of abortions. *See, e.g.*, Djerassi, "Abortion in the United States: Politics or Policy," 42(1) *Bulletin Atomic Scientists* 38, 39–40 (1986) (using California data to estimate oversupply of adoptive children were abortion forbidden). The second approach attempts to estimate the potential pool of adoptive parents by examining the prevalence in the population of characteristics associated with adoptive parents, such as marriage, age, desire for children, and an impairment in fertility. Finally, I shall note procedural barriers to adoption that support my claim.

The statistics that follow have substantial limitations, especially those since 1975 when the federal government ceased its systematic and ongoing collection of adoption statistics. *See* National Committee for Adoption, *Adoption Factbook* (Washington, D.C., 1985), pp. 5, 154. The statistical extrapolations from samples that follow also suffer in particular from the fact that adoption is, in the statistical sense, a rare event.

Actual Adoption Statistics

The data demonstrating the limited number of adoptions, especially adoptions by nonrelatives, do not justify optimistic predictions about the size of the pool of potential adoptive parents. Nor do data on the number of children, and especially minority and handicapped children, who are presently available for and in need of adoption but remain unadopted.

The pre- and post-*Roe* statistics concerning the actual number of adoptions describe a level of adoption in this country that has never come close to the present number of abortions. Nor do they describe a level that comes close to many estimates of the number of illegal abortions before *Roe*. Between 1951 and 1970, the number of adoptions rose from 72,000 to 175,000, an all-time high. A subsequent decline in adoptions leveled off in 1975 and the number has remained fairly constant since then. In 1982, there were an estimated 141,861 adoptions, compared with more than ten times that number of abortions. *Id.* at 13–14, 54; *see supra* note 58 (reporting number of abortions).

These numbers of annual adoptions, moreover, substantially overstate the extent of adoption by counting adoptions by both relatives and nonrelatives. In 1982, there were only 50,720 unrelated adoptions, as compared with 91,141 related adoptions. *See Adoption Factbook, supra,* at 13–14, 54. The number of unrelated adoptions amounted to about 3.2 percent of the number of abortions in 1982. Related adoptions are far less probative than nonrelated or stranger adoptions with respect to the prediction that a large pool of potential adoptive parents exists. Indeed, most relative adoptions are by step-parents and are irrelevant to this subject. *Cf.* Bachrach, "Adoption Plans, Adopted Children, and Adoptive Mothers," 48 *J. Marriage & Family* 243, 244 (1986) (step-parent adoptions constituted about 56 percent of all adoptions in 1975).

The balance between related and unrelated adoptions has shifted since *Roe*, but that shift does not alter the inference that may be drawn from the low number of unrelated adoptions. When the nationwide number of adoptions reached a high of 175,000 in 1970, relatives adopting children constituted slightly less than one-half of all adoptions: 85,800 by relatives and 89,200 by nonrelatives. Since then, the number of related adoptions has increased slightly, while the number of unrelated adoptions has dropped; as a result, adoptions by relatives have come to constitute substantially more than half of all adoptions. *See Adoption Factbook, supra,* at 13–14, 101–103 (although the total number of adoptions declined only 4.6 percent between 1972 and 1982, unrelated adoptions declined 22.4 percent). However, even if it were assumed that a prohibition of elective abortion would cause a return to the pre-*Roe* nearly one-to-one ratio of related to unrelated adoptions, that increased number of unrelated adoptions (91,000) would be only 5.8 percent of the present number of abortions. (It may be noted that the data on the ratio of related and unrelated adoptions are consistent with an increased number of remarriages occasioning step-parent adoption and with a decreased availability of unrelated children, which appears to be attributable partly to the deregulation of abortion and partly to the increased likelihood that unmarried mothers will keep their infants.)

Despite this reported decrease in the number of unrelated adoptions since 1972, there is contrary evidence that the percent of ever-married women between the ages of 15 and 44 who have adopted a child, other than a step-child, remained constant between 1973 and 1982, at slightly more than 2 percent. Bachrach, *supra*, at 245. This is not consistent with the claim that *Roe* created a large unmet demand for adoptive children and deprived substantial numbers of persons of an opportunity to adopt that they would otherwise have had. One explanation for this apparent inconsistency in the two statistics is that the 1982 data are less reliable than the earlier 1973 federal data and may overstate the decline in unrelated adoptions. *Cf. Adoption Factbook, supra*, at 154 (suggesting that the recent data it reports may undercount the number of unrelated adoptions).

Data concerning foreign adoptions may also be usefully considered. The resort to foreign-born children might be treated as indicative of the availability of potential parents ready to adopt additional children born in the United States should they become available. But the absolute number of such foreign adoptions does not suggest a large reservoir of adoptive parents awaiting more United States children. Although the number of foreign adoptions has doubled in the last decade, it fluctuates substantially from year to year and accounted for only 5707 adoptions in 1982 and 8327 adoptions in 1984. *Id.* at 14, 28.

Finally, other evidence such as a low level of applications to adopt and the fickleness of requests to adopt do not justify optimistic predictions either. But because of difficulties in their collection and interpretation, such data do not warrant further attention. *See, e.g.*, California Health & Welfare Agency, Department of Social Services, Statistical Services Branch, *Adoptions in California, Statistical Series, Adop 1* (Sacramento: State of California, 1970–1986).

Turning now from the absolute numbers of adoptions to the numbers of children currently left unadopted, it is clear that optimism cannot be justified by statistics on the actual treatment of children. Our society does not presently evidence a capacity to care for the children it has. Nor does it evidence a capacity to provide adoptive parents for those who need them. This is especially the case for minority and handicapped children.

In 1982, according to one study, 274,000 children were in foster care, and 425,000 children spent at least one day in the foster care system. Over half of these suffered family abuse or neglect. Yet that system is substantially strained and adequate care is not provided in many instances. Moreover, many children in that system are presently available for adoption but go unadopted. Of these foster care children, one study estimates that 36,000 are legally free and awaiting adoption. *Adoption Factbook, supra*, at 32, 42.

Substantial numbers of minority children, handicapped children, and other so-called "hard-to-place" children presently are available for adoption but go unadopted. In 1977, only 37 percent of those black children who were free for adoption received adoptive homes. Other studies report that among black children in substitute care only 33.4 percent in 1982 and 36.6 percent in 1983 had adoptions finalized. *Id.* Yet another study estimated that 40,000 of 100,000 children in out-of-home placements who were eligible for adoption were nonwhite. *See* Rita Simon & Howard Altstein, *Transracial Adoption: A Follow-up* (Lexington, MA: Lexington Books, 1981), p. 67; *see also* Beal v. Doe, 432 U.S. 438, 456 (1977) (Marshall, J., dissenting) ("Many thousands of unwanted minority and mixed-race children now spend blighted lives in foster homes, orphanages, and 'reform' schools").

This pool of hard-to-place children has substantial numbers of older children, who, if they first became available for adoption after infancy, are outside the scope of the optimistic claim, which pertains only to the potential demand for infants. But the interests of older children in adoption should not be discounted and disadvantaged in favor of increasing the supply of infants by an abortion prohibition. Indeed, their present relative scarcity benefits adoptive children and especially the hard-to-place, even as it "disadvantages" potential adoptive parents. *See, e.g.,* Cohen, "Posnerism, Pluralism, Pessimism," 67 *B.U.L. Rev.* 105 (1987).

Finally, it has been suggested that the absolute numbers of unadopted children and especially unadopted minority children might grow if an increase in the number of adoptions were to lead to the popular belief that children had a greater chance of being adopted; for then, more minority mothers who presently fear discrimination against their children might place them for adoption. *See* Charles Zastrow, *Outcome of Black Children—White Parents Transracial Adoptions* (San Francisco: R&E Research Associates Inc., 1977), pp. 2–3.

In summary, the data concerning actual adoptions and unadopted and hard-to-place children suggest that the number of abortions vastly surpasses the capacity of the child-care system to provide parents for children.

Defining a Pool of Potential Parents

Criticizing this approach, some claim that actual adoption behavior does not begin to indicate the potential demand for healthy infants. They argue that the relative scarcity of healthy adoptive infants is so discouraging, as is the rebuff of adoption agencies (acting in response to this scarcity of children), that most potential parents simply do not register their interest in adoption in a manner that our data can reflect. Some also argue that, because this relative scarcity long predated 1973, a comparison of adoption statistics before and after *Roe* will not disclose striking differences that would support a claim that *Roe* has deprived substantial numbers of couples of an opportunity to adopt. Accordingly, they reject statistics based on actual adoption levels in favor of data attempting to define a pool of persons who might be motivated to adopt.

This approach involves trying to define a pool of potential adoptive parents by reference to characteristics that are logically and empirically associated with a motivation to adopt, such as fertility impairment, marital status, age, wish for a child, number of children in family, and the like. The size of that pool is then compared with the annual number of abortions. I shall show that even with excessively generous assumptions about the size of that pool, it does not begin to compare with the annual number of abortions. Because defining the pool is a long process, I shall begin by merely asserting three definitions of the pool: an apparently reasonable definition, an excessively large definition, and an exceedingly large definition. Then I shall compare their sizes with the number of abortions. (In this comparison, I shall assume that, given the present annual 1.59 million abortions, a fully enforced abortion prohibition would result in 1.59 million more infants. However, such a prohibition would probably reduce the frequency with which those who have repeat abortions now become pregnant, and would change the sexual and contraceptive behavior of some, thus somewhat reducing the 1.59 million number.) Finally, I shall explain in some detail how the exceedingly and excessively large pools may be defined.

The first definition of the pool comes from Judge Richard Posner, recently appointed to the United States Court of Appeals for the Seventh Circuit and a well-known scholar at the University of Chicago Law School. He has proposed that such a pool consists of 148,000 married couples. These couples represent the 54 percent who have not yet adopted among the 274,000 currently married couples, with a wife between the ages of thirty and forty-four, who have not had and are unable to have a child. Judge Posner urges this definition of the pool as part of his long-standing proposal to partially deregulate and encourage a freer legal market in adoption. His goals are to eliminate the excessive prices of the black market in adoptions and to induce mothers to increase the supply of healthy infants to a legal adoption market so as to spare would-be adoptive parents the delays and disappointments that he believes certain state regulations cause. Accordingly, Posner has no interest in minimizing the size of the pool he proposes; indeed, his argument benefits from defining the pool as substantially as he reasonably can. *See* Posner, "The Regulation of the Market in Adoptions," 67 *B.U.L. Rev.* 59, 68–69 (1987); *see also* Landes & Posner, "The Economics of the Baby Shortage," 7 *J. Legal Stud.* 323, 336 (1978) (proposing a pool of 130,000 couples adopting two children each, but suggesting that this pool would replenish itself annually, a suggestion Posner has apparently dropped). (It may be noted that, as he discusses the use of market incentives to encourage young mothers to bear children and place them for adoption, Posner demonstrates some of the risks of the logic of separateness that his individualistic market-oriented language involves.)

This apparently reasonably defined pool could provide parents for less than 10 percent of those who would be born in one year if not earlier aborted. However, it could provide care for nearly all of those children who are currently eligible for adoption and in great need of adoptive parents.

But others suggest that the pool of potential adoptive parents is very much greater, between 1 to 3 million couples. I shall later review the data that can be used to define a pool in this range in order to show what kind of exceedingly generous assumptions are necessary to support such numbers. Here, I shall merely assert, based upon this subsequent analysis, that a second definition of the pool would consist of one-half of the following group: the approximately 1 million married women who have impaired fecundity and have sought medical fertility services, plus the 1.7 million married women who are surgically sterile for noncontraceptive reasons and express a wish for a child. Half of these approximately 2.7 million couples *might* be motivated to act to enlarge their families by adoption. This pool of 1.35 million could not supply enough parents to outstrip the present number of abortions even in the first year.

Finally, the third, broadest, and most generously constructed pool would consist of all 2.7 million couples. Such a pool would be able to supply adoptive parents for less than 1.7 years to those 1.59 million infants who would be born if not earlier aborted. Thereafter, the supply of infants would quickly outstrip the size of this adoptive pool. If it were instead assumed that each couple would adopt two children, it would take 3.4 years to exhaust the pool. This assumption is especially generous in that a majority of couples in the pool already have or will have their own children.

But the pool is not static; new women enter it. Some who make optimistic predictions seem to assume that any such pool would completely replenish itself afresh each year. But based as it is on data about women over a thirty-year age range from fifteen through forty-four, this proposed pool does not gain many new members annually. Using a simple linear model in which successive age cohorts join it, the pool would gain new members at the rate of 3.3 percent annually. I shall instead somewhat arbitrarily assume that the pool adds new members at the rate of 7 percent annually in order to allow for the fact that the pool consists primarily of women in the second two-thirds of this age range, for increased population growth, and for a possible recent increase in impaired fecundity among those who have never had children, *see* Aral & Cates, "The Increasing Concern with Infertility: Why Now?," 250 *JAMA* 2327 (1983).

Even assuming two adoptions and a 7-percent growth rate, the number of infants would outstrip the pool in about 4.5 years. Thus, with extraordinarily generous and counterfactual assumptions about the pool of potential adoptive parents, its yearly growth, and the number of children adopted per family, this pool could not, even in the short run, provide care for all the infants who would hypothetically become available.

Having argued that, under any of three definitions, the pool could not provide sufficient adoptive parents, I shall show the very generous assumptions needed to construct the second and third definitions of the pool. It should be remembered that I am indulging in generous assumptions in order to test my hypothesis. I am also assuming that all of the couples in each pool would be deemed acceptable by adoption agencies, an assumption that is substantially inconsistent with present adoption practice. Finally, although the pool is defined as *possible* adoptive parents, I am assuming, contrary to fact, that all in the pool would adopt if the opportunity were available.

For data on impaired fertility, one can turn to the 1982 National Survey of Family Growth, conducted by the National Center for Health Statistics. It studied women of childbearing ages fifteen through forty-four; all subsequent data reported here are restricted to that age range. Several measures identify those who have difficulty bearing children. The "infertile" are those married women who by self-report have engaged in regular unprotected intercourse for one or more years without a resulting pregnancy. Those with "impaired fecundity" identify themselves as having difficulty either conceiving or safely bearing a pregnancy to term. As such, the impaired comprises a larger group than the infertile. But it does not include those who have not yet identified themselves as impaired, such as virgins and those using contraception who have never tried to conceive. In addition to these two overlapping groups are the surgically sterile for either noncontraceptive or contraceptive reasons. Data on these four groups are reported in terms of the fecundity status of women; but, if married, a woman's status reports the couple's status and is determined either by her condition or her husband's. The following data are estimated from a sample; all numbers are rounded.

How many suffer fertility impairment? Of the 54.1 million women of childbearing age, 4.5 million (or 8.4 percent) are classified as having impaired fecundity; another 4.2 million (or 7.8 percent) are surgically sterile for noncontraceptive reasons. These numbers include those who have never been married and who are presently divorced. *See* Mosher, "Reproductive Impairments in the United States, 1965–1982," 22 *Demography* 415, 417 table 1 (1985).

Because the pool of adoptive parents of unrelated children comes overwhelmingly from the population of presently married persons, data on presently married women provide more useful evidence. *See* Bachrach, *supra*, at 247 table 3 (99.3 percent of the 615,000 women of childbearing age who ever adopted an unrelated child were married at the time of adoption). Of the 28.2 million married women in the relevant age group, 2.4 million (or 8.5 percent) are infertile; and 3.05 million (or 10.8 percent) report impaired fecundity. Moreover, 3.1 million (or 11 percent) are surgically sterile for noncontraceptive reasons. *See* Mosher, *supra*, at 417 table 1, 423 table 5.

But not all of these women, when asked, express an intention to have, or a wish for, another baby. Based on extrapolations from the women studied, 2.7 million of any marital status with impaired fecundity wish for another baby. Focusing on the currently married with impaired fecundity, 1.8 million women (or 59.1 percent) have such a wish. Among the 3.1 million married women who are surgically sterile for noncontraceptive reasons, 1.7 million wish for another baby. *Id.* at 417 table 1, 419 table 2. These last two groups constitute the source of women for the hypothesized pool.

While a negative response to an inquiry about wanting a baby is a good reason for excluding someone from the pool of potential adopters, is an affirmative wish for a baby reason for including her in that pool? The expression of a wish is after all costless, whereas the adoption process is arduous.

[In determining how seriously to take this expression of a wish for a baby, it may be instructive to note that among those 7.85 million couples with a spouse who is sterilized for contraceptive reasons, 1.9 million women (or 24.7 percent) still wish for a baby. *Id.* This may evidence that an expression of a desire for another baby in this survey does not predict that a woman will act to make or enlarge a family, for these women have acted in a manner contrary to their wish. (Alternatively, it may show marital disagreement over procreation, which would make the group of the contraceptively sterile unlikely adopters, for adoption presumably requires greater agreement between partners than does either pregnancy or sterilization; or it may show a change of heart, changed family circumstance such as the death of a child, or that the sterilization occurred prior to marriage.) It is also instructive to note that the wish for a baby varies with the number of children already born. Approximately 916,000 (or 82.8 percent) of married women with impaired fecundity and no children wish for a birth; while only 886,000 (or 45.6 percent) with one child or more have that wish. Among the married who are noncontraceptively sterile, of the 270,000 who are childless, 174,000 (or 64.5 percent) wish for a child; and among the 2.85 million who have children, 1.5 million (or 53.4 percent) want a child. Mosher, *supra*, at 417 table 1, 419 table 2. Among the 2.6 million infertile married women, of the 791,000 who have never been pregnant, 551,000 want a baby; of the 1.8 million who have been pregnant, 870,000 want an infant. *See* Hirsch & Mosher, "Characteristics of Infertile Women in the United States and Their Use of Infertility Services," 47 *Fertility & Sterility* 618, 620 table 1, 622 table 2 (1987).]

The wish for a baby does not even lead many couples who may be benefited to take the less difficult step of seeking medical advice for impaired fertility. Seeking such help may serve, better than a mere wish, as an indicator of the motivation for a child that might lead to adoption. Accordingly, the resort to medical services for fertility advice or treatment will be used to determine who among those with impaired fertility expressing a wish for a baby should be included in the pool.

Of the 791,000 married infertile women who have never been pregnant, 399,000 (or about 50 percent) have at some time sought infertility services. Of the 1.8 million married infertile women who have been pregnant at least once, 404,000 (or about 22.3 percent) have sought such services. Thus, 803,000 married infertile women have sought services. *See* Hirsh & Mosher, *supra*, at 620 table 1, 622 table 2.

Other data suggest that 1 million ever-married women seek private medical fertility treatment each year. *See* Mosher, *supra*, at 415; *see also* Aral & Cates, *supra*, at 2327 table 1 (suggesting figure of 900,000 women). This group would seem to evidence both a present wish for a child and a willingness to take action. However, it includes both the presently and formerly married and may include persons who, while defining themselves as having an impairment, are not within the definition of impaired fecundity. Nonetheless, rather than the figure of 803,000 married infertile women, I shall use this much more generous number of 1 million to define one component—married women with impaired fecundity seeking medical service—of the pool of potential adoptive parents. Of course, the same women in this group may seek treatment over the course of several years.

Limiting the group of married women with impaired fecundity to those who use medical services is partially underinclusive and partially overinclusive for defining the impaired-fecundity component of the pool. It is underinclusive in that some wanting an infant might adopt but not seek medical services for reasons of ignorance, discomfort, and cost. Among married infertile nonusers of medical services, of those who have never been pregnant 196,000 (or 51.5 percent) report wanting an infant; and of those who have been pregnant, 549,000 (or 39.3 percent) want an infant. *See* Hirsch & Mosher, *supra*, at 422 table 2. While little is known about why such couples do not seek medical help, it may be hypothesized that, with the diffusion of knowledge about fertility treatment, increasingly the seeking of medical treatment is a likely first, although often final, stop for the impaired on a road leading to adoption.

The group is overinclusive in that not all of those who have ever sought help will continue to want a baby. This is clear from data on married infertile women who have ever used medical services: of those who have never been pregnant 352,000 (or 88 percent) still want an infant; and among those who have been pregnant 319,000 (or 79 percent) still want an infant. *Id.* Of greater importance, many will eventually have children after medical consultation and treatment. One physician has recently estimated that, in addition to those who spontaneously improve, roughly 50 percent of those who seek advice or treatment successfully bear children without resort to the new birth technologies. *See* statement by Dr. Robert Stillman, George Washington University Medical Center, in *Hearings Before the House Select Committee on Children, Youth, and the Family,* 100th Cong., 1st Sess. (May 21, 1987); *see also* Bachrach, *supra,* at 249 (after an adoption, 13 percent of women gave birth for the first time). Without more data, I shall ignore both its over- and underinclusiveness and include in the pool the group of married women users of medical services with impaired fecundity wanting a baby.

Because not all persons with a fertility impairment can be treated, the use of medical services as evidence of a motivation to adopt may exclude those, like the surgically sterile, whose condition is not amenable to treatment. To the extent women believe, correctly in most cases, that their surgical sterility is irreversible, they may not use medical services (although this is not ascertainable from the reported data). Therefore, those in the group of the surgically sterile for noncontraceptive reasons who express a wish for another child are also candidates for inclusion in the pool.

We cannot test the strength of their motivation as simply as we could with the other component of the pool. But it may be hypothesized that those married sterile women who already have children will be less strongly motivated to realize their wish for a baby through adoption. Among noncontraceptively surgically sterile married women, 272,000 have no children; and of these, 175,000 (or 64.5 percent) want a baby. There are 388,000 with one child, of whom 276,000 (or 71.1 percent) want a baby. There are 1.1 million with two children, of whom 530,000 (or 49.9 percent) want a baby. Finally, there are 1.4 million with three or more children, of whom 713,000 (or 51.2 percent) want a child. Thus, of the 1.7 million married noncontraceptively sterile women wishing for another baby, 1.24 million (or over 73 percent) have two or more children, and more than 700,000 have three or more children. *See* National Center for Health Statistics, Public Health Service, W. D. Mosher & W. F. Pratt, "Fecundity, Infertility, and Reproductive Health in the United States, 1982," Vital & Health Statistics, Series 23, No. 14,

DHHS Pub. No. 11 (PHS) 87–1990 (Washington D.C.: U.S. Government Printing Office, 1987), p. 23 table 3. The hypothesis that those with children are less highly motivated to adopt is consistent with actual adoption behavior: among ever-married women, 5.2 percent of those who have never given birth have adopted a child other than a step-child; 2.5 percent of those who have once given birth have adopted; 1.4 percent with two births have adopted; and 1.2 percent with three or more births have adopted. *See* Bachrach, "Adoption as a Means of Family Formation: Data from the National Survey of Family Growth," 45 *J. Marriage & Family* 859, 861 table 1 (1983).

Accordingly, this component of the pool could reasonably be reduced by excluding the 73 percent with two or more children or the 41 percent with three or more children. Nonetheless, applying a rule of very generous construction, I shall assume that all 1.7 million might adopt if given the opportunity.

In summary, married persons who have impaired fecundity and have sought medical services (approximately 1 million) and married persons who are surgically sterile for noncontraceptive reasons and express a wish for a child (1.7 million) together may be used to define very roughly a pool of 2.7 million persons who *might* be motivated to act to enlarge their families.

This combined pool is overinclusive and underinclusive in ways other than those noted above; and in the absence of sufficient data I shall again assume that these conflicting tendencies cancel each other out. It is underinclusive in that it excludes nonmarried persons who may seek to adopt. *See id.* at 860 (of all children adopted by unrelated persons in 1975, 97.5 percent were adopted by married persons). It excludes those who could bear another child but instead choose to adopt. *Cf.* Christine Bachrach, "Adoption Plans, Adopted Children, and Adoptive Mothers: United States, 1982," Working Papers Series No. 22 (Hyattsville MD: National Center for Health Statistics, 1985), table 3 (of the 18.5 million fecund ever-married women of childbearing age, 166,248, or .9 percent, have adopted). Finally, it excludes persons who have been sterilized for contraceptive reasons but change their minds. *Cf. id.* (of the 9.2 million ever-married women of childbearing age who are contraceptively sterile, 101,200, or 1.1 percent, have adopted, whether before or after being sterilized; for comparison, it may be noted that 359,100, or 7.5 percent, of the noncontraceptively sterile have adopted).

This pool is overinclusive in that it includes persons who will absolutely not consider adoption and others who for idiosyncratic reasons will not adopt if given the opportunity. Survey data from 1973 indicate that only 48.2 percent of currently married women over eighteen intending to have additional children say that they would adopt if unable to achieve their desired family size. For several reasons this may overstate the number who would actually adopt. First, the percentage of women indicating a willingness to adopt declines with age down to

31 percent; and it is relatively older women who adopt, with the average age at first adoption being 28.5 years. *See* Bonham, "Who Adopts: The Relationship of Adoption and Social-Demographic Characteristics of Women," 39 *J. Marriage & Family* 295, 300–301 & table 3 (1977) (51.6 percent between the ages of fifteen and twenty-four indicate they would adopt; 48 percent between the ages of twenty-five and twenty-nine so indicate; 41.7 percent between the ages of thirty and thirty-four so indicate; and 31.1 percent between the ages of thirty-five and forty-four so indicate). Second, to predict that 48 percent of women wishing another child would actually adopt assumes that husbands will agree with their wives' wishes in every case (or that husbands and wives will equally persuade opposing spouses in favor of adoption). Third, the fact that the decline in expressed willingness to adopt is associated with age seems inconsistent with a psychological hypothesis that people become amenable to adoption when confronted by the hard reality of not conceiving their desired number of children; to the contrary, life experience including childbearing may be associated, through the variable of age, with a reduced openness to adoption. If so, then the gap may be substantial between the number of women who say they would adopt and the number who would in fact adopt when confronted with the opportunity. Of course, experience may change the minds of those who say they would not adopt.

However, in addition to the rule of generous construction, there are two additional reasons I shall not reduce the pool of potential parents by 52 percent, to 1.3 million, to exclude those who would not adopt. First, it is possible, although unlikely, that the 52 percent who would not consider adoption are not randomly distributed throughout the population of the noncontraceptively sterile wishing for a baby; for the expression of a wish for a baby by a woman who has no hope of conceiving might for some constitute an implicit expression of a willingness to adopt. Second, the decreased willingness to adopt is associated not only with age but also with an increased number of born children, a factor which, although relevant, I have already decided not to take into account. *See* Bonham, *supra*, at 300 table 3 (of those married women with no children, 62.1 percent indicate they would adopt to reach a desired family size; with one child, 41.9 percent so indicate; with two children, 29.6 percent so indicate; and with three or more children, 22.4 percent so indicate).

The foregoing illustrates the extraordinary assumptions underlying the excessively large pool of 2.7 million women. The reasons previously noted for reducing each component of this pool by approximately 50 percent provide the bases for constructing the exceedingly large pool of 1.35 million. Even that smaller pool seems very excessive in size.

Procedural Barriers To Adoption

Finally, many states have procedural rules governing adoption that involve time-consuming requirements of notice to interested parties and a substantially delayed period of maternal consent. These postpone immediate transfer of the neonate at birth. Even assuming available adoptive parents, such procedural rules may not satisfy the minimal requirement of assuring a continuity of care similar to that of the biological mother.

69. On most kibbutzim, parental involvement in child care is a strong tradition that reasserted itself when the rigors of desert life in the early Zionist period passed. Similarly, the Chinese peasantry apparently resisted with some success Mao's attempts to make infant care a strictly communal enterprise.

70. Robert Bellah, Richard Madsen, William Sullivan, Ann Swidler & Steven Tipton, *Habits of the Heart: Individualism and Commitment in American Life* (Berkeley, Los Angeles, London: University of California Press, 1985), p. 277; *cf. id.* ("though the processes of separation and individuation were necessary to free us from the tyrannical structures of the past, they must be balanced by a renewal of commitment and community if they are not to end in self-destruction"); Michael Sandel, *Liberalism and the Limits of Justice* (Cambridge: Cambridge University Press, 1982), p. 183 ("Not egoists but strangers . . . make for citizens of the deontological republic").

71. If the relationship is sundered after birth, the biological parent may lose some of her special status. *See* Joseph Goldstein, Anna Freud & Albert Solnit, *Beyond the Best Interests of the Child* (New York: The Free Press, 1979).

72. By virtue of present technology, one woman as genetic mother can donate an ovum, an anonymous man can donate sperm, another woman as gestational mother can provide the womb and gestational environment, and a third woman, the intended mother, can raise the child by herself and in conjunction with others.

Some treat such possibilities as opportunities for an increase in liberty. *See, e.g.,* Robertson, "Procreative Liberty and the Control of Conception, Pregnancy and Childbirth," 69 *Va. L. Rev.* 405, 410 (1983) ("Procreative freedom includes the right to separate the genetic, gestational, or social components of reproduction and to recombine them in collaboration with others"); *id.* at 424 ("Some men and women, for example, may be unable to find a suitable spouse, be unwilling to marry, or object to heterosexual intercourse, and yet still wish to conceive, bear, and rear a child. Other men and women may want the satisfaction of transmitting their genetic heritage without taking on the responsibilities of gestation or rearing. Finally some women may wish to conceive a child and to parent, but may be unwilling or physically unable to bear and give birth to the child"); *cf.* Tushnet, "An Essay on Rights," 62 *Texas L. Rev.* 1363, 1365–1369 (1984).

For a discussion of new social arrangements for custody that also support the disaggregation of the parent-child relationship, *see* Bartlett, "Rethinking Parenthood As An Exclusive Status: The Need for Legal

Alternatives When The Premise of The Nuclear Family Has Failed," 70 *Va. L. Rev.* 879 (1984).

Tom Grey appropriately views *Roe* as affirming traditional family stability in contradistinction to such trends. *See* Grey, "Eros, Civilization and the Burger Court," 43 *Law & Contem. Prob.* 83, 90 (1980) (Court has "consistently protected traditional familial institutions, bonds and authority against the centrifugal forces of an anomic modern society").

73. *Roe* v. Wade, 410 U.S. at 153. Justice White gives this passage a truncated reading when he asserts that the only interest *Roe* protected was the woman's interest in avoiding "post-birth burdens of rearing a child." Planned Parenthood of Mo. v. Danforth, 428 U.S. 52, 94 (1976) (White, J., dissenting).

74. Similarly, in wrongful birth cases, courts have not imposed a duty to mitigate damages by inquiring why the mother has not put the child up for adoption. *See supra* note 33.

75. *See generally* Otto Kernberg, *Object Relations Theory and Clinical Psychoanalysis* (New York: Jason Aronson, 1976) (describing the psychic achievement at one year of fusing hostile and loving images of the "bad," "frustrating" mother with the "good," "satisfying" mother into one integrated and more realistic mental representation of mother); D. W. Winnicott, "The Development of the Capacity for Concern," in *Maturational Processes, supra* note 15, at 73 (describing the growing capacity toward the end of the first year of life to accept the mother, or other caretaker, as a whole person and not merely as a "part-object" existing only for meeting the infant's needs).

76. On the instinctuality of procreation, *see* Erikson, "On the Generational Cycle: An Address," 61 *Int'l J. Psychoanalysis* 213 (1980); Erikson, *The Life Cycle Completed, supra* note 2, at 67.

On pre-conceptive fantasies, *see* D. W. Winnicott, *supra* note 31, at 51–52. ("The beginning of children is when they are conceived of [in pre-conceptive fantasies]. They turn up in the play of many children of any age after 2 years. It is part of the stuff of dreams and of many occupations. After marriage there comes a time when the idea of children begins to appear"); Feder, *supra* note 54.

On the relationship of intercourse to a parent's relationship with offspring, *see* D. W. Winnicott, "Integrative and Disruptive Factors in Family Life," in *The Family and Individual Development* (New York: Basic Books, 1965) (accompanying intercourse are particular fantasies about her sexual partner and about the fantasied effects of intercourse that shape a parent's response to the resulting offspring).

On the fusion of intercourse, *see* Balint, *supra* note 21.

On the fuller identification with one's parents and identification with the fetus, *see* Pines, *supra* note 31; Pines, "Pregnancy and Motherhood: Interaction Between Fantasy and Reality," 45 *British J. Med. Psychol.* 333 (1972).

77. For the woman's identification of the fetus with her inner fantasy world, *see* D. W. Winnicott, "The Relationship of a Mother to Her Baby at the Beginning," in *The Family and Individual Development, supra* note 76, at 15; Benedek, *supra* note 10, at 395. Technically, this fantasy world is a world of inner objects and, in particular, internalizations of the woman's infantile relationship with her mother. *See generally* W. Ronald Fairbairn, *Psychoanalytic Studies of the Personality* (London: Routledge & Kegan Paul, 1952).

The psychoanalytic emphasis upon the centrality of internal objects for psychic structure evidences the constitutive nature of the mother-infant relationship for the self.

For the heavy, unpleasant, and risky burdens of pregnancy, in contrast to the emphasis in text, *see* Regan, *supra* note 66, at 1579–1583.

78. D. W. Winnicott, "From Dependence Towards Independence in the Development of the Individual," in *Maturational Processes, supra* note 15, at 83, 85.

79. *Id.* at 85–86; *see also* Benedek, *supra* note 10, at 392–397; Deutsch, *supra* note 31, at 153.

80. Winnicott, *supra* note 78, at 85. This primary maternal preoccupation, in health, lasts only a few months:

> The mother will grow up out of this state of easy devotion, and soon she will be back to the office desk, or to writing novels, or to a social life along with her husband, but for the time being she is in it up to the neck. The reward . . . is that the infant's process of development is not distorted.

Id. at 88.

81. The foregoing discussion should have made clear the close relationship between a form of bodily autonomy and what *Roe* protects. Bodily autonomy as an aspect of the negative freedom of nonconstraint has dominated the literature. *See supra* chapter 1 note 48. But bodily autonomy is also an essential aspect of identity. A person is first defined and self-defined by the body the "I" inhabits. It is a basic principle of psychoanalysis that the ego is "first and foremost a bodily ego." Sigmund Freud, "The Ego and the Id" (1923), in *Standard Edition*, vol. 19, *supra* note 4, at 26.

It may be that bodily autonomy has a different meaning for females because of their procreative potential. For this potential can be activated by the male even in a passive, nonconsenting, or resisting female; and her own active sexual wishes may overwhelm her procreational intentions. *See* Erik Erikson, "The Inner and Outer Space: Reflections on Womanhood" (1964), *reprinted in modified form in* Erik Erikson, *Identity: Youth and Crisis* (New York: W. W. Norton & Co., 1968), p. 261 (attempting to delineate the nature of the woman's procreative body for her identity); Harrison, *supra* note 49, at 196–198 (staking out a claim for a person's body-right).

That men's bodies have been conscripted for millenia in war, as well as in work, may have led the *Roe* Court to discount the woman's bodily autonomy claim. *See* Roe v. Wade, 410 U.S. at 154 ("it is not clear to us that the claim . . . that one has an unlimited right to do with one's body as one pleases bears a close relationship to the right of privacy"); Regan, *supra* note 66. But the exploitation of a man's body usually leaves his germ plasm and procreative function unexploited. Perhaps the mentality that "walls do not a prison make," which identifies creativity and identity exclusively with the mind, is a male concept that fails to appreciate the intimate link between body and creativity and between intimate association and identity.

82. For examples of such narcissism, *see* Robertson, *supra* note 72:

People want their child to be . . . perfect rather than imperfect. In addition, a person's interest in conceiving and rearing may rest largely on the child's being of a certain gender or having certain physical characteristics. . . . [P]arents often select mates in part with an eye to the vigor or beauty of their expected offspring and . . . go to extraordinary lengths through education and rearing to mold children to their image of perfection.

Id. at 429–430.

83. *See* Karst, *supra* note 43, at 641 n.90; Tribe, *supra* note 43, at 924 & n.19.

84. The empirical speculation of regulators that abortion undermines family integrity invites counter-hypotheses and questions: To further its own interest in the next generation, should the state refrain from injuring the woman's procreative choice and her potential for future maternal attachment, and instead respect her special predisposition to assume her dyadic office by trusting her with abortion-choice? Would a state policy that lessens the importance of biological parenthood by denying it a privileged status undermine some of the cultural meanings that support the commitment of adoptive parents to recreate as far as possible the rooted symbiosis of the biological tie? Do those who pursue procreation through alternative technological means and family relationships draw meaningful psychological models and support from reproduction in the nuclear heterosexual family?

85. The feelings of at least some women who place their children out for adoption appear, from the reports, to be more painful and conflicted than the typical feelings of women who abort; and those women appear to have a greater potential for experiencing the adoption as a mutilation of the self. *See infra* notes 125–128.

For a compelling discussion of the experiences of some birth-mothers and adopted children, *see* Betty Jean Lifton, *Lost and Found: The Adoption Experience* (New York: Dial Press, 1979); *see also* Arthur Sarosky, Annette Baran & Reuben Pannor, *The Adoption Triangle: The Effects of the Sealed Record on Adoptees, Birth Parents, and Adoptive Parents* (Garden City, NY: Doubleday, 1978), p. 56 (likening parents' placing a child for adoption to "psychological amputation"); Millen & Roll, "Solomon's Mothers: A Special Case of Pathological Bereavement," 55 *Am. J. Orthopsychiatry* 411, 413 (1985) (describing ongoing pain and mourning from placing child for adoption as akin to "loss of self or mutilation"); Deykin, Campbell & Patti, "The Postadoption Experience of Surrendering Parents," 54 *Am. J. Orthopsychiatry* 271 (1984) (ascribing some disturbances in fertility and subsequent parenting to prior placing of child for adoption); Rynearson, "Relinquishment and its Maternal Complications: A Preliminary Study," 139 *Am. J. Psychiatry* 338 (1982).

With respect to the assertion that the actual number of children and parents who seek each other out is quite small, *see Adoption Factbook, supra* note 68, at 66 (only 1 percent of adopted parents and children search).

It appears that for a child the constitutive element of his origins may involve more than knowing his genetic source. The origins of self can include the human intentions of parents that led to one's creation through sexual union and gestation. *Cf.* Hamilton, *supra* note 20.

86. *See* Planned Parenthood of Mo. v. Danforth, 428 U.S. 52, 67–72 (1976) (denying husband a veto of woman's abortion choice). *But cf.* Levy, "Abortion and Dissenting Parents: A Dialogue," 90 *Ethics* 162 (1980) (querying why one parent should have greater say than another in abortion decision); Harris, "Fathers and Fetuses," 96 *Ethics* 594 (1986). Harris argues that a father has an interest in the fetus apart from his interest in ethical treatment by his mate. But Harris' examples suggest that the two interests may not be so easily separated: it is usually within the context of making a procreative unit with a woman that the man acquires an interest in the fetus—through his interest in having his mate treat him honestly and respect his procreative interests, for the realization of which he is relying on her. It is his interest in honesty and respect and his reliance on her for procreation to which the woman should give substantial consideration. Put somewhat differently, she becomes obligated to consider his interests by virtue of a joint procreative unit they have agreed to undertake.

The presumption in favor of the biological mother over the father as the privileged decision maker and interpreter of the dyad requires further consideration and experience before firm conclusions can be reached concerning its applicability to the new relationships occasioned by *in vitro* fertilization and related techniques. For example, a dispute may arise during a divorce between the genetic father and genetic mother over the disposition of a frozen zygote created *in vitro*. To maintain a consistent legal rule and because both genetic mother and father had intended for her to enter the dyad through the gestational process, the presumption in favor of the biological mother as dyadic representative might apply in such a case. An alternative rule might permit either party to compel the destruction of the unimplanted embryo because it was formed as part of a procreative community's joint undertaking which has since failed. This latter rule might reflect the conclusion that in the absence of intercourse, internal fertilization, and gestation, the woman has no greater dyadic relationship with the zygote than the father.

A dispute between a gestational (surrogate) mother and the genetic and intended mother and father who have contracted with her to carry their embryo requires a clarification of the meaning of "mother," even given the presumption in her favor. In this case it could be argued that the genetic mother and father (or intended parents if different) do not have a sufficient present dyadic relationship with the fetus to overcome the presumption in favor of the gestational mother as its representative.

Whatever the rules in cases such as these, they do not diminish the appropriateness of the presumption favoring the natural mother who begets through sexual intercourse. The fact that technology can disaggregate begetting, bearing, and rearing does not make analyses of procreation that assume this disaggregated state somehow "truer" or more accurate. Our concepts need not be slaves to our technology.

87. *See, e.g.,* Schneider, "Moral Discourse and the Transformation of American Family Law," 83 *Mich. L. Rev.* 1803, 1812 (1985); Luker, *supra* note 58, at 282 n.17; Jagger, "Abortion and a Woman's Right to Decide," in *Women and Philosophy: Toward a Theory of Liberation,* ed. Carol Gould & Mary Wartofsky (New York: Putnam, 1976), p. 34 (arguing for abortion-choice because in our culture burdens of childrearing fall primarily to the mother). For a discussion of female-headed households, *see* Daniel Patrick Moynihan, *Family and Nation: The Godkin Lectures* (San Diego: Harcourt Brace Jovanovich, Publishers, 1986); Bachrach, "Children in Families: Characteristics of Biological, Step-, and Adopted Children, 45 *J. Marriage & Family* 17 (1983).

88. *See, e.g.,* Ross, "Fathering: A Review of Some Psychoanalytic Contributions on Paternity," 60 *Int'l J. Psychoanalysis* 317, 321 (1979); Benedek, *supra* note 10, at 399 (father achieves specific involvement with infant through identification with his wife during pregnancy, in addition to a general wish for fatherhood that grows from his identification with his father).

89. *But see* Dorothy Dinnerstein, *The Mermaid and the Minotaur* (New York: Harper & Row, 1976) (advising that it is best to minimize or, as she would have it, eliminate such differences between fatherhood and motherhood); *see also* Chodorow, *supra* note 29.

90. *See* Thornburgh v. American College of Obst. & Gyn., 106 S. Ct. 2169, 2200 (1986) (White, J., dissenting) (denying that burdens of pregnancy differ from burdens, such as required vaccinations, that the state may impose to further a significant interest); Meredith Michaels, "Abortion and the Claims of Samaritanism," in *Abortion: Moral and Legal Perspectives,* ed. Jay Garfield & Patricia Hennessey (Amherst: University of Massachusetts Press, 1984), p. 213. Examples such as vaccination or the draft may be distinguished both by the nature and impact of the burden imposed and the type of benefit conferred on society. The burdens

of vaccination obviously are not comparable to pregnancy; and at present there is no draft in this country. For one acceptable but not compelling attempt to distinguish the burdens of pregnancy from the burdens of the draft, *see* Regan, *supra* note 66, at 1605–1606 (arguing that pregnancy benefits only the fetus and thus must be assimilated to the law of good samaritanism whereas the draft affords a public good); *see also* Tushnet & Seidman, "A Comment on Tooley's *Abortion and Infanticide*," 96 *Ethics* 350, 355 (1986); *supra* chapter 1 notes 23–24, 27–28.

91. It is not appropriate here to try to allocate the reasons for the privileged position of motherhood (and fatherhood) among biological, psychological, and cultural sources, lest an imagined theoretical hold on the subject induces a mistaken belief that one can immediately constitute an alternative system that would equally assure offspring a continuity of committed care.

92. Should society, in a utopian (or antiutopian) future, ever cease through new technology or social arrangements to use women for bearing and rearing children, *see, e.g.,* Shulamith Firestone, *The Dialectic of Sex* (New York: Morrow, 1970); Margaret Atwood, *The Handmaid's Tale* (Boston: Houghton Mifflin Co., 1986), and should it try to disconnect the social meanings of impregnation, pregnancy, birth, and infant care from the woman's generative needs—and this might involve a very deep alienation indeed—then the argument set forth in text for the woman's privileged status as representative of the dyad would be weakened. Her bodily autonomy claims would remain in full force.

93. *Cf.* Michael Tooley, *Abortion and Infanticide* (New York: Oxford University Press, 1983) (asserting that the absence of cognitive indications of personhood permits infanticide for some brief postpartum period); *supra* chapter 1 note 4.

Although the position advanced here locates separate personhood at a time after birth and denies that the fetus exists as a separate being, it does not suggest, as does Tooley, that the fetus is nothing, or mere potential. Rather the fetus-infant is in a relational field, a part of a whole to the extent that the woman chooses.

94. *See* Sigmund Freud, "Civilization and its Discontents" (1930), in *Standard Edition*, vol. 21, *supra* note 4, at 59; Erik Erikson, *Toys and Reasons: Stages in the Ritualization of Experience* (New York: W. W. Norton & Co., 1977), pp. 82–83; Erik Erikson, *Gandhi's Truth: On the Origins of Militant Nonviolence* (New York: W. W. Norton & Co., 1969).

Its emphasis on the pervasiveness of ambivalence is one of the important contributions of psychoanalysis. In particular, analysis has explored in detail the ambivalences between parents and children. *See* Erik Erikson, *Life History and the Historical Moment* (New York: W. W. Norton & Co., 1975), p. 223; Erikson, *Childhood and Society, supra* note 2, at 25; *cf.* Feder, *supra* note 54. However, recent criticism of Freud has asserted that he systematically failed to credit parental hostility to children. *See* Janet Malcolm, *In the Freud Archives* (New York: Knopf, 1984) (discussing claims that Freud suppressed the truth of adult ambivalence toward children by making infantile oedipal strivings the centerpiece of his psychology); Alice Miller, *Thou Shalt Not Be Aware: Society's Betrayal of the Child* (New York: Farrar, Straus & Giroux, 1984); Virginia Abernethy, "Children, Personhood, and a Pluralistic Society," in *Abortion: Understanding Differences*, ed. Sidney Callahan & Daniel Callahan (New York: Plenum Press, 1984), p. 131 (discussing the eighteenth-nineteenth century European practice of abandoning children to orphanages, where mortality rates ran about 90 percent for those under two, amounting to socially approved infanticide).

95. Bernard Haring, *The Law of Christ*, vol. 3 (Westminster, MD: Newman Press, 1966), p. 209, *quoted in* Callahan, *supra* note 56, at 421.

96. *See* C. Everett Koop, "The Road to Auschwitz," in Ronald Reagan, *Abortion and the Conscience of the Nation* (Nashville, TN: T. Nelson, 1984), p. 59.

97. *Cf.* Callahan, *supra* note 56, at 258–277 (considering case of Japan). Against the claim of a slippery slope are cross-cultural data suggesting that, in a society with legalized abortion, the abortion rate reaches a plateau, a trend toward earlier and earlier abortion develops, and contraceptives, as they become more available, partially tend to replace abortion. *See, e.g.,* "General Discussion 1: Abortion Law and Abortion Services in Japan and Other Countries," in *Abortion: Medical Progress and Social Implications*, *supra* note 54, at 32.

A counter-hypothesis to the slippery-slope hypothesis can be developed. Maria Piers identifies as a precondition to infanticide the capacity of mothers (and fathers) in extremity to retreat into a condition of estrangement and withdrawal from attachment which she calls "basic strangeness." Maria Piers, *Infanticide* (New York: W. W. Norton & Co., 1978), pp. 21–24. Might the chosen child tend in extremity not to become quite so basically strange as the unchosen one, because the woman who chooses pregnancy will open herself to the growing opportunity for attachment that pregnancy and infant care afford?

However, a decision not to abort does not necessarily contain and control parental ambivalence. *See* Hunter, Kilstrom, Kraybill & Loda, "Antecedents of Child Abuse and Neglect in Premature Infants: A Prospective Study in a Newborn Intensive Care Unit," 61 *Pediatrics* 629, 630 (1978) (parents of premature infants who subsequently abuse them distinguished from nonabusing parents by: having seriously considered aborting the child, their own history of abuse as children, failures to visit and bond with premature infant in hospital, social isolation, and other evidence of pathology).

98. *Cf.* Magda Denes, *In Necessity and Sorrow* (Middlesex, England: Penguin Books, Ltd., 1976), pp. 1–2 (describing her own ambivalence about having an abortion).

99. *See* Fletcher, "Abortion, Euthanasia and Care of Defective Newborns," 292 *New Eng. J. Med.* 75, 77 (1975) (relying on Erikson in arguing against euthanasia of handicapped newborns because "the task of mothering is strengthened . . . by a world view based on confidence that life is good, even though death and tragedy are part of life"); *see also supra* note 63 (discussing why it is appropriate to exclude some women from third trimester abortions); *cf.* Regan, *supra* note 66, at 1643 (justifying third trimester abortion prohibition by a theory of waiver).

Where a woman accepts the symbiotic relationship by choosing birth over abortion, as prescribed by law, may the law properly set some outer limits on the pregnant woman's aggression, narcissism, and autonomy for the benefit of the later-individuated child and others? The extent to which such lesser restrictions on the activities of women are consistent with a regime of procreative choice and female equality is beginning to be debated. *See, e.g., supra* Preface note 4; Robertson, *supra* note 72, at 437–458.

100. *Cf.* Malcolm Potts, "Medical Progress and the Social Implications of Abortion: Summing-Up," in *Abortion: Medical Progress and Social Implications, supra* note 54, at 263, 267 (dividing psychological states of aborting women into three categories: first, "my period is late," associated with the use of a contragestational agent like RU 486 and menstrual extraction, and lasting from implantation up to organ formation at about seven weeks; second, "I am pregnant," associated with a D&C abortion and lasting approximately from six or seven to twelve weeks; and third, "I'm having a baby," associated with "late abortion" after fourteen weeks LMP, which typically involves a woman's sense of "extreme threat" to herself or the fetus, as in an abortion that is therapeutic or that follows amniocentesis).

101. The Supreme Court recognized the importance of firm boundaries and confirmation in human relationships in an analogous context of "nonassociation" in Boddie v. Connecticut, 401 U.S. 317 (1971) (assuring access to court's divorce decree for indigent persons unable to pay court fees so that they would not be deprived of a legal confirmation of divorce).

102. The phrase is from Herman Melville, *Moby Dick, or, The Whale,* chapter 41, last paragraph (describing Starbuck, who repeatedly would have turned back from Ahab's voyage because of thoughts of his own family). It may be noted that the incompetence of one's unaided virtue and more generally the potential for mistaken, irrational, or self-destructive decisions provides no general justification in the law for paternalistic intervention.

103. *See supra* text accompanying chapter 2 note 1. For Luker's description, *see* Luker, *supra* note 58, at 158–175.

104. Hans Loewald, *Psychoanalysis and the History of the Individual* (New Haven: Yale University Press, 1978), p. 16.

For a discussion of the concept of freedom in psychoanalysis, *see, e.g.*, Peter Gay, "Freud and Freedom: On a Fox in Hedgehog's Clothing," in *The Idea of Freedom: Essays in Honour of Isaiah Berlin*, ed. Alan Ryan (Oxford: Oxford University Press, 1979), p. 41; Abramson, *supra* note 4, at 114–123, 131–138.

These competing attitudes toward autonomy have led at different times to competing therapeutic attitudes with respect to the potential freedom women can enjoy through the psychoanalytic process. *See, e.g.*, Juliet Mitchell, *Psychoanalysis and Feminism* (New York: Pantheon Books, Random House, 1974). Similarly, it has led to different evaluations of abortion by psychoanalysts. *See supra* note 31.

105. Sigmund Freud, "On Narcissism: An Introduction" (1914), in *Standard Edition*, vol. 14, *supra* note 4, at 67, 85.

106. *See, e.g.*, Winnicott, *supra* note 15, at 37 (discussing ego's capacity to bring external trauma within the ego's sphere of personal omnipotence); Erikson, *Identity: Youth and Crisis, supra* note 81, at 208–260 (stressing the central role of ideology in enabling the ego to respond with vitality not only in the realm of play but of necessity); *cf* Sullivan, *supra* note 22, at 92–98, 280–296 (exploring person's integration of complex motivational dynamisms).

For a discussion of the integration of a variety of procreational motivations, see Wyatt, "The Psychoanalytic Theory of Fertility," 4 *Int'l J. Psychoanalytic Psychotherapy* 568 (1975).

107. *See, e.g.*, Bellah et al., *supra* note 70, at 275–296 (even while urging a return to more communal traditions, recognizing that such traditions must be experienced as given, transcending the self, in order to bear the burden of obligation that a greater communal solidarity requires; and suggesting that this country has only two traditions, puritan and republican, which have a sufficient objective existence to provide a communal ethos); Sandel, *supra* note 70, at 59–65.

108. Sandel, *supra* note 70, at 151–152; *see also id.* at 162–165. In describing the "interlocking claims of moral theory and philosophical anthropology on which deontological liberalism has been seen to depend," Sandel writes:

> We are distinct selves first, and *then* we form relationships and engage in co-operative arrangements with others; hence the priority of plurality over unity. We are barren subjects of possession first, and *then* we choose the ends we would possess; hence the priority of the self over its ends.

Id. at 133.

109. Robert Burt, *Taking Care of Strangers* (New York: The Free Press, 1979); *id.* at 168 (a collaborative process would provide for mutual acknowledgment of "alternating power and powerlessness and thereby of fundamental equality" between doctor and patient, and minimize the coercive power that comes from the allocation to either of exclusive decision making); *cf.* Willard Gaylin, ed., *Doing Good: The Limits of Benevolence* (New York: Pantheon Books, 1978).

By way of example, Burt discusses mental patients, whose behavior threatens the social conventions that maintain our separate identities.

The law's current efforts to increase the exclusive decision-making power of patients by limiting involuntary commitment has led the same patients to suffer as the homeless, extruded by a hostile society to its periphery, allowed to die with less succor than in the back-wards of a hospital. So long as the law permits disengagement from mutual interaction, through the exclusive allocation of power to doctor or patient, this vicious cycle will continue, Burt believes.

He similarly analyzes a physician's decision to deny assistance to a severely burned patient in his wish to die, since the wish was deemed to be incompetent because it was the product of depression. If the law were instead to have informed the staff that they are pawns in the hands of a patient who is vested with the exclusive legal power to decide about his treatment, Burt suggests, the staff would still have had the power to induce the patient to choose death. His pain and grotesque appearance initiate the staff's suppressed wish to be done with him. The staff may nonverbally communicate this wish by withdrawing from emotional involvement with him. If given the power to terminate his treatment, the patient might well choose to die in order to implement the sense of worthlessness and hopelessness that the (death) wishes of the staff convey. For Burt, this evidences the incoherence of identifying an exclusive decision maker, where heightened dependency makes the boundaries of identity especially permeable.

Because of this permeability, truth includes not only static facts, but what can be actualized between individuals in an interpersonal context. *See* Erikson, *Insight and Responsibility, supra* note 3, at 159–214 (distinguishing empirical fact from actuality, what may be actualized among persons). In Burt's case studies, truth involves determining whether the famous plaintiff, Catherine Lake, was truly endangered on the streets, or whether her growing senility merely invited fantasies of disintegration which threatened the coherent identities of the police officer and judge who incarcerated her. The search for truth requires clarification of whether a severely burned patient wanted to die, or voiced his wish in compliance with the unverbalized wishes of his caretakers that he and his extraordinarily painful injuries disappear. And it involves the question whether Karen Quinlan's father, asked to make a treatment decision that she would have made, should decide as if his daughter were a selfish person choosing to remain alive in a comatose state, or instead the loving and other-regarding daughter he knew, who would take into consideration the pain of her family; and, in choosing the latter characterization of her, whether the father should therefore take into consideration his own wants in determining her treatment.

110. Burt, *supra* note 109, at 167–168; *see also id.* at 144–173 (discussing cases of Quinlan and of Saikewicz, who was institutionalized because profoundly retarded and from whom the Supreme Judical Court of Massachusetts agreed chemotherapy treatment for cancer might be withheld).

In an unconvincing part of his argument concerning "silent patients," Burt proposes that the law decline to "regularize death's dispensation"; instead it ought to remain silent and refuse to issue declaratory judgments, even while it continues to threaten criminal retribution should a decision to forgo treatment be unjust. He writes:

> The law should not offer to relieve everyone's mutual distress if some among us will assume an identity, as exclusive choice maker for all others, that none can coherently exercise. This fictitiously bestowed identity cannot effectively allay anyone's distress.

Id. at 168–169. Because Burt believes that the product of a consensus of interested participants is likely to be just, he argues that the participatory process, which he proposes, will protect participants from prosecution. This proposal has been reasonably criticized as leading not to greater personal involvement by physicians but rather to a retreat into professional roles that leads to rigidity, not communication. Burt's threat of legal sanction may well be greater than most professionals and family members would want to risk. In considering the applicability of Burt's analysis to abortion, I do so, for this and other reasons, without considering such a threat, although Burt believes it is necessary to assure consultation.

While Burt is silent on the applicability of his analysis of "silent patients" to the subject of abortion, he has criticized the *Roe* Court for designating an exclusive winner in the abortion context and foreclosing political debate on a matter of fundamental communal concern, namely membership. *See* Burt, "The Constitution of the Family," 1979 *Sup. Ct. Rev.* 329, 371–374; Burt, *supra* note 47, at 488 ("the question . . . whether fetuses or profoundly retarded people or animals are equal participants in this social dialogue, with consequent claims to full-fledged substantive entitlements, cannot coherently depend on some a priori application of the notion of equality or dialogue itself. . . . [I]f fetuses speak to me in ways that you cannot hear, that does not mean that your deafness defines the permissible (or the actually present) participants in the dialogue between us. I see three participants and you see two").

111. Burt, *supra* note 109, at 167.

Burt's analysis might be read as casting radical doubt on the very existence of an individuated self. Yet his entire moral enterprise of seeking to assure better medical and life-sustaining treatment, and the psychoanalytic literature on which he relies, favor a less radical reading of him.

Whatever the implications of his analysis, the object-relations account discussed here is consistent with the existence of an individuated self, albeit one with vulnerabilities and potentialities for regression to a more fused state. However, this account dates the beginnings of the individual self at a period substantially after birth, and treats the fused symbiotic relationship as its precondition and the caregiver as a constituent of that self. To the extent that object-relations theory provides a theory for analyzing relationships such as families and groups, as well as individuals, *see, e.g.*, Henry Dicks, *Marital Tensions* (New York: Basic Books, 1967), it nonetheless assumes that healthy adults in relationship have a core self. Thus the language of rights is appropriate for them. *See supra* text following note 31.

112. In addition to the one in the text, four other entirely speculative questions about possible psychological motivations for adopting particular positions in the abortion debate may be noted here.

a. Does the debate discussed in chapter 1 entail such different and incompatible approaches to the fetus and its relationship with the woman in part because our understandings of the "inside and outside" of the body and of the nature of the "other" cannot be taken for granted but are instead achievements of childhood maturation that are heavily burdened with fantasy? Images of one's own body and one's mother's body are especially burdened and enriched. Do those who deny the fetus any sort of meaningful existence until well after birth, and appear to see nothing at all when they "look inside" the woman, seek to avoid self-other quandaries altogether? (Given their approach, they should treat the involvement of women and men in a wanted pregnancy and infant as excessive anticipation of mere potential.) By contrast, for others the "insideness" of the fetus is irrelevant. They see the conceptus—deep within a woman, its bulk mostly from her own ovum, first floating along with other cells that are a part of her, then buried with cells that constitute her womb—as clearly separate, not-her, residing as in some great cavern carved out of her. *See supra* note 17.

b. Is the debate's focus on the fetus either as a person separate from the woman or as almost nothing at all in part a defensive denial of a feared dependence on a woman? For a discussion of the fantasy of being self-made, *see* Erikson, *Dimensions of a New Identity: The 1973 Jefferson Lectures in the Humanities, supra* note 31; *cf.* Sigmund Freud, "A Special Type of Choice of Object Made by Men" (1910), in *Standard Edition*, vol. 11, *supra* note 4, at 163, 173 (referring to boy's "wish to be his own father").

c. Does the effort to prohibit abortion partially express a wish to control the power of women which is experienced as awesome by the small child? Does the contrary deregulatory position seek to deny this fear and simultaneously acquiesce in the demands of the mother-aggressor? Psychoanalysis has alerted us to a general fear of the power of woman. It relates this fear to the adult's denial of his former, absolute fused dependence on his mother, a return to which threatens his ego with annihilation: "[t]he general failure of recognition of absolute dependence at the start contributes to the fear of WOMAN that is the lot of both men and women." D. W. Winnicott, "Primary Maternal Preoccupation," in *Through Paediatrics to Psycho-analysis, supra* note 5, at 304; *cf. supra* note 24 (discussing analyst's anxiety when nearing the symbiotic fused state); Dinnerstein, *supra* note 89 (because infants separate from women under our present cultural arrangements, there is a reservoir of rage against them); Adrienne Rich, *Of Woman Born* (New York: W. W. Norton & Co., 1976), p. 188 ("Somehow her relationship to him is connected with death. Is it simply that in looking at his mother (or any mature women) he is reminded, somewhere beyond repression, of his existence as a mere speck, a weak, blind, clot of flesh growing inside her body? Remembering a time when he was nothing, is he forced to acknowledge a time when he will no longer exist?").

Alice Balint has argued that this general fear of women is exacerbated by the fact of abortion:

> The institution of abortion is a paramount factor in the relation between mother and child. Women all over the world know of artificial abortion, so that it is women who have the final say about the existence or non-existence of a child. (This fact is undoubtedly one of the reasons why the mother appears sometimes so weird and gruesome to the child, whose life depends in the truest sense of the word on whether it pleases her or not.) The undeniable fact of psychogenic sterility points to another fact, namely that *the child who is born is always the child who was wanted by the mother.* Moralizing condemnation or penal prosecution of artificial abortion are probably only defensive measures against the dangerous, absolute power of the woman.

Balint, "Love for the Mother and Mother-Love," *supra* note 11, at 255 (emphasis in original).

One may also wonder whether the totalitarian image that some regulators use to describe a woman's choice is the modern equivalent of more ancient, mythical maternal monsters, and whether behind it is the fear of the awesome mother, experienced by the child as coldly indifferent and awesomely powerful when she acts as a person with her own interests. *See infra* text accompanying chapter 4 note 14; Erikson, *Childhood and Society, supra* note 2, at 338–339 (discussing Hitler's maternal imagery).

d. Does the emphasis that some place upon the innocence of the fetus and newborn, and the privileged status this confers, reflect our adult response to the fused, preambivalent symbiotic stage in which the receptivity of the suckling infant is not yet "contaminated" with its later-developed sadistic and punitive wishes against a separated mother of the subsequent "oral sadistic stage," as classical analysts name it? The absence of ambivalence within the infant sets it apart from most other human beings and permits the fusion which adults, as well as their infants, cherish. *See* Fairbairn, *supra* note 77, at 3, 24 (preambivalence coincides with the pristine ego prior to splitting). *But cf.* Winnicott, "The Sense of Guilt," in *Maturational Processes, supra* note 15, at 22–24 (describing preambivalent infantile love as a ruthless, devouring, totally incorporative love, and noting that the infant does not yet suffer guilt over its ruthlessness).

113. For some data on the prevalence of abortion in other cultures and times, *see, e.g.,* Devereux, *supra* note 31; Richard Feen, "Abortion and Exposure in Ancient Greece," in *Abortion and the Status of the Fetus, supra* note 53, at 283.

For a discussion of psychogenic miscarriage, *see* Deutsch, *supra* note 31, at 188–194; Kaffman, Elezar & Harpaz, "An Epidemic of Spontaneous Abortion: Psychosocial Factors," 19 *Israel J. Psychiatry & Related Stud.* 239 (1982); Hunter et al., *supra* note 97.

114. *See* John Noonan, Jr., *A Private Choice: Abortion in America in the Seventies* (New York: The Free Press, 1979), pp. 38–40; Stone, "Justices As Medical Decision-Makers: Is the Cure Worse than the Disease," 34 *Clev. St. L. Rev.* 579, 580 (1986). The claim that the justices believed that physicians would, after *Roe*, continue to deny abortion to substantial numbers of women appears questionable given the evidence then available from the liberalization of abortion laws in California, *see* Luker, *supra* note 58, at 94 ("By 1971, women in California had abortions because they wanted them, not because physicians agreed they could have them").

115. Only 43 percent of all providers of abortion services perform abortions after twelve weeks gestation LMP; this is up from 33 percent in 1982. Only 32 percent of abortion providers perform abortions after fourteen weeks; 24 percent after sixteen weeks; and 7 percent after twenty weeks. Second trimester abortions are performed by only 13 percent of providers who are private physicians, and only 46 percent of hospital providers. Many providers restrict even first trimester abortions to the first ten weeks (47 percent of private physicians and 20 percent of hospitals), eight weeks (21 percent of physicians and 11 percent of hospitals), or six weeks (4 percent of physicians and 2 percent of hospitals). *See* Henshaw et al., "Abortion Services in the United States, 1984 and 1985," *supra* note 58, at 68–69 & table 7.

The interpersonal process of physician and patient appears to show that many physicians do not experience fetuses in late second trimester abortions as persons, but that the growing similarity of a fetus to the neonate leaves grave distress where the woman's reasons do not seem significant or her response to the interpersonal confrontation is inadequate. *See, e.g.,* Jonathan Imber, *Abortion and the Private Practice of Medicine* (New Haven: Yale University Press, 1986), pp. 77–93; *id.* at 74 (quoting one physician as saying: "It's disgusting pulling out arms and legs"); Denes, *supra* note 98, at 245 ("Abortion is an abomination unless it is experienced as a human event of great sorrow and terrible necessity"); Kaltreider, Goldsmith & Margolis, "The Impact of Midtrimester Abortion Techniques on Patients and Staff," 135 *Am. J. Obstet. & Gynecol.* 235, 236–237 (1979).

116. *See* Planned Parenthood of Mo. v. Danforth, 428 U.S. 52, 65–67 (1976) (upholding requirement that woman evidence consent in writing); *id.* at 67 n.8 (woman must be informed "as to just what would be done and as to its consequences"); *id.* at 67 ("The decision to abort, indeed, is an important, and often a stressful one, and it is desirable and imperative that it be made with full knowledge of its nature and consequences"). For other cases upholding a state's imposition of a general informed consent requirement on abortion-providers, see Bellotti v. Baird (II), 443 U.S. 622, 639 (1979) (requiring parental or judicial involvement to assure as competent a decision as possible by minor); cf. Bellotti v. Baird (I), 428 U.S. 132, 147 (1976) (noting risk that adolescents can not give informed consent).

But as states have increasingly attempted to regulate the dialogue of physician and patient with specific requirements, the Court has carefully scrutinized all efforts to treat abortion in a manner that differs from state regulation of other medical procedures. As a result, it has struck down informed consent regulations that make abortion more costly, less available, and less safe because postponed, or that require the physician to discourage a woman from choosing an abortion.

For example, to prevent increased costs the Court has held that the state may not require that the aborting physician must be the one among a clinic's staff to provide the information necessary for informed consent. The state however may require the physician to verify compliance with consent requirements and may establish standards for abortion counselors. Akron v. Akron Center for Reproductive Health, 462 U.S. 416, 448–49 (1983).

Nor, typically, may a state impose a mandatory twenty-four hour waiting period between the giving of informed consent and the performance of the abortion. The Court found that the defendant government had failed to show that the delay enhanced the quality of the woman's consent or her health. Indeed, a lower court had found that the waiting period increased the cost of an abortion and imposed a higher health risk on the woman because problems in scheduling a second visit postponed many abortions until later in pregnancy. Id. at 449–450. Such waiting periods more heavily burden working women, the young, and those living in rural areas, for all of whom repeated access to medical services may be especially difficult.

Nor may a state "officially structure" the dialogue of woman and physician. Thornburgh v. American College of Obst. & Gyn., 106 S. Ct. 2169, 2180 (1986). Even information that generally is objective and relevant to the abortion decision may not be mandated in such detail as to "place the physician in an undesired, uncomfortable straightjacket" and prevent the tailoring of disclosure to the particular needs and circumstances of each patient. Planned Parenthood of Mo. v. Danforth, 428 U.S. at 67 n.8; see also Akron v. Akron Center for Reproductive Health, 462 U.S. at 445–46. As a result, a state may not in every case mandate the disclosure of "all particular medical risks" of an abortion and of the statement that there may be "detrimental physical and psychological effects" which are not accurately foreseeable. Thornburgh v. American College of Obst. & Gyn., 106 S. Ct. at 2180.

Nor may the state mandate that the physician disclose information or beliefs "designed to influence" or "persuade" the woman to desist from an abortion. The Court's prohibition includes: statements that the "unborn child is a human life from the moment of conception," Akron v. Akron Center for Reproductive Health, 462 U.S. at 444; "dubious" information, such as the assertion that abortion is a "major surgical procedure," *id*; "speculative" information concerning such matters as fetal "pain, perception[s] or response," *id*. at 444 n.34; anatomical and physiological characteristics of the fetus at two week increments, Thornburgh v. American College of Obst. & Gyn., 106 S. Ct. at 2179 ("This is not medical information that is always relevant to the woman's decision, and it may serve only to confuse and punish her and to heighten her anxiety, contrary to accepted medical practice"); facts about adoption and support for women choosing that course; and facts about keeping custody of the child, including information that medical assistance may be available and that the father is financially responsible for the child, *id*. at 2180 (describing this information as irrelevant for therapeutic abortion, "gratuitous" with respect to a rape victim, and "cruel and destructive" of the physician-patient relationship). The state's placement of such specified information in a pamphlet that the physician must offer to the patient does not save the requirement from being "an outright attempt to wedge the Commonwealth's message discouraging abortion into the privacy of the informed-consent dialogue between the woman and her physician." *Id*. at 2179.

(It may be noted that private associations and possibly the state can reach women and men with information and ideas, including anti-abortion ideas, in a multiplicity of contexts outside the doctor-patient relationship.)

Although these decisions may partially reflect a commitment to the egalitarian values of *Roe* and *Doe* (that safe abortion should not only be available to the well-to-do), they, along with most of the Court's abortion decisions, may be usefully analyzed in terms of their impact on the interpersonal dialogue of the pregnant woman and her physician. *See, e.g., infra* text accompanying notes 118–121.

117. Research on informed consent provides some support for the Court's preference for general informed consent standards over detailed regulation. *See* Charles Lidz, Alan Meisel, Eviatar Zerubavel, Mary Carter, Regina Sestak & Loren Roth, *Informed Consent: A Study of Decisionmaking in Psychiatry* (New York: Guilford Press, 1984), p. 323 (studying informed consent to psychiatric treatment); *id*. at 324 ("another barrier to the informed consent doctrine is inherent in the mechanisms chosen to implement that doctrine. . . . [I]t was in the setting most governed by [state] . . . regulations . . . that informed consent worked least well. . . . [T]here were less disclosure (or disclosure more perfunctorily performed), less comprehension by patients, more reliance on form than on substance, and more pressures placed on patients to make the 'right' decisions"); *cf.* Jay Katz, *The Silent World of Doctor and Patient* (New York: The Free Press, 1984) (describing process of informed consent as depending on personal dialogue).

118. With respect to the law of parental consent, *see* Planned Parenthood Ass'n v. Ashcroft, 462 U.S. at 490–93 (opinion by Powell, J., joined by Burger, C.J.); *id.* at 503–04 (Blackmun, J., dissenting); Akron v. Akron Center for Reproductive Health, 462 U.S. at 439–42; Bellotti v. Baird (II), 443 U.S at 637–39 (Powell, J., plurality op.); Planned Parenthood of Mo. v. Danforth, 428 U.S. at 72–75; *id.* at 90–91 (Stewart, J., concurring); *cf.* Bellotti v. Baird (I), 428 U.S. 132 (1976).

These cases provide that a state may require an immature minor to obtain consent for an abortion from either her parents or from a state-sponsored decision maker, provided that each is constrained to act in the minor's best interests. To prevent an absolute parental veto, the Court insisted that the state provide an alternative state-sponsored decision maker, whether of a judicial or administrative nature, who would make a determination of:

    a. whether the minor is emancipated or otherwise mature and thus entitled to give consent without parental veto or notice; or, if not,

    b. whether an abortion is nonetheless in her best interest and parental notice is not, in which case the state decision maker must authorize an abortion and withhold notice.

The Court justified the allocation of this qualified veto to parents or the state by: the special vulnerability of minors and their lack of decisional competence; the state interest in assuring that the minor reaches an informed decision; and the state interest in protecting, and its duty to respect, traditional parental authority over and responsibility for children. The state's interest in aiding the minor's decisional competence overlaps, for practical reasons, its interest in deferring to parents; for parental involvement is the "traditional way by which States have sought to protect children from their own immature and improvident decisions." Planned Parenthood of Mo. v. Danforth, 428 U.S. at 95 (White, J., concurring in part and dissenting in part). The process of assuring wise decisions for children, "in large part, is beyond the competence of impersonal political institutions," especially with respect to a decision that by its nature is so personal and private. Bellotti v. Baird (II), 443 U.S. at 638 (Powell, J., plurality op.). Indeed,

> affirmative sponsorship of particular ethical, religious or political beliefs is something we expect the State *not* to attempt in a society constitutionally committed to the ideal of individual liberty and freedom of choice. Thus "It is cardinal with us that the custody, care and nurture of the child reside first in the parents, whose primary function and freedom include *preparation for obligations the state can neither supply nor hinder.*"

Id. (emphasis in original) (quoting Prince v. Massachusetts, 321 U.S. 158, 166 (1944)). *But cf.* Burt, "The Constitution of the Family," *supra* note 110, at 337–340 (interpreting Burger Court's decisions on the family as reinforcing state authority over children).

The Court addressed the issue of notice, as distinguished from consent, in the procedurally troubled case of *H.L. v. Matheson*, 450 U.S. 398 (1981). It held that a state could require a physician to use reasonable efforts to notify one or both parents, prior to performing a nonemergency abortion on an unemancipated and immature minor, provided that such notification was not contrary to the minor's best interests. Although the plaintiff in that case purported to represent a class of all pregnant minors, the Court found she lacked standing to assert the rights of the following classes: minors who were emancipated (those whom by virtue of marriage, childbirth, court declaration, and the like, state law treats as emancipated); minors who were mature (that is, capable of giving informed consent by virtue of having the capacity to comprehend and intelligently make an abortion decision); and minors whose best interests would have been injured by virtue of adverse parental reaction to notice. Accordingly, the Court appeared to reserve decision with respect to these other classes of minors. *Id.* at 406–07.

Subsequently the Court has assumed that it is settled law that notice cannot be required in the case of a mature or emancipated minor. Akron v. Akron Center for Reproductive Health, 462 U.S. at 441 n.31; *cf.* H.L. v. Matheson, 450 U.S. at 420 (Powell, J., concurring); *id.* at 428 n.3 (Marshall, J., dissenting); Bellotti v. Baird (II), 443 U.S. at 647 (Powell, J., plurality op.) (a court may decline to give consent to an immature minor until it notifies and consults with parents, should it find such consultation in the child's best interests). *But see* Akron v. Akron Center for Reproductive Health, 462 U.S. at 469 n.12 (O'Connor, J., dissenting) (denying that Court has reached the notice issue).

The Court has been closely split on the matter of parental consent and notice. At present four Justices, Blackmun, Brennan, Marshall, and Stevens, would prohibit all consent requirements that permit an absolute parental or judicial veto, as an impermissible intrusion on the minor's privacy with respect to a decision whose consequences she bears most directly. Planned Parenthood Ass'n v. Ashcroft, 462 U.S. at 503–04 (Blackmun, J., dissenting). Others would allow more parental involvement than the Court now permits. Because the vote of Justice Powell, now retired, has been necessary to constitute a majority, his position has governed: it permits a state to mandate parental involvement provided that an alternative state procedure exists by which involvement may be avoided in certain circumstances.

In practice, the burdens of the alternative state-administered consent process may encourage some minors to endure parental notice rather than seek a state-sponsored alternative, to desist from seeking an abortion, to seek an illegal abortion, or to travel to a jurisdiction without such requirements. For a study of the implementation of the Massachusetts parental consent requirement, *see* Robert Mnookin, "*Bellotti v Baird*: A Hard Case," in *In the Interest of Children: Advocacy, Law Reform, and Public Policy*, ed. Robert Mnookin (New York: W. H. Freeman & Co., 1985), p. 149.

119. Reasons for not requiring notice even to a father who has evidenced by his actions a willingness to maintain a family with the pregnant woman include: substantial difficulties in enforcing the requirement, because the physician would necessarily have to rely on the woman to determine whether there is such a male; the extent of male violence against women; male desertion of women because of pregnancy; the interest in preserving families intact by minimizing conflict; the female's interest in her own bodily autonomy and privacy; and the male's interest in informational privacy.

When the pregnancy does not occur within an ongoing relationship with the father, then dialogue with him would be of no benefit. Establishing and enforcing a standard for distinguishing between the male who is both father of the fetus and in a substantial relationship with the woman from the male who meets neither requirement would be very difficult.

120. Planned Parenthood of Mo. v. Danforth, 428 U.S. at 67–72 (striking down law permitting spousal veto).

For lower court cases addressing spousal notice, *see* Planned Parenthood of Rhode Island v. Board of Medical Review, 598 F. Supp. 625, (D.R.I. 1984) (Pettine, J.); Scheinberg v. Smith, 550 F. Supp. 1112 (S.D. Fl. 1982), *on remand from* 659 F.2d 476 (5th Cir. 1981); *cf.* Doe v Deschamps, 461 F. Supp. 682, 686 (D. Mont. 1976).

121. The Court has recognized that the requirements of due process may be satisfied by informal dialogue between two persons. *See, e.g.,* Goss v. Lopez, 419 U.S. 565 (1975) (mandating dialogue between student and school disciplinarian prior to certain punishments); *cf.* Bellotti v. Baird (II), 443 U.S. at 643 n.22 (noting with respect to minors seeking a state alternative to parental consent that "much can be said for employing procedures and a forum less formal than those associated with a court of general jurisdiction").

Such informal procedures serve, among other purposes, to protect the woman's interest in informational privacy in making a procreative choice, an interest that the Court has repeatedly stressed. *See, e.g.,* Thornburgh v. American College of Obst. & Gyn., 106 S. Ct. at 2178–84; Planned Parenthood of Mo. v. Danforth, 428 U.S. at 80 ("Recordkeeping and reporting requirements that are reasonably directed to the preservation of maternal health and that properly respect a patient's confidentiality and privacy are permissible"); *see also* H.L. v. Matheson, 450 U.S. at 437–38 (Marshall, J., dissenting) (notice to parents "effectively cancels her right to avoid disclosure," "publicizes her private consultation with her doctor and interjects additional parties in the very conference held confidential in *Roe"*); Bellotti v. Baird (II), 443 U.S. at 655 (Stevens, J., concurring).

122. The Court has prevented the states from inhibiting the growth of abortion clinics in several ways. Most important is its holding that states may not require that abortions be performed solely in hospitals prior to the sixteenth week LMP. Akron v. Akron Center for Reproductive Health, 462 U.S. at 434–39; Doe v. Bolton, 410 U.S. at 193–95.

Other decisions have helped clinics keep their costs low by striking down costly state regulations. For example, the Court struck down a requirement that the physician rather than her agent (such as an abortion counselor) provide the information needed for informed consent. Akron v. Akron Center for Reproductive Health, 462 U.S. at 470–71; *supra* note 116 (concerning the relationship of the Court's holdings on informed consent and clinics). For other costly regulations that have been stuck down, *see supra* chapter 1 note 52.

Such holdings as these have protected the provision of low-cost abortions, as the medical profession organized a substantial portion of the delivery of such services through clinics. *See* Imber, *supra* note 115, at 69–70 (while many abortions are performed by gynecologists as part of their private practice for women with whom they have an ongoing professional relationship, substantial numbers are performed in clinics that have intermittent patient contact).

The Court protected the establishment of such clinics to protect the equal opportunity of women who are not well-to-do to exercise the right of procreative choice that *Roe* recognized, although doing so undercut its initial assumption that an abortion decision would be made in the context of an ongoing doctor-patient relationship. The following description by the Court of a clinical encounter illustrates this initial assumption:

> [T]he obstetrician . . . is concerned with the physical and mental welfare, the woes, the emotions, and the concern of his female patients. He, perhaps more than anyone else, is knowledgeable in this area of patient care, and he is aware of human frailty, so-called "error," and needs. The good physician . . . will have sympathy and understanding for the pregnant patient that probably are not exceeded by those who participate in other areas of professional counseling.

Doe v. Bolton, 410 U.S. at 196–97 (companion case to *Roe*).

Moreover, the Court has protected the establishment of low-cost clinics although at least some justices believe that such clinics do not adequately meet their informed consent obligations and in fact lead to the abortion decision being a solitary and private choice. *See, e.g.,* Planned Parenthood of Mo. v. Danforth, 428 U.S. at 91 & n.2 (Stewart, J., concurring) ("It seems unlikely that . . . [the pregnant minor] will obtain adequate counsel and support from the attending physician at an abortion clinic"); Bellotti v. Baird (II), 443 U.S. at 641 n.21; H.L. v. Matheson, 450 U.S. at 420 n.8 (Powell, J., concurring) (at urban clinics, abortions may be obtained "on demand"); Singleton v. Wulff, 428 U.S. 106, 130 n.7 (1976) (Powell, J., concurring in part and dissenting in part) (deriding description of physician-patient relationship as a "confidential one" because an abortion case "often is set in an assembly-line type abortion clinic"). Indeed, the perception that, as a consequence of *Roe*, the woman has become the sole decision maker appears to have led Chief Justice Burger to indicate, shortly before he retired, that he would be prepared to reconsider *Roe*. *See* Thornburgh v. American College of Obst. & Gyn., 106 S. Ct. at 2190 (Burger, C.J., dissenting) ("every member of the *Roe* Court rejected the idea of abortion on demand").

It should be noted that nonlegal factors may also contribute to an impairment of the informed consent process, especially in clinics. Technological developments in medicine may diminish the importance of the physician-patient relationship in the view of the physician. Other changes which turn many physicians from professionals into carefully regulated employees or into entrepreneurs whose overhead requires high volume may also undermine dialogue. *See* Executive Board of The American College of Obstetricians and Gynecologists, *Statement of Policy: Further Ethical Considerations in Induced Abortion* (December 1977), p. 2 ("there may be a tendency for the physician to act solely as a technician. Such action denies the physician's traditional role in utilizing medical and ethical judgment as a counselor and advisor. Physicians have an ethical responsibility to assure quality counseling is provided"). Other critics, who may accept the professional nature of medical decision making, instead discount the importance of doctor-patient dialogue by asserting that physicians make medical decisions by paternalistic fiat rather than through dialogue.

123. The threat of malpractice tort actions should help to assure that counseling leads to an adequately informed consent and to an appropriate interpersonal process. There appear to be few reported malpractice cases. However, antiabortion groups include women who assert that they were pressured into having abortions and not informed about the potential severe negative sequelae which they have endured.

124. Recent psychologies of women place primary emphasis upon the feminine capacity and inclination to think in relational terms and to make moral choices in light of the ethical imperatives of relationship. *See, e.g,* Carol Gilligan, *In a Different Voice: Psychological Theory and Women's Development* (Cambridge, MA: Harvard University Press, 1982), pp. 75–150 (discussing the manner in which the interviewed women reached abortion decisions); *id.* at 76 (quoting a subject: "I started feeling really good about being pregnant instead of feeling really bad, because I wasn't looking at the situation realistically. I was looking at it from my own sort of selfish needs, because I was lonely. Things weren't really going good for me, so I was looking at it that I could have a baby that I could take care of or something that was part of me, and that made me feel good. But I wasn't looking at the realistic side, at the responsibility I would have to take on"); *id.* at 77 (quoting a subject: "What I want to do is to have the baby, but what I feel I should do, which is what I need to do, is have an abortion right now, because sometimes what you want isn't right. Sometimes what is necessary comes before what you want, because it might not always lead to the right thing"); *id.* at 78 (quoting a subject: "I think you have to think about the people who are involved, including yourself"); *id.* at 92 (quoting a subject: "I don't need to pay off my imaginary debts to the world through this child, and I don't think that it is right to bring a child into the world and use it for that purpose"); *id.* at 117 ("her thinking is complicated by the fact that what seems the 'responsible thing to do,' namely paying for one's mistakes by having the child, suddenly appears also to be 'selfish,'—bringing a child into the world 'to assuage my guilt.' Given these apparent contradictions, she is unable to find the good or self-sacrificing solution, since either way she can construe her actions as serving not only others but also herself").

For additional evidence of such other-regarding decision making, *see* Friedlander, Kaul & Stimel, "Abortion: Predicting the Complexity of the Decision-Making Process," 9 *Women & Health* 43, 51 (1984) (finding that women engage in a more complex and lengthy decision-making process when they are in a stable relationship with a partner).

Burt conceptualizes an essential quality of the inner dialogue Gilligan describes when he argues that rigid conceptions of self and other fail to take into account that the caretaking self is dependent upon and defined by the dependent other; and that the needs and interests of the dependent self cannot but be affected by its caretaker. *See supra* notes 109–110.

125. *See* Theodore Lidz, "Reflections of a Psychiatrist," in *Therapeutic Abortion*, ed. Harold Rosen (New York: Julian Press, 1954), pp. 276, 279 (noting that a great many women have abortions with great relief and with little if any subsequent disturbance, but stating that "the fetus is an integral part of themselves, and removal . . . can be felt as a serious assault upon the integrity of the body and a tremendous threat to the integrity of the ego"); David Wilson, "The Abortion Problem in the General Hospital," in *Therapeutic Abortion, supra*, at 189, 196 ("the woman who experiences an abortion, whether therapeutic or criminal, is traumatized by the act to such a degree that the memory becomes a potent factor in her future behavior pattern"); May Romm, "Psychoanalytic Considerations," in *Therapeutic Abortion, supra*, at 209, 209 ("Therapeutic abortion, except in emergency situations, should be considered as the treatment of choice only after the personality of the patient has been studied and evaluated, so that the abortion itself may not prove more dangerous . . . than the psychological traumata of pregnancy and childbirth"); Flanders Dunbar, "A Psychosomatic Approach to Abortion and the Abortion Habit," in *Therapeutic Abortion, supra*, at 22; Calef, "The Hostility of Parents to Children: Some Notes on Infertility, Child Abuse, and Abortion," 1(1) *Int'l J. Psychoanalytic Psychotherapy* 76 (1972); Ney, "A Consideration of Abortion Survivors," 13 *Child Psychiatry & Human Development* 168 (1983) (hypothesizing without data: that unresolved guilt from a prior abortion impedes a woman's bonding with a child carried to term and increases that child's risk of abuse; and that children are preconsciously aware that their mothers have aborted potential siblings and egocentrically assume responsibility with consequent survivor guilt and with fear of a similar fate should they cease to please their parents); *cf.* Feder, *supra* note 54, at 167 ("Parents who questioned their children's rights for survival will breed children who will in turn question the parents' right to survive"). *See generally* Potts et al., *supra* note 54, at 178; Betty Sarvis & Hyman Rodman, *The Abortion Controversy* (New York: Columbia University Press, 1973), pp. 102–106; Callahan, *supra* note 56, at 48–90; Roberta Kalmar, ed., *Abortion: The Emotional Implications* (Dubuque: Kendall/Hunt Publishing Co., 1977).

Interestingly, the psychiatric literature emphasized more the self-destructive aspects of abortion prior to the legalization of elective abortion. *Cf.* David, *supra* note 59, at 151; Baluk & O'Neil, "Health Professionals' Perceptions of the Psychological Consequences of Abortion," 8 *Am. J. Community Psychology* 67 (1980); Fingerer, "Psychological Sequelae of Abortion: Anxiety and Depression," 1 *J. Community Psychology* 221 (1973) (finding that women report less stress from abortion than graduate students applying psychoanalytic theory predict they will experience).

126. *See, e.g.,* Janet Mattinson, "The Effects of Abortion on a Marriage," in *Abortion: Medical Progress and Social Implications, supra* note 54, at 165, 168; "Discussion," *id.* at 173, 174; Kumar & Robson, "Previous Induced Abortion and Ante-Natal Depression in Primiparae: Preliminary Report of a Survey of Mental Health in Pregnancy," 8 *Psychological Medicine* 711, 714 (1978) (hypothesizing that a prior abortion had been incompletely mourned only in the small subsample of women who, during a subsequent pregnancy to term, experienced increased depression and anxiety about the health of the fetus carried to term, and guilt and fear of retribution because of the prior abortion) (recommending that women be encouraged to confront and work through guilt or remorse attendant on abortion); Cavenar, Maltbie & Sullivan, "Aftermath of Abortion: Anniversary Depression and Abdominal Pain," 42 *Bull. Menninger Clinic* 433 (1978) (reporting symptoms of abdominal pain and nausea in one case and depression, crying spells, and suicidal ideation in another where prior abortion had not been mourned; but brief psychotherapy led to remission and insight into preexisting interpersonal difficulties with fathers of aborted fetuses) (reaction may occur on an anniversary of an abortion or on an anniversary of when fetus would have been born).

127. Adler, "Abortion: A Social-Psychological Perspective," 35 *J. Social Issues* 100 (1979) (review article); Da Silva & Johnstone, "A Follow-Up Study of Severe Puerperal Psychiatric Illness," 139 *British J. Psychiatry* 346, 353 (1981) (two of the three psychoses that followed abortion, in the studied group of pregnant women, occurred in woman who had become psychotic after childbirth as well); Brewer, "Post-Abortion Psychosis," in *Mental Illness in Pregnancy and the Puerperium,* ed. Merton Sandler (Oxford: Oxford University Press, 1978), p. 52; Belsey, Greer, Lal, Lewis & Beard, "Predictive Factors in Emotional Response to Abortion: King's Termination Study-IV," 11 *Soc. Sci. & Medicine* 71, 80–81 (1977); Brewer, "Incidence of Post-Abortion Psychosis: A Prospective Study," 1 *British Medical J.* 476, 477 (1977) (calculating incidence of postabortion psychosis at 0.3 per 1000 terminations and the incidence of psychosis following childbirth at 1.7 per 1000 deliveries; with the one woman actually suffering a postabortion psychosis having suffered two prior postpartum psychoses); Lask, "Short-term Psychiatric Sequelae to Therapeutic Termination of Pregnancy," 126 *British J. Psychiatry* 173, 174 (1975); Ewing & Rouse, "Therapeutic Abortion and a Prior Psychiatric History," 130 *Am. J. Psychiatry* 37 (1973) (finding that majority reported relief following abortion, without major psychiatric symptoms, but those women with prior psychiatric illness reported more symptoms, ambivalence, and regret than the others in sample); Simon, Senturia & Rothman, "Psychiatric Illness Following Therapeutic Abortion," 124 *Am. J. Psychiatry* 59, 65 (1967).

Even among women at risk for experiencing an unusually severe reaction, negative effects tend to dissipate in the half-year following an abortion and do not preclude a net sense of satisfaction with the decision. Payne, Kravitz, Notman & Anderson, "Outcome Following Therapeutic Abortion," 33 *Arch. General Psychiatry* 725, 733 (1976).

By contrast, the negative consequences of giving birth and caring for an unwanted child appear to be more long-lasting, although comparisons are difficult and the evidence is somewhat contradictory for certain subgroups of aborting women. For example, in a sample of thirty women refused a therapeutic abortion, approximately one-third still regretted having the baby one year later and acknowledged feelings of resentment toward the child. Pare & Raven, "Follow-up of Patients Referred for Termination of Pregnancy," 1970 *Lancet* I:635, 636. In another followup of women denied abortion, Visram reported that roughly half of the seventy-three who gave birth had not adjusted well after more than one year. Visram, "A Follow-up Study of 95 Women Who Were Refused Abortion on Psychiatric Grounds," in *Proceedings of Third International Congress of Psychosomatic Medicine in Obstetrics & Gynaecology, London, 1971,* ed. Norman Morris (Basel, Switzerland: Karger, 1972). *But see* David, *supra* note 59, at 155 (finding that among never-married and married women in Denmark, rates of psychiatric hospital admission were the same postabortion and postbirth; but that rate of admission was much higher postabortion for women who were separated, divorced, or widowed; and hypothesizing that many of these aborted pregnancies had been pregnancies desired by women who then lost important social support and an important love relationship); David, Rasmussen & Holst, "Postpartum and Postabortion Psychotic Reactions," 13 *Family Planning Perspectives* 88, 89–91 (1981) (finding higher rates of psychiatric admission for Danish women receiving abortions than for those giving birth, with the difference largely contributed by women seeking abortions after the dissolution of a love relationship); Grimes, *supra* note 59, at 263 (noting very small number of possible postabortion suicides); Handy, "Psychological and Social Aspects of Induced Abortion," 21 *British J. Clinical Psychology* 29 (1982); Hamill & Ingram, "Psychiatric and Social Factors in the Abortion Decision," 1 *British Medical J.* 229, 230–231 (1974) (four cases of psychiatric sequelae among eighty-four women receiving abortions; three cases of depressive reaction among forty-eight women refused abortion, two of which were precipitated by relinquishment of child for adoption).

128. For evidence concerning the capacity of a woman to integrate an abortion without self-destructive sequelae, *see* Richard Schwartz, "Abortion on Request: The Psychiatric Implications," in *Abortion, Medicine and Law*, ed. J. Douglas Butler & David Walbert (New York: Facts on File Publications, 1986), p. 323; Lazarus, "Psychiatric Sequelae of Legalized Elective First Trimester Abortion," 4 *J. Psychosomatic Obstet. & Gynaecol.* 141, 147–148 (1985); Adler, *supra* note 127; Nadelson, "The Emotional Impact of Abortion," in *The Woman Patient: Medical and Psychological Interfaces*, vol. 1, *Sexual and Reproductive Aspects of Women's Health Care*, ed. Malkah Notman & Carol Nadelson (New York: Plenum Press, 1978), p. 173; Brewer, *supra* note 60; Payne et al., *supra* note 127 (aborting women show pattern of crisis and resolution with relief or normal mourning, but not pathological grief); Greer, Lal, Lewis, Belsey & Beard, "Psychosocial Consequences of Therapeutic Abortion: King's Termination Study-III," 128 *British J. Psychiatry* 74, 78–79 (1976); Osofsky & Osofsky, "The Psychological Reaction of Patients to Legalized Abortion," 42 *Am. J. Orthopsychiatry* 48, 57 (1972); Ford, Castelnuovo-Tedesco & Long, "Abortion: Is It a Therapeutic Procedure in Psychiatry?," 218 *JAMA* 1173 (1971) (postabortion psychiatric symptoms remit for all but psychotic women); Patt, Rappaport & Barglow, "Follow-Up of Therapeutic Abortion," 20 *Arch. General Psychiatry* 408, 412–413 (1969) (despite sadomasochistic aspects of pregnancy-abortion sequence, most women in psychiatric group improved or stabilized); Kretzschmar & Norris, "Psychiatric Implications of Therapeutic Abortion," 98 *Am. J. Obstet. & Gyn.* 368, 370 (1967); Peck & Marcus, "Psychiatric Sequelae of Therapeutic Interruption of Pregnancy," 143 *J. Nervous & Mental Disease* 417, 423–424 (1966); *cf.* Luker, *supra* note 58, at 66–91 (prior to *Roe*, among physicians, psychiatrists often advocated legalization of abortion and made it more available to women by certifying that their mental health was in jeopardy).

Those few studies which have considered adolescents separately suggest that serious, long-term psychiatric complications are also rare for this younger group, although adolescents appear to have more negative responses than adults. This may be partially related to delay in seeking an abortion. *See* Nancy Adler & Peggy Dolcini, "Psychological Issues in Abortion for Adolescents," in *Adolescent Abortion: Psychological and Legal Issues*, ed. Gary Melton & Lois Weithorn (Lincoln: University of Nebraska Press, 1986), pp. 74, 83–92; Olson, "Social and Psychological Correlates of Pregnancy Resolution Among Adolescent Women," 50 *Am. J. Orthopsychiatry* 432 (1980); Perez-Reyes & Falk, "Follow-Up After Therapeutic Abortion in Early Adolescence," 28 *Arch. General Psychiatry* 120, 123 (1973). *But see* Wallerstein, Kurtz & Bar-Din, "Psychosocial Sequelae of Therapeutic Abortion in Young Unmarried Women," 27 *Arch. General Psychiatry* 828, 831 (1972) (finding that half of sample of young women showed a decline in psychosocial functioning in the six months following abortion; but noting their small sample size of 22 and the high rate of nonresponse, 92 of 114, as potentially skewing results).

Of course, unpleasant feelings may be associated with an abortion for some period of time. *See, e.g.*, Freeman, "Abortion: Subjective Attitudes and Feelings," 10 *Family Planning Perspectives* 150, 153 (1978) (finding that roughly 42 percent of 106 women had not resolved negative feelings concerning abortion at four-month followup, with lack of support from male partner a related factor).

The abortion decision may be a "crisis," in the Eriksonian sense of a turning point in psychological development that can have either integrative and maturing results, or the opposite. The evidence that the abortion decision is a painful one with feelings of loss that may persist for some period, even years, is not evidence that abortion is psychologically destructive. Pain, loss, and often guilt are part of any significant choice, for no important choice can be made without loss of something emotionally significant.

One relevant type of evidence with respect to its maturational consequences would be increased contraceptive use following an abortion. While the evidence is not as encouraging as one would hope, it is clear that the experience of abortion often leads to improved contraceptive responsibility. *See* Howe, Kaplan & English, "Repeat Abortions: Blaming the Victims," 69 *Am. J. Public Health* 1242, 1243–1244 (1979) (approximately one-half of sample of 255 women seeking repeat abortions were contracepting as compared to approximately one-third of those seeking a first abortion; and the repeaters were twice as likely to have been using more effective forms of contraception); Freeman, *supra* note 128; Beard, Belsey, Lal, Lewis & Greer, "King's Termination Study II: Contraceptive Practice Before and After Outpatient Termination of Pregnancy," 1 *British Medical J.* 418, 420 (1974); Bracken, Hachamovitch

& Grossman, "Correlates of Repeat Induced Abortions," 40 *Obstet. & Gynecol.* 816, 823 (1972) (repeaters more likely to have been using contraception at time of conception).

129. *See* Frederick Jaffe, Barbara Lindheim & Philip Lee, *Abortion Politics* (New York: McGraw-Hill Book Co., 1981), pp. 31–35.

In 1985, 60 percent of abortions occurred in abortion clinics, 23 percent in other free-standing clinics such as surgical centers, 13 percent in hospitals, and 4 percent in private physicians' offices. *See* Henshaw, et al., "Abortion Services in the United States, 1984 and 1985," *supra* note 58, at 67 table 5.

130. For reasons to be indicated in the text, the efforts of philosophers to apply the golden rule or categorical imperative to the problem of abortion—*see, e.g.*, Hare, "Abortion and the Golden Rule," 5 *Phil. & Pub. Aff.* 201, 207–208 (1975); *cf.* Alisdair MacIntyre, *After Virtue* (Notre Dame: University of Notre Dame Press, 1981), p. 7—are problematic. *See* Quinn, "Abortion: Identity and Loss," 13 *Phil. & Pub. Aff.* 24, 52 n.31 (1984) (arguing that the morality of benevolence governs abortion because the morality of respect is meaningless in the case of a fetus which lacks a will to respect; and asserting that a "future retrospective" view of the will of the fetus does not succeed in creating a morality of respect); *cf.* Harrison, *supra* note 49, at 256–257 (discussing query, "Would you have wanted your mother to abort you?"). In a more abstract version of the golden-rule dialogue, one could imagine persons in the Rawlsian original fetal position. This approach has been used to inquire into views about abortion prior to gender assignment. *Id.* at 44–45. But inquiry into a person's views prior to his potential assignment to the class of abortuses will be no more fruitful or conclusive than the golden-rule approach.

131. The difficulty in recreating a conversation with the fetus may in part relate to the problem of using ordinary language for this task. As Balint once noted, psychoanalysis needed to develop a more adequate language for describing preverbal experiences in order to understand them. Because words cease to be reliable means of communication in the area of the basic fault, interpretation fails to cure and leads to a "confusion of tongues," with resulting therapeutic difficulty. Rather, Balint noted, stability, protection, and witnessing are essential. The analyst must become like a basic element such as air: essential, indestructible, all pervasive, and utterly taken for granted. *See* Balint, *supra* note 10, at 29 (referring to "comparative uselessness of adult language").

The difficulty in recreating a conversation probably does not arise from the fact that adults are survivors, unlike the abortus. Empathy with a person at risk of death, although painful, is certainly possible.

The imagined conversations that a pregnant woman does have with her fetus can play an important internal role in preparing for the mother-infant relationship, but such conversations are unique to each parent. They consist in part of inner dialogues with one's own parents, with one's self at various stages of one's past, and, to use a technical psychoanalytic term, with one's inner-objects. Of course, such dialogues may differ markedly among women of different classes, cultures, marital status, and age. A woman who has borne several children may speak differently from one who is pregnant for the first time.

132. For the natural tendency of different persons to hear different sounds, *see* Sigmund Freud, "The Dynamics of Transference" (1912), in *Standard Edition*, vol. 12, *supra* note 4, at 99.

The attempt to construct an imaginary dialogue requires caution to avoid projecting onto the fetus feelings from a much later stage of development. Might not the feelings which some associate with an anonymous fetus relate to the feelings of vulnerability, anxiety, and anger associated with the later struggle to maintain a newly discovered separate existence from the mother? *Cf. supra* note 17.

For a compelling if tenuous example of one who hears screams, *see* Virgil, *The Aeneid*, book VI, trans. Robert Fitzgerald (New York: Random House, 1983), p. 174 ("Now voices crying loud were heard at once—/The souls of infants wailing. At the door/Of the sweet life they were to have no part in/Torn from the breast, a black day took them off/And drowned them all in bitter death").

133. *See* T. S. Eliot, "The Love Song of J. Alfred Prufrock," in *The Complete Poems and Plays* (New York: Harcourt, Brace & World, 1962), pp. 3, 4–5 ("Do I dare disturb the universe?/ . . . So how should I presume?/ . . . And how should I presume?/ . . . And should I then presume?"). These questions, as applied to the present matter, involve us in an elemental form of guilt: separate existence apart from the mother.

134. The woman has been called a "representative" of the dyad in this chapter, thus drawing upon legal and political concepts that imply the existence of interests capable of being represented. She may also be treated as the "interpreter" of the dyad, and enjoy a privileged status as its interpreter. For it is through dyadic and family relationships that meaning for the infant develops: what the infant means and who he is come to exist.

For one autobiographical account of the way parents afford meaning to their children, consider the description of the writer Joseph Brodsky, comparing the meaning of his life as a child with the meaning he has made for himself as an adult. The adult, he writes, is concerned with

> manufacturing his own reality. . . . [W]hen the new reality is mastered . . . he . . . learns that the old nest is gone. . . . [But he discovers] the reality of his own manufacture . . . is less valid than the reality of his abandoned nest. . . . Because it was built by *others*, by those who gave him life, and not by him who knows only too well the true worth of his own labor, who, as it were, just *uses* the given life. . . . Yet for all his skill, he'll never be able to reconstruct that primitive, sturdy nest that heard

his first cry of life. Nor will he be able to reconstruct those who put him
there. An effect, he can't reconstruct his cause.

Brodsky, "In a Room and a Half," 33(3) *New York Review of Books* 40, 44
(February 27, 1986).

4. CODA: COMMUNAL ATTACHMENTS

1. *Cf.* California Federal Savings & Loan Ass'n v. Guerra, 107 S. Ct.
683 (1987); Littleton, "Reconstructing Sexual Equality," 75(4) *Calif. L.
Rev* (July 1987) (forthcoming).

2. Ronald Reagan, *Abortion and the Conscience of the Nation* (Nashville, TN: Thomas Nelson, 1984). As noted at the outset, Noonan repeats
these analogies, in far more sophisticated form, as do many others opposed to abortion-choice. *See supra* Introduction note 4.

3. One appealing to the natural order might argue that once an individual surrenders to sexual union, he cannot interrupt the phylo-
genetic processes without undermining a more natural order—whether
it be called sociobiological, instinctual, communal, or religious. That
person might further suggest that such undermining may operate on
the unconscious of women, men, and children to create a sense of vulnerability and hostility, and otherwise weaken the affective bonds of society. *See supra* chapter 3 note 125. This point of view might also claim
that the process of demystification is not readily reversible, so that respect for children and for life generally depends on maintaining a sacred attitude to all beings that resemble persons and to the procreative
process, regardless of logical discussions about personhood and regardless of a society's actual practices regarding life and death. *Cf.*
Jerome Kagan, *The Nature of the Child* (New York: Basic Books, 1984),
pp. 121–122, 149 (distinguishing between moral standards maintained
by strong affect of guilt and fear and mere social convention).

While we have again learned in this generation that caution in interfering with biological processes is appropriate in many cases, there
is evidence that warrants not accepting any simple claim about abortion and the natural order. For example, the abundance, variety, and
functions of the human sexual drive suggest that procreation is not the
only component of its nature. Certainly, only a few would deny a woman
autonomous control over reproduction through either chastity or contraception. Also, abortion has been around for such a long time and
ranges through so many cultures that it may be accepted as a fact of
female reproductive behavior that is socially institutionalized. *See*
George Devereux, *A Study of Abortion in Primitive Societies: A typological, distributional, and dynamic analysis of the prevention of birth in 400
preindustrial societies*, rev. ed. (New York: International Universities
Press, 1976). Moreover, modern societies such as Japan and Scandi-
navia that differ substantially with respect to the importance of tradi-

tion and social solidarity have allowed abortion-choice and removed some of the social controls that have characterized other cultures. Finally, psychological studies of women—although of limited duration—suggest that abortion is not incompatible with either mental health or healthy family and reproductive lives.

4. *See, e.g.,* Kommers, "Liberty and Community in Constitutional Law: The Abortion Cases in Comparative Perspective," 1985 *B.Y.U.L. Rev.* 371 (describing the decision of the West German Federal Constitutional Court striking down legislative abortion deregulation as valuing "community" more than "liberty," which the U.S. Supreme Court "overvalued" in *Roe*); Sidney Callahan, "The Impact of Religious Beliefs on Attitudes Toward Abortion," in *Defining Human Life: Medical, Legal, and Ethical Considerations,* ed. Margery Shaw & A. Edward Doudera (Ann Arbor, MI: AUPHA Press, 1983), pp. 279–291; Rice, "Overriding *Roe v. Wade*: An Analysis of the Proposed Constitutional Amendments," 15 *B.C. Indus. & Com. L. Rev.* 307, 340 (1973); *cf.* Schneider, "Moral Discourse and the Transformation of American Family Law," 83 *Mich. L. Rev.* 1803 (1985) (treating *Roe* as a paradigmatic case of a liberal, individualistic mentality in family law that has forsaken any effort to develop a common language of moral discourse based on a shared community of values and sense of mutual obligation).

A different argument comes from those who criticize *Roe* on constitutional grounds. They see it as injuring the interests of the majority in regulating its affairs and as a judicial intrusion on democratic politics unwarranted by constitutional text, structure, or history. This is a claim not on behalf of some larger communal order but rather on behalf of a particular transient majority, an aggregation of individuals. These constitutional critiques address the role of the Court and not the place of abortion in a democratic society. From this constitutional perspective, deregulation of abortion by the legislature would be as appropriate and valid an exercise of legislative power as regulation. As Justice White has said: "[I]t seems apparent to me that a free, egalitarian, and democratic society does not presuppose any particular rule or set of rules with respect to abortion." Thornburgh v. American College of Obst. & Gyn., 106 S. Ct. 2169, 2196 (1986) (White, J., dissenting). *See generally* Ely, "The Wages of Crying Wolf: A Comment on *Roe v. Wade*," 82 *Yale L.J.* 920 (1973); John Ely, *Democracy and Distrust* (Cambridge, MA: Harvard University Press, 1978).

Related to this critique is Burt's argument that the question of abortion is especially unsuited to a judicial resolution because it prevents the community from defining itself by struggling politically with the question of its own membership, a question that abortion poses. The absence of self-definition through debate diminishes a society's communal solidarity. *See supra* chapter 3 note 110.

5. A class deserving of such special fourteenth amendment protection, and strict judicial scrutiny of state action with respect to it, is referred to as a "footnote four class" after the theory of judicial review set forth by Chief Justice Stone in United States v. Carolene Products Co., 304 U.S. 144, 152 n.4 (1938).

For a political-psychological account of why such special protection is appropriate, *see* Ely, *Democracy and Distrust, supra* note 2, at 157–159 (discussing we-they psychology and the special judicial role in protecting the "theys" when the political process cannot be relied upon to protect their interests because it is dominated by the us").

For an argument that the fetus might arguably be a footnote four class, *see* Ely, "The Wages of Crying Wolf: A Comment on *Roe v. Wade,*" *supra* note 4, at 933–937.

For a procedural claim about the lack of representation of the fetus in *Roe, see* Gorby, "The 'Right' to an Abortion, the Scope of Fourteenth Amendment 'Personhood,' and the Supreme Court's Birth Requirement," 1979 *S. Ill. U.L.J.* 1, 8–9 (1979) (suggesting that the adjudication of *Roe* lacked a necessary party, a guardian *ad litem* for fetus).

6. As with Noonan, Brody makes the common and unsupported assumption that abortion is tolerated only by treating the "fetus, hidden and unknown, as a being alien from humanity and . . . [by giving] no more thought to its destruction. . . . "Baruch Brody, *Abortion and the Sanctity of Human Life* (Cambridge, MA: MIT Press, 1975), p. 132.

7. *See* Forbath, "The Ambiguities of Free Labor: Labor and the Law in the Gilded Age," 1986 *Wis. L. Rev.* 767.

8. For a discussion of the myth of the self-made man in American society, *see* Erik Erikson, *Childhood and Society,* 2d ed. (New York: W. W. Norton & Co., 1963), pp. 285–325; Erik Erikson, *Dimensions of a New Identity: The 1973 Jefferson Lectures in the Humanities* (New York: W. W. Norton & Co., 1974); Erik Erikson, *Identity: Youth and Crisis* (New York: W. W. Norton & Co., 1968); *cf.* Forbath, *supra* note 7.

For a discussion of the ways that modern industrial societies overcome the regressive pulls of dependency of an agrarian and feudal past, *see* Erikson, *Childhood and Society, supra,* at 304–306, 359–402.

9. *See, e.g.,* United States v. Blyew, 80 U.S. (13 Wall.) 581 (1871); United States v. Reese, 92 U.S. 214 (1876); United States v. Cruikshank, 92 U.S. 542 (1876); United States v. Harris, 106 U.S. 629 (1882); Civil Rights Cases, 109 U.S. 3 (1883); *cf.* Plessy v. Ferguson, 163 U.S. 537 (1896).

10. Civil Rights Cases, 109 U.S. at 25. The Supreme Court did not overcome the disabling effects of that case until the moral suasion of the civil rights movement of the 1960s led to Katzenbach v. McClung, 379 U.S. 294 (1964); Heart of Atlanta Motel v. United States, 379 U.S. 241 (1964); United States v. Guest, 383 U.S. 745 (1966); Jones v. Alfred H. Mayer Co., 392 U.S. 409 (1968).

11. Lochner v. New York, 198 U.S. 45, 61 (1905). *But cf.* Muller v. Oregon, 208 U.S. 412, 418 (1908) (with respect to women, accepting vision of state as "pater familias," quoting Lochner v. New York, 198 U.S. at 62).

12. *See, e.g.*, Roe v. Wade, 410 U.S. 113, 174 (1973) (Rehnquist, J., dissenting). *Roe*, understood as recognizing and accepting dependency (of the fetus), stands in stark contrast to *Lochner*. From this perspective, *Roe* is not *Lochner's* logical successor. *But see* Ely "The Wages of Crying Wolf: A Comment on *Roe v. Wade*," *supra* note 4, at 937–943.

13. *Cf.* Morris Eagle, *Recent Developments in Psychoanalysis* (New York: McGraw-Hill, 1984). Eagle writes:

> If his [the adult's] universalism is truly human, it will have emerged organically from this early matrix [of concrete and parochial experience]. . . . The relationship between mother and child is always concrete and parochial. . . . Any universalism which overlooks this fact has permitted ideology to dominate flesh and bone and usually leads to the treatment of man as an object and his subjection as a means to an end.

Id. at 212.

14. C. Everett Koop, "The Slide to Auschwitz," in Reagan, *supra* note 2, at 49–50 (quoting J. Engelbert Dunphy); *see also id.* at 50 ("History shows clearly the frighteningly short steps from 'the living will' to 'death control' to 'thought control' and finally to the systematic elimination of all but those selected for slavery or to make up the master race") (quoting J. Engelbert Dunphy); Malcolm Muggeridge, "The Humane Holocaust," in Reagan, *supra* note 2, at 75; *supra* Introduction note 4; *cf.* Lawrence Lader, *Abortion II* (Boston: Beacon Press, 1973) p. 161 *et seq.* Even Magda Denes, who staunchly favors deregulation and who apparently was a refugee from totalitarian forces, nonetheless considers the same analogy. Magda Denes, *In Necessity and Sorrow* (Middlesex, England: Penguin Books, Ltd., 1976), pp. 60, 235.

15. Leaving aside the most obvious flaws in this analogy—including the failure to distinguish heinous state coercion, linked with a racist ideology, from private choice—these differences should be noted: Nazi Germany glorified Aryan motherhood in propaganda, presumably for the purpose among others of using women to breed soldiers for the state and using images of mother to inspire them to fight. *See, e.g.*, Erikson, *Childhood and Society, supra* note 8, at 343–344. It also had a highly restrictive abortion policy. *See* Hans Bleuel, *Sex and Society in Nazi Germany*, ed. Heinrich Fraenkel, trans. J. Maxwell Brownjohn (Philadelphia: J. B. Lippincott Co., 1973), pp. 213, 237; *cf.* Malcolm Potts, "Medical Progress and the Social Implications of Abortion: Summing-up," in *Abortion: Medical Progress and Social Implications*, Ciba Foundation Symposium 115, ed. Ruth Porter & Maeve O'Connor (London: Pitman, 1985), pp. 263, 266 (reporting that in Vichy France, a woman was guillotined for having an abortion in 1943); Adrienne Rich, *Of Woman Born* (New York: W. W. Norton & Co., 1976), pp. 270–273 (discussing Soviet Union and Peron's Argentina, which restricted contraceptives in order to increase population growth).

16. For an argument concerning the breakdown of the rule of law in the regulatory state, *see, e.g.,* Friedrich Hayek, *The Road to Serfdom* (Chicago: University of Chicago Press, 1976).

For a comparison of two theories of totalitarianism, and for the phrase in text "totalitarian temptations," *see* Michael Sandel, "Introduction," in *Liberalism and Its Critics,* ed. Michael Sandel (New York: New York University Press, 1984). Sandel writes:

> Liberals often argue that a politics of the common good, and the moral particularity it affirms, open the way to prejudice and intolerance. . . . Any attempt to govern by a vision of the good is likely to lead to a slippery slope of totalitarian temptations.
>
> Communitarians reply that intolerance flourishes most where forms of life are dislocated, roots unsettled, traditions undone. In our day, the totalitarian impulse has sprung less from the convictions of confidently situated selves than from the confusions of atomized, dislocated, frustrated selves, at sea in a world where common meanings have lost their force.

Id. at 7.

For a discussion of the breakdown of communal values and traditions in American culture, dominated as it is by individualism and its associated myth of the self-made person, *see* Robert Bellah, Richard Madsen, William Sullivan, Ann Swidler & Steven Tipton, *Habits of the Heart: Individualism and Commitment in American Life* (Berkeley, Los Angeles, London: University of California Press, 1985). Bellah and his colleagues remark:

> What we fear above all, and what keeps the new world powerless to be born, is that if we give up our dream of private success for a more genuinely integrated societal community, we will be abandoning our separation and individuation, collapsing into dependence and tyranny. What we find hard to see is that it is the extreme fragmentation of the modern world that really threatens our individuation; that what is best in our separation and individuation, our sense of dignity and autonomy as persons, requires a new integration if it is to be sustained.

Id. at 286.

17. Where do culture and communal sentiment reside in each of us? According to Winnicott, they are to be found in the developing space between the mother and individuating infant. *See* D. W. Winnicott, *Playing and Reality* (London: Tavistock Publications, 1980), p. 95 (treating cultural phenomena as the heir of transitional phenomena and locating cultural experiences in that part of the mind which is between me and not-me). The capacity to form deep attachments, those that link us firmly to the fundamental associations of a community, the family and the church, is ontologically linked, some analysts claim, to the attachment capacities learned first with the mother.

18. The modern privacy doctrine begins with the protection of the contraceptive choices made within the marriage relationship. Griswold v. Connecticut, 381 U.S. 479, 486 (1965) ("We deal with a right of privacy older than the Bill of Rights—older than our political parties. . . . Marriage is a coming together . . . intimate to the degree of being sacred. It is an association that promotes a way of life, not causes; a harmony in living, not political faiths; a bilateral loyalty, not commercial or social projects"). While it took an individualistic turn in Eisenstadt v. Baird, 405 U.S. 438 (1972), many privacy cases continue to protect relationships more than individual autonomous choice. *See supra* chapter 1 note 49; *supra* chapter 3 note 43. *Compare* the Nazi boast: "The only person who is still a private individual in Germany is somebody who is asleep," *quoted in* Hannah Arendt, *The Origins of Totalitarianism* (New York: Harcourt Brace Jovanovich, 1973), p. 339, *with* Poe v. Ullman, 367 U.S. 497, 522 (1961) (Harlan, J., dissenting) (urging Court to strike down law prohibiting married couple's use of contraceptives as interference with the privacy of that relationship in the bedroom). As Heymann and Barzelay have written:

> Our political system is superimposed on and presupposes a social system of family units, not just of isolated individuals. No assumption more deeply underlies our society than the assumption that it is the individual who decides whether to raise a family. . . . Any sharp departure from this assumption would cut as deeply at the underlying conditions of acceptance of our society and governing institutions as a broad restriction on the right to vote or hold office. . . . [T]he family unit does not simply co-exist with our constitutional system; it is an integral part of it. In democratic theory as well as in practice, it is in the family that children are expected to learn the values and beliefs that democratic institutions later draw on to determine group directions. The immensely important power of deciding about matters of early socialization has been allocated to the family, not to the government. Thus, if a state government decided that all children would be reared and educated from birth under such complete control of a state official that the parental role would be minimal, the effect on our present notions of democratic government would be immense. . . . [The family is] the most basic substructure of our society and government.

Heymann & Barzelay, "The Forest for the Trees: *Roe v. Wade* and Its Critics," 53 *B.U.L. Rev.* 765, 772–773 (1973).

   19. While the medical profession of course is not entitled to anything resembling automatic deference, its close connection to our natural and fourteenth amendment liberty interests in health, broadly conceived, appears to have led the Court to give it some legal deference. Thus the Court has taken care to protect the medical profession's independence in a number of cases. It has allowed the state to defer to medical conclusions without turning those conclusions into state action. *See* Blum v. Yaretsky, 457 U.S. 991 (1982). It has in a number of cases instructed courts to defer to medical judgment in determining whether civil rights have been infringed by the acts of physicians. *See, e.g.,* Regents of the University of Michigan v. Ewing, 106 S. Ct. 507 (1985) (deferring to medical faculty's dismissal of student, provided that faculty in fact exercised professional judgment); Youngberg v. Romeo, 457 U.S. 307 (1982) (deferring to medical judgment in evaluating retarded pa-

tient's right to habilitation and treatment); Parham v. J.R., 442 U.S. 584
(1979) (right of child to hearing prior to institutionalization by parent
only includes effective psychiatric exam). The Court has also attempted
to protect physicians from state control by forbidding a state from requiring them to mouth sentiments on its behalf. *See* Akron v. Akron
Center for Reproductive Health, 462 U.S. 416, 443–45 (1983); Thornburgh v. American College of Obst. & Gyn., 106 S. Ct. 2169, 2179–80
(1986) (holding unconstitutional a state's attempt to "wedge . . . [its]
message discouraging abortion into the privacy of the informed-consent
dialogue," and describing statute that required physicians to provide
certain information as "state medicine imposed upon the woman").

The abortion cases clearly evidence the belief that some deference is
appropriate to the physician-patient relationship and to medical judgments as a means of resolving difficult legal issues. *See, e.g.,* Doe v.
Bolton, 410 U.S. 179, 219 (1973) (Douglas, J., concurring) (asserting that
"right of privacy has no more conspicuous place than in the physician-
patient relationship, unless it be in the priest-penitent relationship,"
thereby implying the moral-ascriptive aspect of "health"); *cf.* United
States v. 12 200-Ft. Reels, 413 U.S. 123, 127 n.4 (1973) (describing "constitutionally protected privacy, such as that which encompasses the
intimate medical problems of family, marriage, and motherhood");
Thornburgh v. American College of Obst. & Gyn., 106 S. Ct. at 2190
(Burger, C.J., dissenting) (indicating willingness to reconsider *Roe* precisely because medical profession to which Court had seemingly appropriately deferred in *Roe* had failed to maintain its own professional limitations on the performance of abortions).

Dissenting from the special protection the Court afforded the physician-patient relationship in *Thornburgh*, Justice White asserted to the
contrary that the medical profession may be the object of state regulation like any other profession, subject only to a court's most minimal
rational-basis scrutiny:

> [N]othing in the Constitution indicates a preference for the liberty of
> doctors over that of lawyers, accountants, bakers, or brickmakers. Ac-
> cordingly, if the State may not "structure" the dialogue between doctor
> and patient, it should also follow that the State may not . . . [require cer-
> tain disclosures by attorneys].

Id. at 2200–2201; *cf.* Bob Woodward & Scott Armstrong, *The Brethren*
(New York: Simon & Schuster, 1979), p. 416 (Justice White sarcastically
referring to Blackmun's "medical question doctrine").

As an empirical matter, the profession's independence from the
state may have at times served to tame some of the passions of the abortion debate. *Cf.* Kristin Luker, *Abortion and the Politics of Motherhood*
(Berkeley, Los Angeles, London: University of California Press, 1984),
pp. 40–65 (discussing how medical profession mediated conflicting values with respect to abortion from late nineteenth century to *Roe*).

20. The totalitarian analogy suggests important and intriguing questions about the relationship of the inquiry of this essay to psycho-anaysis and its use of individualistic and relational categories.

In his novel *The White Hotel*, the poet D. M. Thomas attempted to convey the Holocaust horror and Nazi mass slaughter that Koop and Muggeridge invoke. For this, Thomas turned to Freud. At the center of this fictionalized version of Freud's *Dora* case study (albeit one that takes into account Freud's later theory of the death instinct but informed with a religious attitude of reconciliation) is the analysis of Thomas' doomed character Lisa Erdman. Her analysis with Freud is the means by which Thomas evokes the individuality or personhood of each of the faceless victims of fascism.

Thomas tells us that, after completing her analysis and reconciling herself to her childless life, Erdman married Berenstein, a Jewish widower with a young son. Sometime thereafter they moved to Kiev. Though her husband later died, Erdman remained there and eventually found herself trapped by the invading Germans. Forgoing a claim that she was Christian, she chose to stand by her Jewish stepson, whom she found she could not abandon as they faced a mass death in the unmarked graves of Babi Yar. Thomas counterpoints the anonymous mound of slaughtered bodies with the unique spirit of each of the victims:

> The soul of man is a far country, which cannot be approached or explored. Most of the dead were poor and illiterate. But every single one of them had dreamed dreams, seen visions and had had amazing experiences, even the babes in arms (perhaps especially the babes in arms). Though most of them had never lived outside the Podol slum, their lives and histories were as rich and complex as Lisa Erdman-Berenstein's. If a Sigmund Freud had been listening and taking notes from the time of Adam, he would still not fully have explored even a single group, even a single person.
>
> And this was only the first day. . . .
>
> The thirty thousand became a quarter of a million.

Thomas, *The White Hotel* (New York: Viking Press, 1981), pp. 294–295.

Thomas' use of psychoanalysis is more than a fortuitous literary device in the hands of a poet. Historically and intellectually, the development of psychoanalysis stands in sharp contrast to the totalitarian society that engineered this mass death. For if fascism is one European product of this century, psychoanalysis is another—the one seeking, at the expense of individuality, the domination and coordination of persons, professions, and institutions, their *gleichshaltung*; the other a small profession strengthening the self in stubborn resistance to the pressures of time and money, conformity and convention. *See* Erik Erikson, *The Life Cycle Completed* (New York: W. W. Norton & Co., 1982). Erikson has written:

> [T]he historical period in which we learned to observe . . . revelations of the inner life was well on its way to turning into one of the most cata-

strophic periods in history; and the ideological division between the "inner-" and the "outerworld" [in analytic theory] may well have had deep connotations of a threatening split between the individualistic enlightenment rooted in Judaeo-Christian civilization and the totalitarian veneration of the racist state. . . . [The efforts of Viennese analysts] stubbornly redoubled, as if a methodological devotion to the timeless pursuits of healing and enlightenment was now needed all the more desperately. *Id.* at 22. *Cf.* William McGrath, *Freud and the Discovery of Psychoanalysis* (Ithaca, NY: Cornell University Press, 1986) (discussing impact of authoritarianism of Austro-Hungarian Empire and antisemitism on Freud's thought); Geoffrey Cocks, *Psychotherapy in the Third Reich: The Göring Institute* (New York: Oxford University Press, 1985) (reporting survival of some analytic work in Nazi Germany).

Interestingly, it was in part over the nature of individuality that Freud and Jung differed. Freud asserted the unique historical aspect of human psychology—that is, individuality. By contrast, Jung sought to achieve therapeutic results not only by teaching a patient to understand himself in the context of his own history but also as part of supraindividual archetypes. Jung's later brief connection with the Nazis, *see* Reuben Fine, *A History of Psychoanalysis* (New York: Columbia University Press, 1979), p. 85, may not be unrelated to the tendency of fascist ideology to subsume individuals within a mass, and to motivate them by supraindividual imagery to the exclusion of themes of individuality.

Given its purpose and historical experience, psychoanalysis has, not surprisingly, yielded a substantial literature attempting to comprehend fascism. These works typically seek to explain the loss of individuality and the capacity of persons to act en masse in destructive ways that individually they would not. The classic account is Erich Fromm, *Escape from Freedom* (New York: Farrar & Rhinehart, Inc., 1941). From a different sociological and political viewpoint, Freud had told a similar story in his "Group Psychology and the Analysis of the Ego" (1921), in *The Standard Edition of the Complete Psychological Works of Sigmund Freud*, vol. 18, ed. and trans. James Strachey et al. (London: The Hogarth Press 1953–1974), p. 65; *see also* Jeffrey Abramson, *Liberation and Its Limits: The Moral and Political Thought of Freud* (New York: The Free Press, 1984), p. 129 ("If the solidity of political community is invariably entwined with the creation of mass individuals, then one must in the end side with the stark antipolitics of *Group Psychology*. The ideal of erotic politics, so utopian-sounding, would but welcome totalitarianism"). Other accounts include Theodore Adorno, Else Frenkel-Brunswick, Daniel Levinson & B. Nevitt Sanford, *Authoritarian Personality-Part One* (New York: W. W. Norton & Co., 1969); Franz Neumann, "Anxiety and Politics," in Franz Neumann, *The Democratic and the Authoritarian State: Essays in Political and Legal Theory*, ed. Herbert Marcuse (Glencoe: The Free Press, 1957), p. 270; Wilhelm Reich, *The Mass Psychology of Fascism*, trans. Vincent Carfagno (New York: Farrar, Straus & Giroux,

1970); *cf.* Martin Jay, *The Dialectical Imagination* (London: Heinemann, 1973).

It is uncertain what the implication is for these accounts of the newer psychoanalytic emphasis upon attachment and fusion, the importance of which is testified to by the strength of Erdman's attachment to her stepson in the face of death. *See, e.g.,* Erikson, *Childhood and Society, supra* note 8, at 326–358.

21. Arendt, *supra* note 18, at 478–479 (footnote omitted).

INDEX

Abnormality, fetal, 18–19, 61, 120 n.42, 175–176 n.61, 178 n.65
Abolitionists, regulators compared to, 93–96
Abortifacients. *See* Abortion techniques
Abortion: accepted, 11–19, 120 n.42; after incest, 18, 119 n.40; after rape, 12, 13, 14, 16, 114 n.26, 119 n.40; alternatives to (*see* Adoption); as best alternative, 163 n.31; contraception distinguished from, 7, 8, 16, 17, 108–109 n.11; contraceptive use after, 216–218 n.128; for convenience, 19; counseling before, 82 (*see also* Consent, informed); decision-making in (*see* Decision-making); denied, 63, 172–173 n.54, 215–216 n.127; discouraged, 58–59; of ectopic pregnancy, 11; as euthanasia, 119–120 n.41; family conditions cause, 18, 19; family affected by, 77–78, 194 n.84; father's rights in, 195–196 n.86 (*see also* Consent, spousal); feelings after, 86–87, 213–214 n.125, 214 n.126, 215–216 n.127, 217 n.128; for fetal abnormalities, 18–19, 61, 120 n.42, 175–176 n.61, 178 n.65; first trimester, 23, 26–27, 60, 61, 82; for gender selection, 175–176 n.61; for health reasons, 11, 26, 125–126 n.51, 126–127 n.52; as homicide, 118–119 n.38; infanticide distinguished from, 107 n.7; infanticide as result of, 71; interpersonal dialogue before, 84; live birth following, 29, 141 n.70, 177–178 n.64; as medical procedure,
80–82, 83–84, 85, 99, 126–127 n.52; for minors, 13, 83, 114 n.25, 208–210 n.118, 217 n.128; as moral issue, 87, 92–93, 218 n.130; natural order disturbed by, 220–221 n.3; numbers of, 25, 59–60, 139–140 n.67, 183 n.68; opinion polls on, 111–112 n.18; placenta affected by, 10; pre- v. postimplantation, 16, 17, 108–109 n.11; as responsible act, 87; safety of, 23, 126–127 n.52; to save mother's life, 11–12, 22; second trimester, 24, 25, 26, 60, 61, 82, 126–127 n.52, 175 n.60, 177–178 n.64, 178 n.65; as self-defense, 11–12, 17–18, 113 n.21; in Sweden, 172–173 n.54, 176–177 n.62; technology affects, 24; third trimester, 29, 177 n.63, 198–199 n.99; totalitarianism compared to, 93, 96–100; and viability of fetus (*see* Viability). *See also* Reasonable period of choice; *Roe* v. *Wade*
Abortion and the Conscience of the Nation, 92–93
Abortion debate, duty-based v. rights-based, 1–3, 5, 32–34, 143–144 n.1. *See also* Deregulators; Regulators
Abortion funding, 57, 102–103 n.2, 119 n.39
Abortion law, vii, viii–ix, 3, 101 n.1. *See also* individual cases by name
Abortion services/clinics, 82, 85, 87, 103 n.3, 176–177 n.62, 205 n.115, 211–212 n.122; pre-*Roe,* 27–28
Abortion techniques, 16–17, 117–118 n.35, 141 n.70, 177–178 n.64

231

Designer: U.C. Press Staff
Compositor: G & S Typesetters, Inc.
Text: 10/13 Aster
Display: Aster
Printer: Haddon Craftsmen
Binder: Haddon Craftsmen